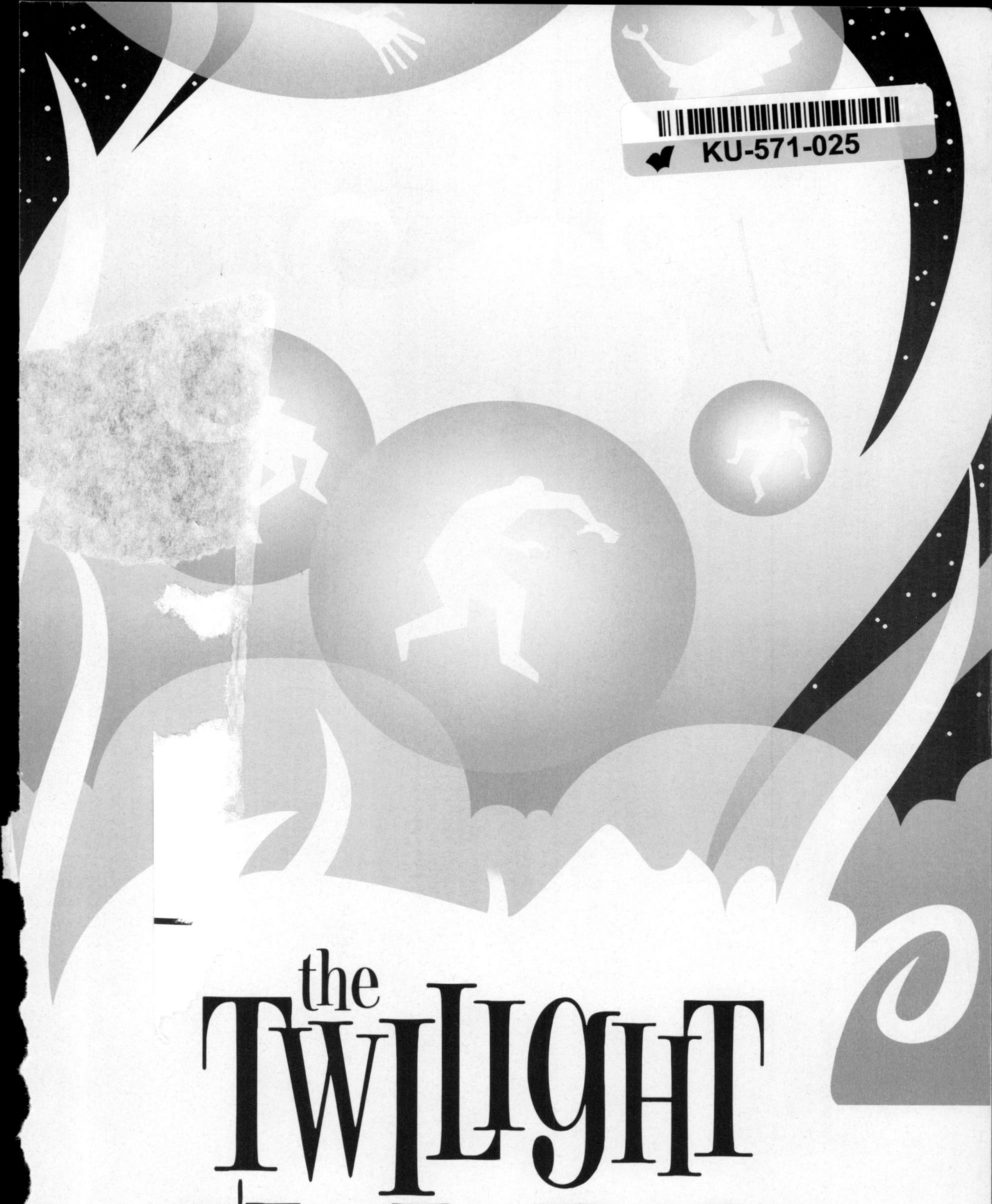

the TWILIGHT CHILDREN

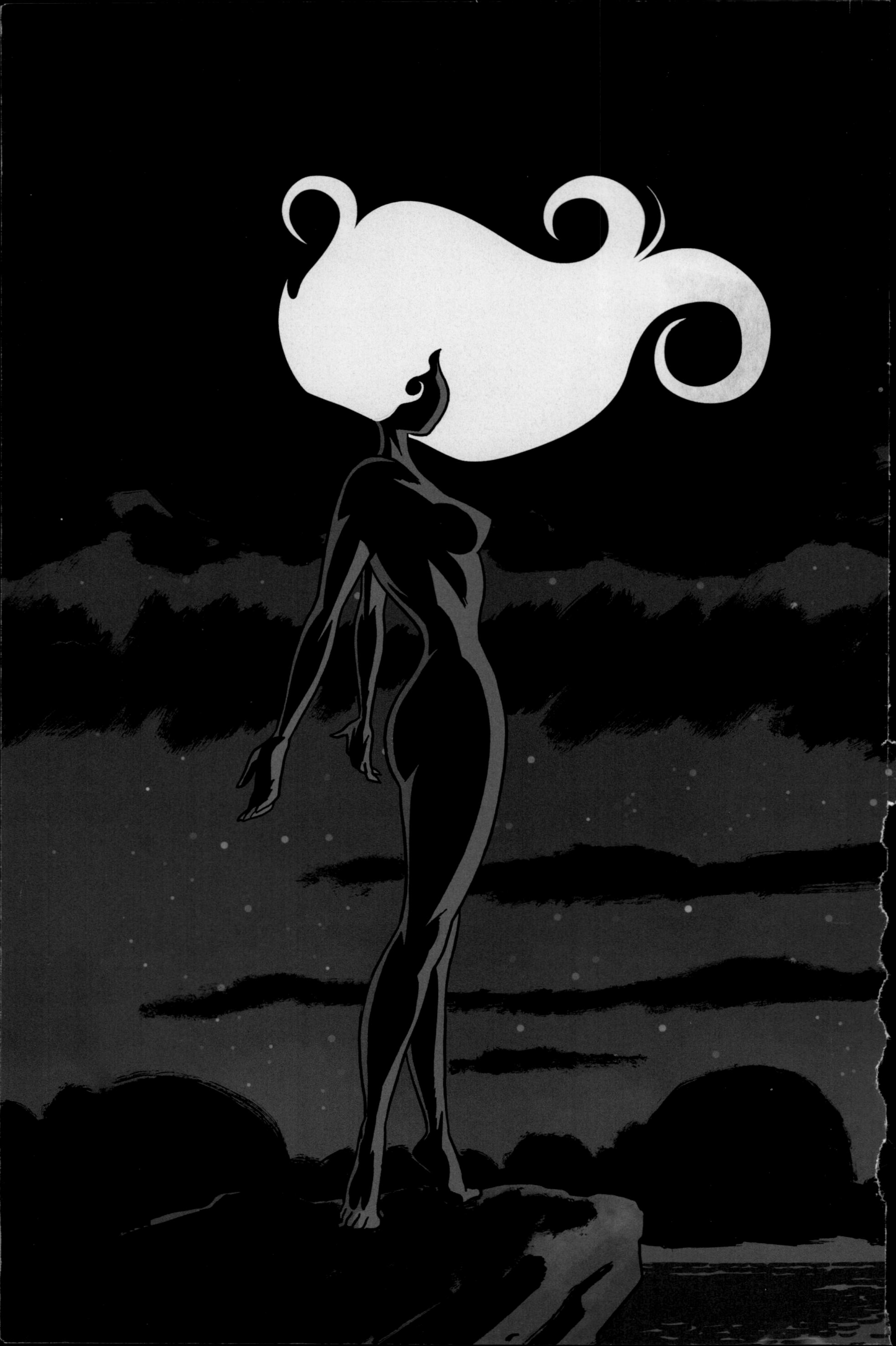

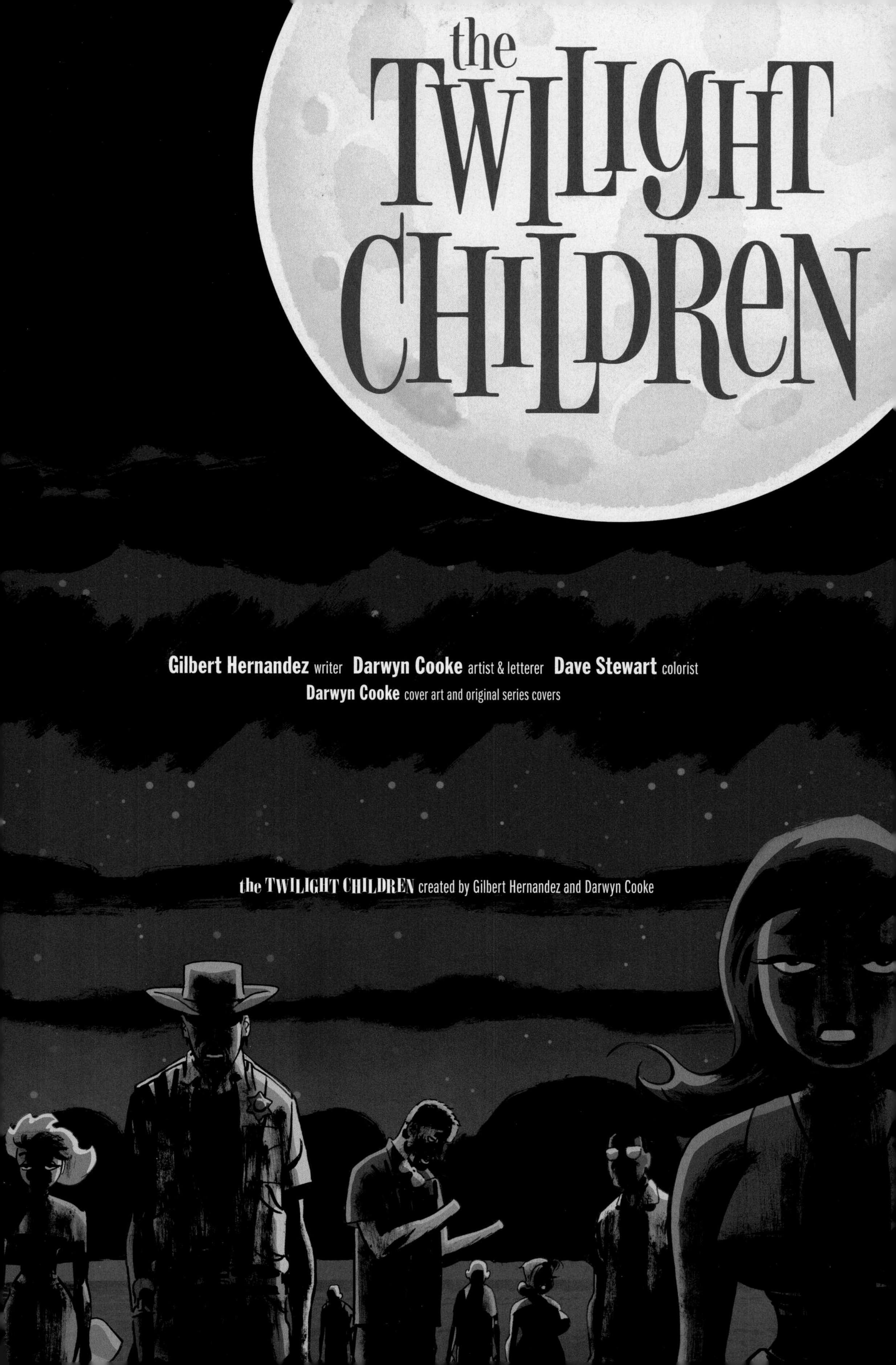

the TWILIGHT CHILDREN

Gilbert Hernandez writer **Darwyn Cooke** artist & letterer **Dave Stewart** colorist
Darwyn Cooke cover art and original series covers

the TWILIGHT CHILDREN created by Gilbert Hernandez and Darwyn Cooke

Shelly Bond VP & Executive Editor – Vertigo, and Editor – Original Series
Rowena Yow Associate Editor – Original Series
Jeb Woodard Group Editor – Collected Editions
Scott Nybakken Editor – Collected Edition
Steve Cook Design Director – Books
Curtis King Jr. Publication Design

Diane Nelson President
Dan DiDio and **Jim Lee** Co-Publishers
Geoff Johns Chief Creative Officer
Amit Desai Senior VP – Marketing & Global Franchise Management
Nairi Gardiner Senior VP – Finance
Sam Ades VP – Digital Marketing
Bobbie Chase VP – Talent Development
Mark Chiarello Senior VP – Art, Design & Collected Editions
John Cunningham VP – Content Strategy
Anne DePies VP – Strategy Planning & Reporting
Don Falletti VP – Manufacturing Operations
Lawrence Ganem VP – Editorial Administration & Talent Relations
Alison Gill Senior VP – Manufacturing & Operations
Hank Kanalz Senior VP – Editorial Strategy & Administration
Jay Kogan VP – Legal Affairs
Derek Maddalena Senior VP – Sales & Business Development
Jack Mahan VP – Business Affairs
Dan Miron VP – Sales Planning & Trade Development
Nick Napolitano VP – Manufacturing Administration
Carol Roeder VP – Marketing
Eddie Scannell VP – Mass Account & Digital Sales
Courtney Simmons Senior VP – Publicity & Communications
Jim (Ski) Sokolowski VP – Comic Book Specialty & Newsstand Sales

THE TWILIGHT CHILDREN

DC Comics
2900 West Alameda Avenue
Burbank, CA 91505
Printed in the USA. First Printing.
ISBN: 978-1-4012-6245-7

Library of Congress Cataloging-in-Publication Data

Names: Hernandez, Gilbert, author. | Cooke, Darwyn, illustrator. | Stewart,
    Dave, illustrator.
Title: The twilight children / Gilbert Hernandez, writer ; Darwyn Cooke,
    artist ; Dave Stewart, colorist.
Description: Burbank, CA : DC Comics/Vertigo, [2016] | "Originally published
    in single magazine form as THE TWILIGHT CHILDREN 1-4"
Identifiers: LCCN 2016006071 | ISBN 9781401262457
Subjects: LCSH: Graphic novels. | Comic books, strips, etc. | BISAC: COMICS &
    GRAPHIC NOVELS / Superheroes.
Classification: LCC PN6727.H477 T87 2016 | DDC 741.5/973—dc23
LC record available at http://lccn.loc.gov/2016006071

PEFC Certified
Printed on paper from
sustainably managed
forests and controlled
sources
PEFC/29-31-75   www.pefc.org

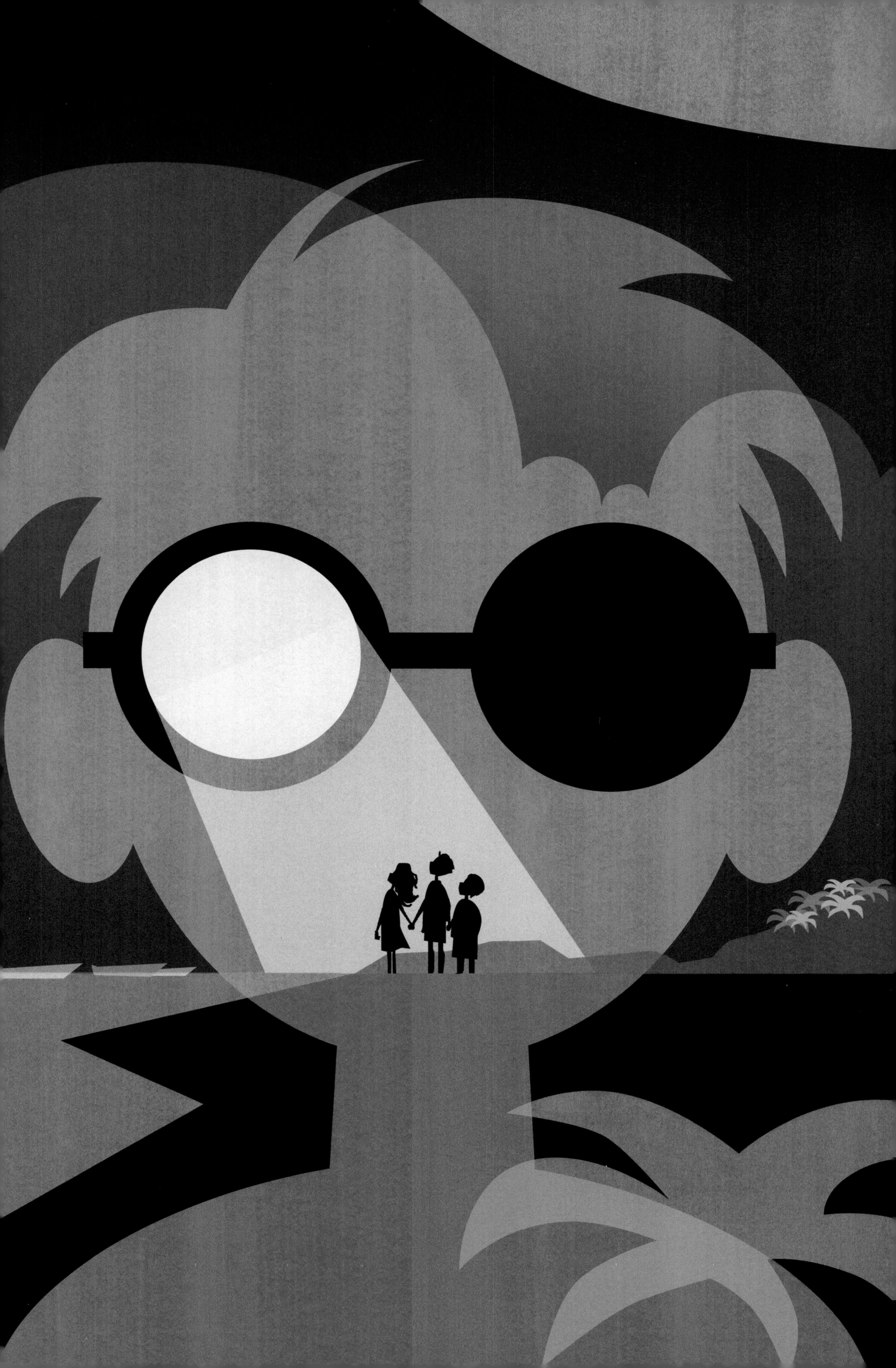

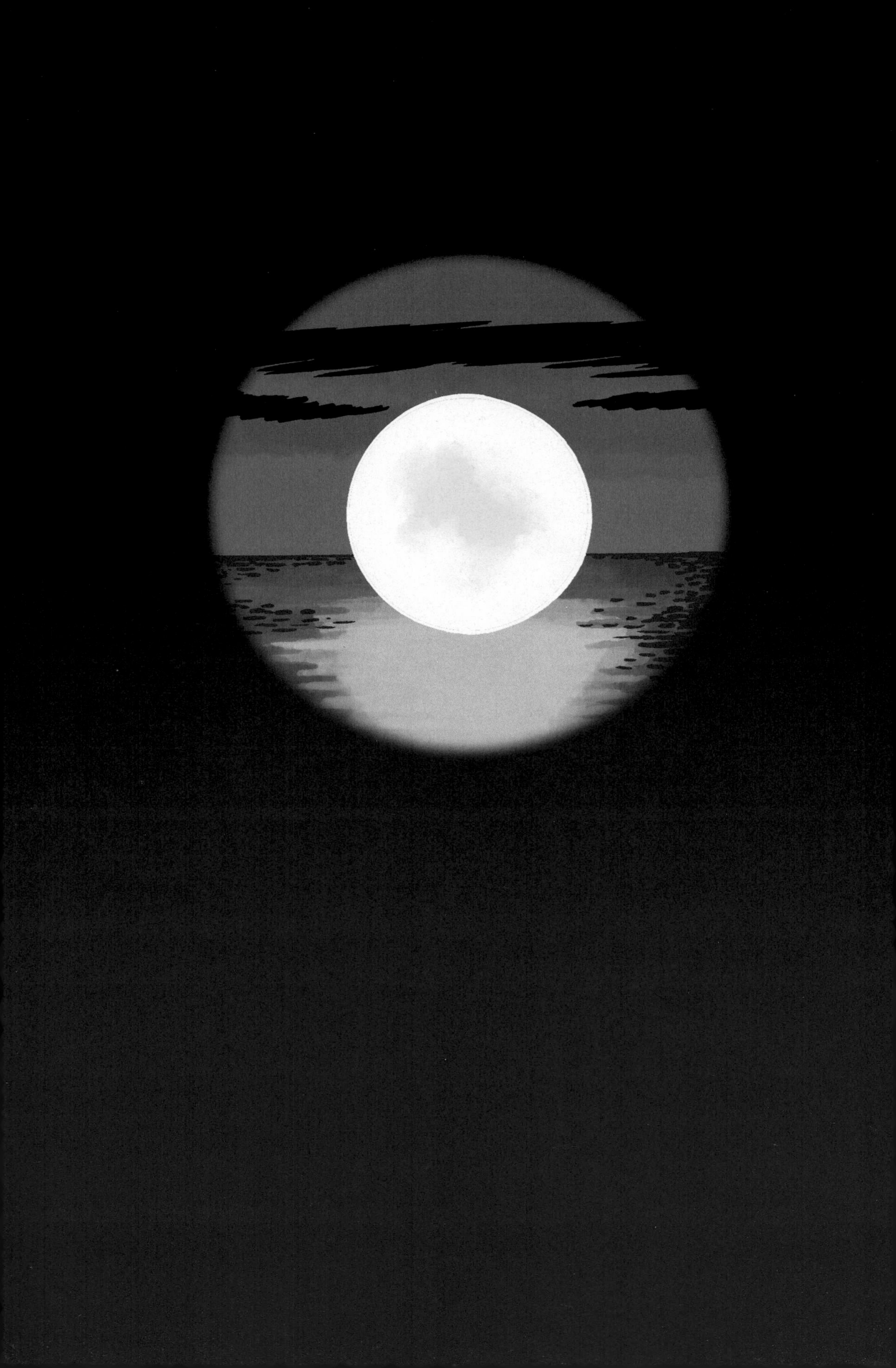

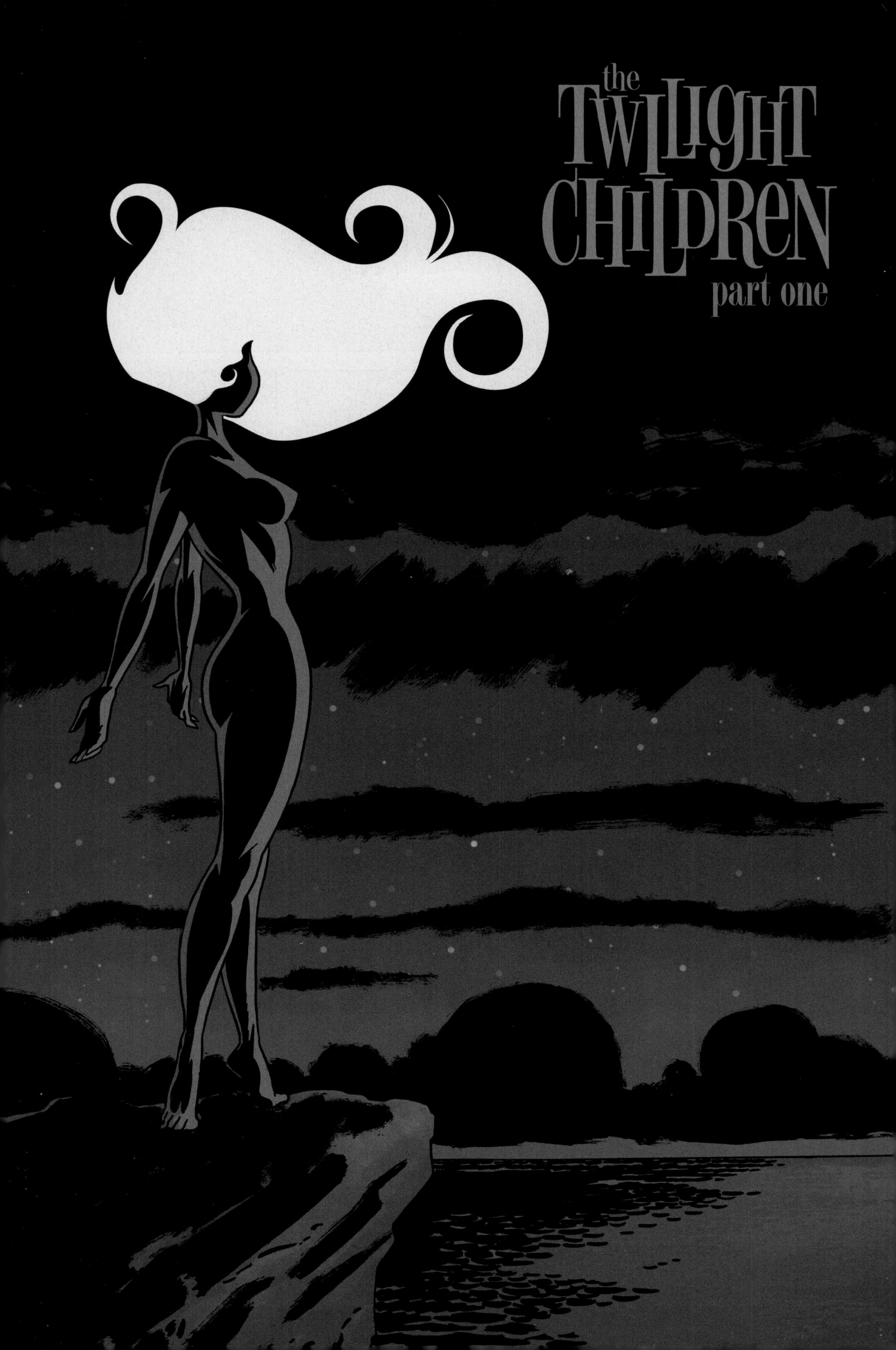
the
TWILIGHT
CHILDREN
part one

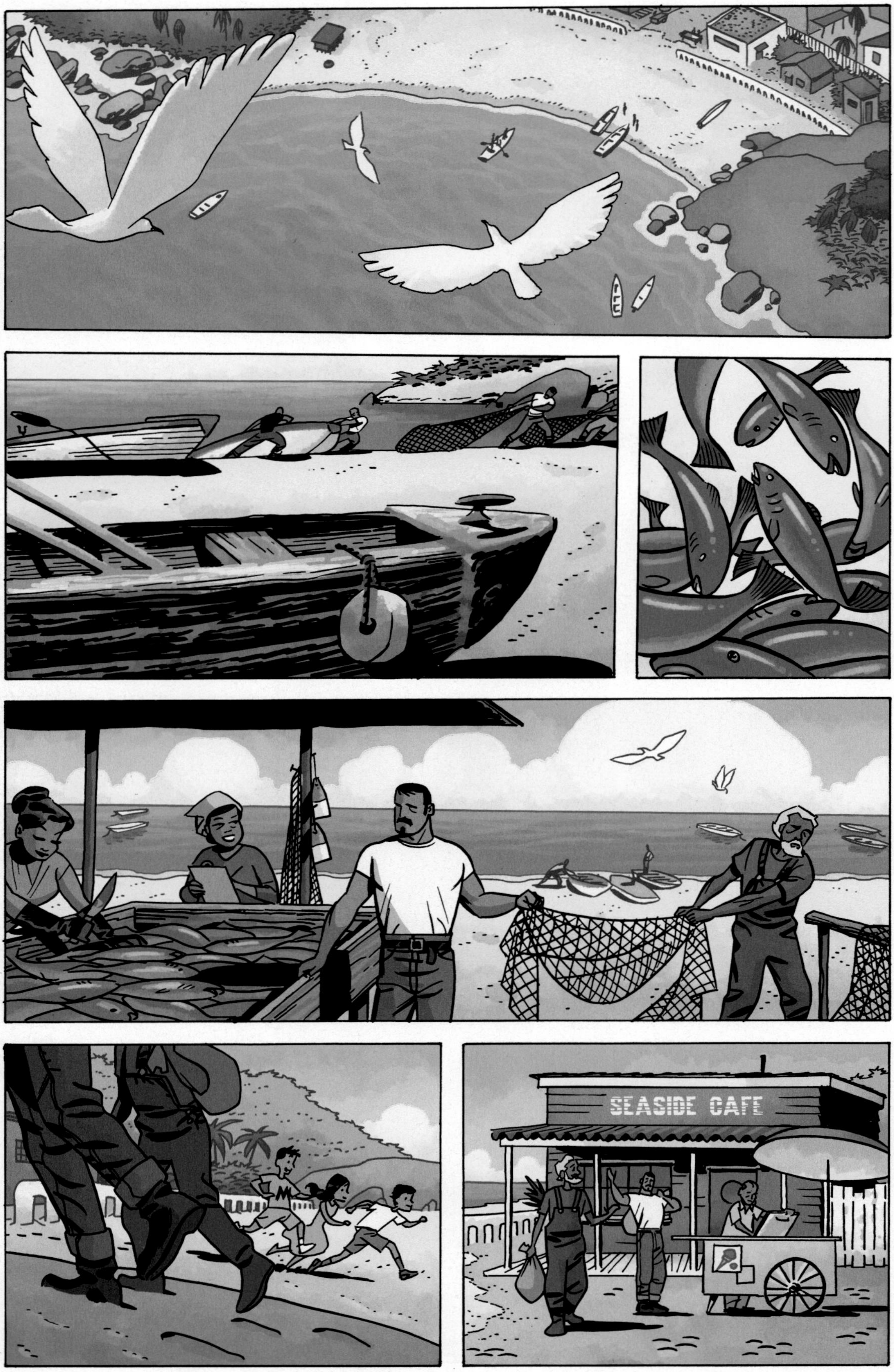
SEASIDE CAFE

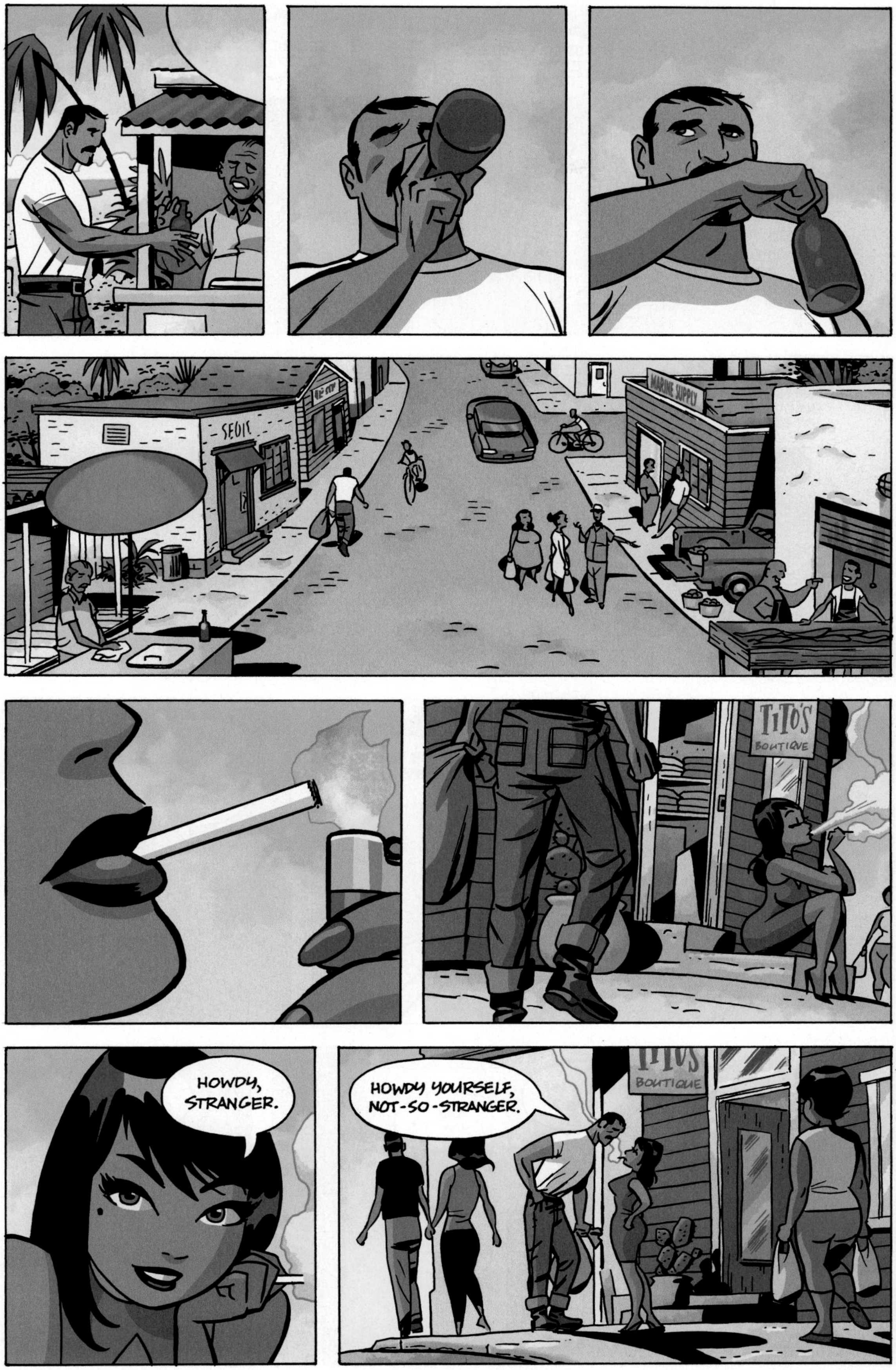
MARINE SUPPLY
TITO'S BOUTIQUE
HOWDY, STRANGER.
HOWDY YOURSELF, NOT-SO-STRANGER.

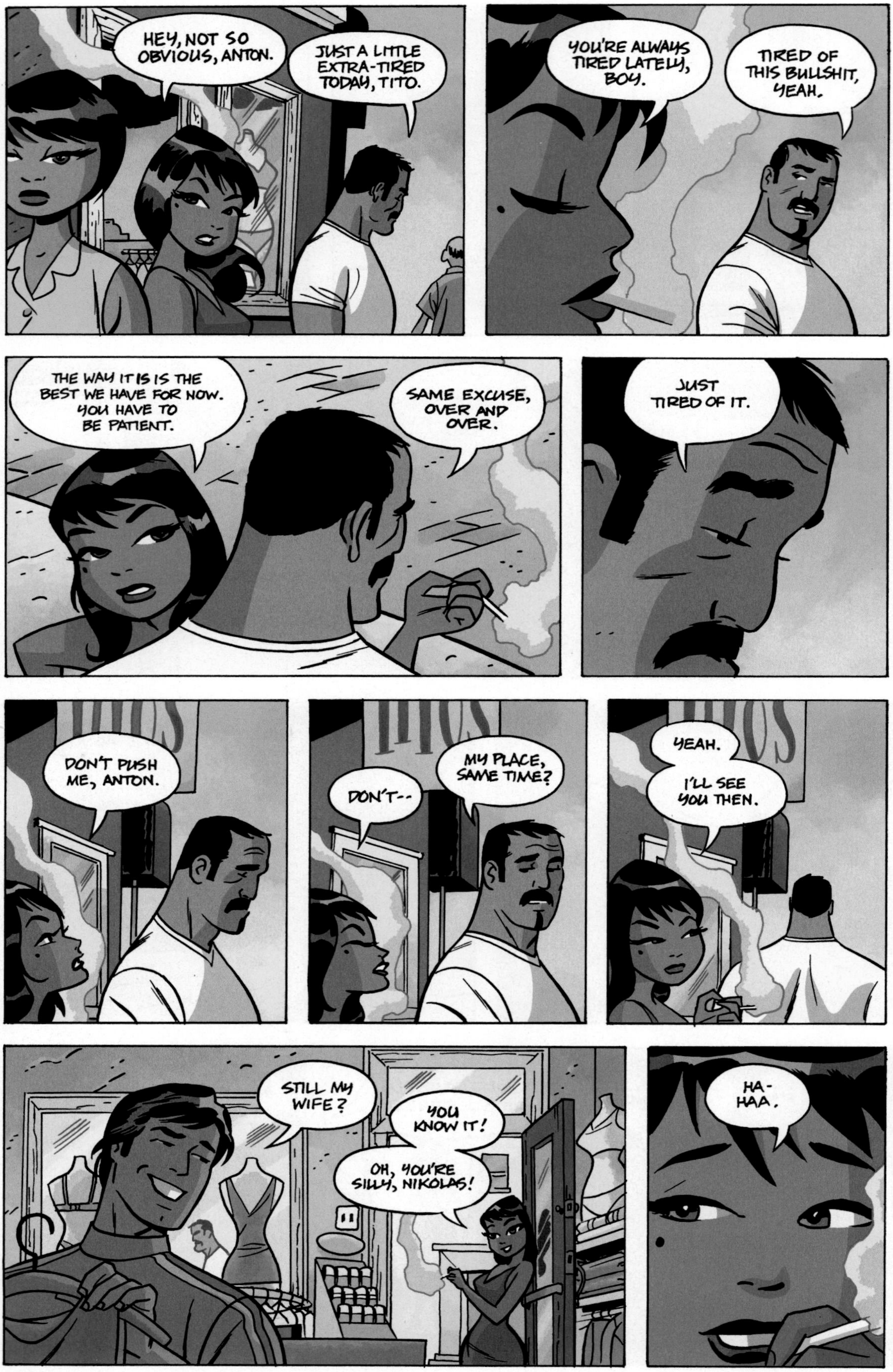
HEY, NOT SO OBVIOUS, ANTON.
JUST A LITTLE EXTRA-TIRED TODAY, TITO.
YOU'RE ALWAYS TIRED LATELY, BOY.
TIRED OF THIS BULLSHIT, YEAH.
THE WAY IT IS IS THE BEST WE HAVE FOR NOW. YOU HAVE TO BE PATIENT.
SAME EXCUSE, OVER AND OVER.
JUST TIRED OF IT.
DON'T PUSH ME, ANTON.
DON'T--
MY PLACE, SAME TIME?
YEAH.
I'LL SEE YOU THEN.
STILL MY WIFE?
YOU KNOW IT!
OH, YOU'RE SILLY, NIKOLAS!
HA-HAA.

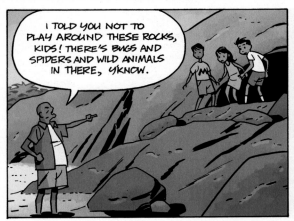

I TOLD YOU NOT TO PLAY AROUND THESE ROCKS, KIDS! THERE'S BUGS AND SPIDERS AND WILD ANIMALS IN THERE, Y'KNOW.

AND LAST I HEARD THEY LIKE MUNCHING ON KIDS THE BEST.

OK, BUNDO. WE'LL STAY AWAY FROM THE ROCKS.

THANK YOU FOR WARNING US AGAIN.

WELL, OK.

ANYTIME YOU NEED MY ADVICE, JUST COME AROUND. I'M ALWAYS AVAILABLE TO HELP YOU WITH ANY PROBLEMS YOU MAY HAVE.

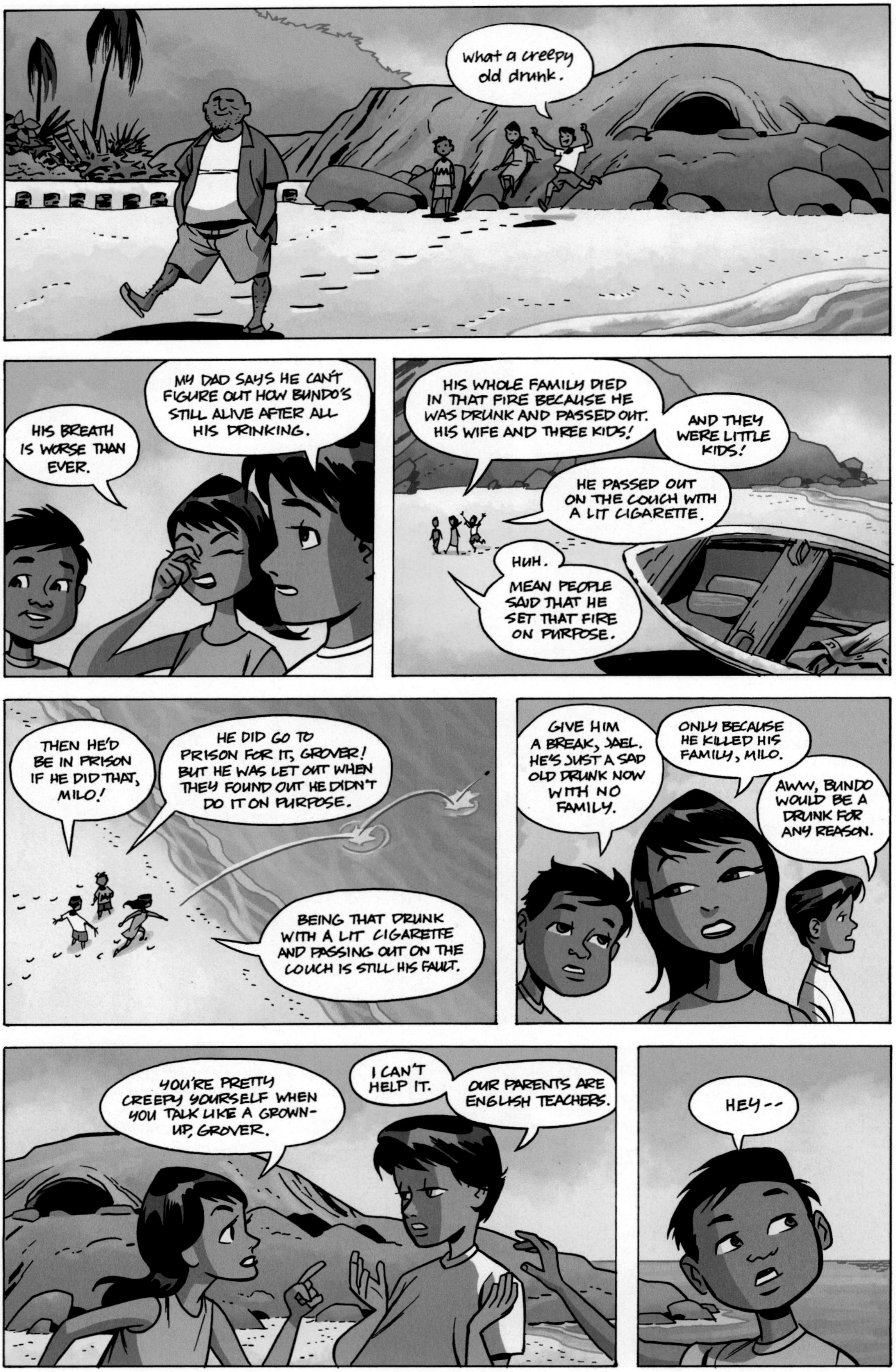
what a creepy old drunk.
HIS BREATH IS WORSE THAN EVER.
MY DAD SAYS HE CAN'T FIGURE OUT HOW BUNDO'S STILL ALIVE AFTER ALL HIS DRINKING.
HIS WHOLE FAMILY DIED IN THAT FIRE BECAUSE HE WAS DRUNK AND PASSED OUT. HIS WIFE AND THREE KIDS!
AND THEY WERE LITTLE KIDS!
HE PASSED OUT ON THE COUCH WITH A LIT CIGARETTE.
HUH. MEAN PEOPLE SAID THAT HE SET THAT FIRE ON PURPOSE.
THEN HE'D BE IN PRISON IF HE DID THAT, MILO!
HE DID GO TO PRISON FOR IT, GROVER! BUT HE WAS LET OUT WHEN THEY FOUND OUT HE DIDN'T DO IT ON PURPOSE.
BEING THAT DRUNK WITH A LIT CIGARETTE AND PASSING OUT ON THE COUCH IS STILL HIS FAULT.
GIVE HIM A BREAK, JAEL. HE'S JUST A SAD OLD DRUNK NOW WITH NO FAMILY.
ONLY BECAUSE HE KILLED HIS FAMILY, MILO.
AWW, BUNDO WOULD BE A DRUNK FOR ANY REASON.
YOU'RE PRETTY CREEPY YOURSELF WHEN YOU TALK LIKE A GROWN-UP, GROVER.
I CAN'T HELP IT.
OUR PARENTS ARE ENGLISH TEACHERS.
HEY--

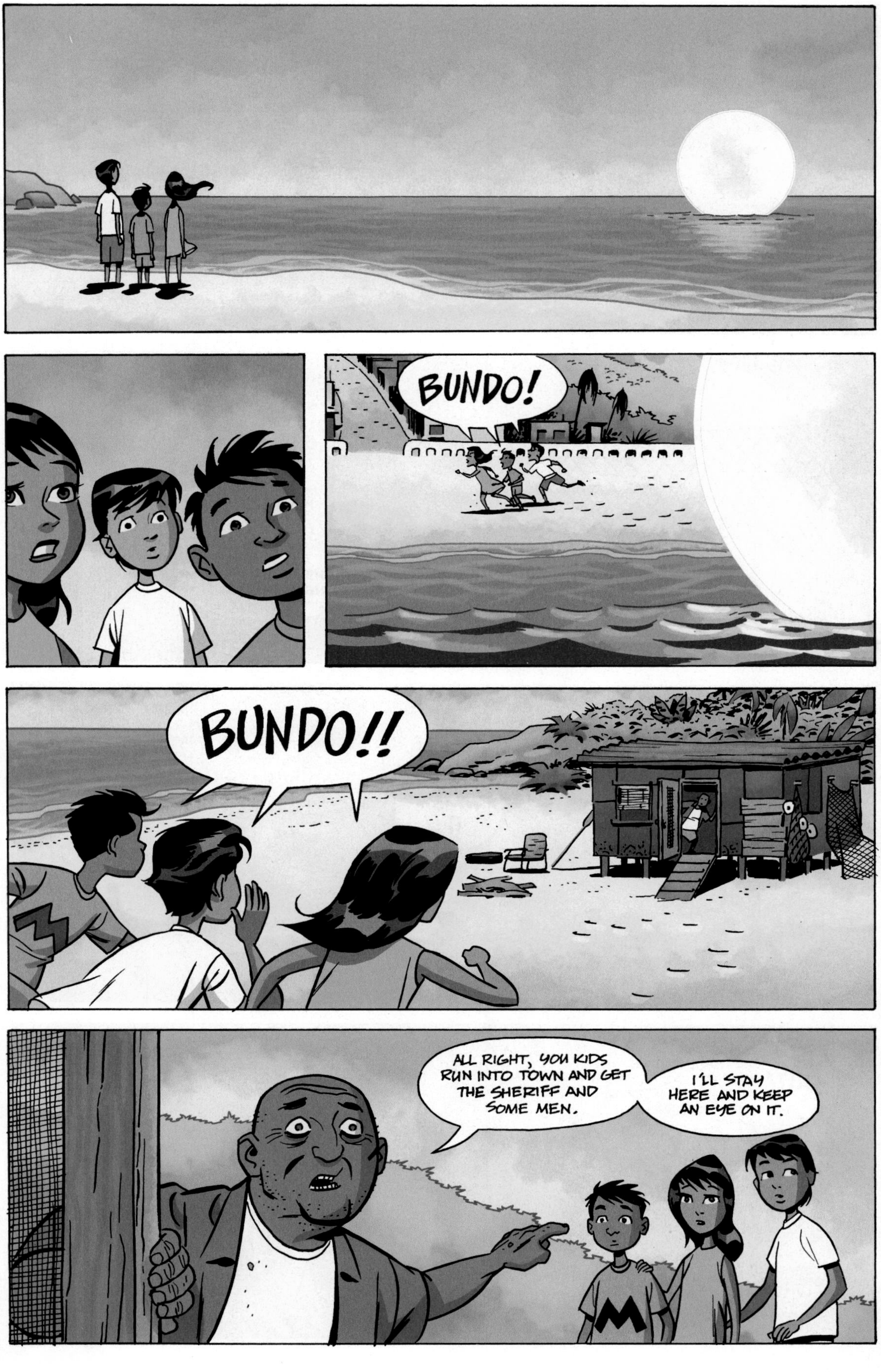
BUNDO!
BUNDO!!
ALL RIGHT, YOU KIDS RUN INTO TOWN AND GET THE SHERIFF AND SOME MEN.
I'LL STAY HERE AND KEEP AN EYE ON IT.

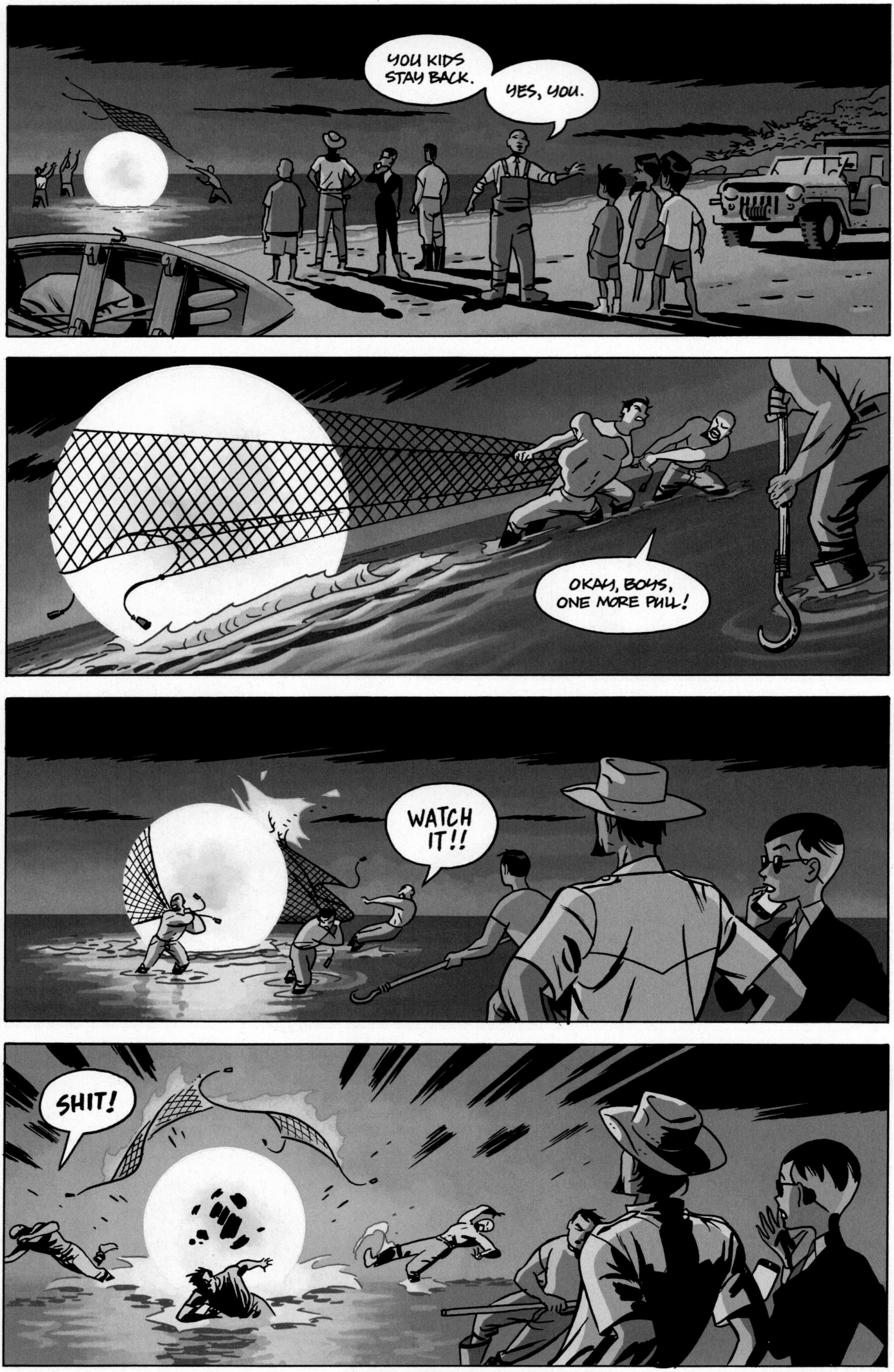
YOU KIDS STAY BACK.
YES, YOU.
OKAY, BOYS, ONE MORE PULL!
WATCH IT!!
SHIT!

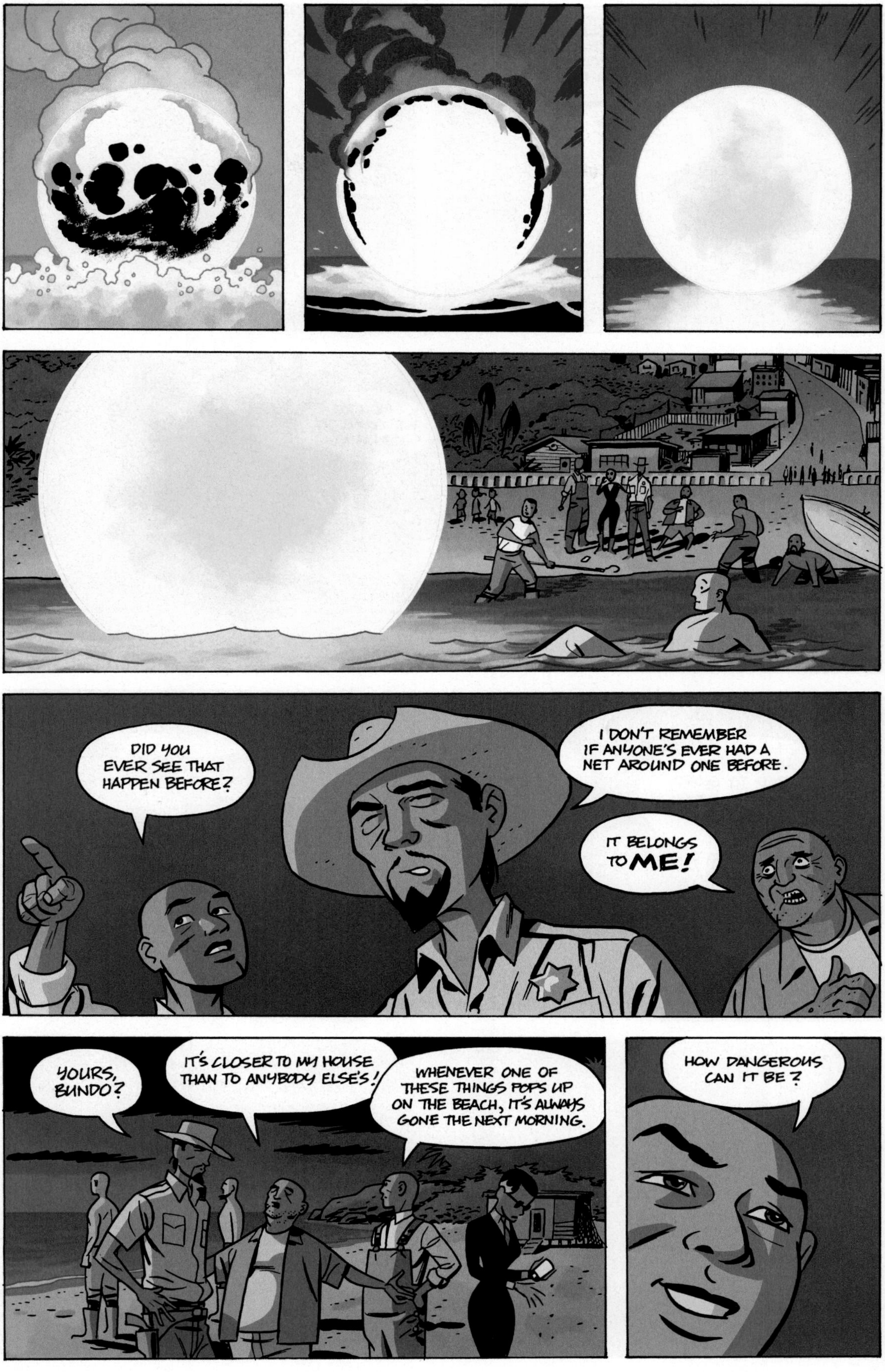
DID YOU EVER SEE THAT HAPPEN BEFORE?
I DON'T REMEMBER IF ANYONE'S EVER HAD A NET AROUND ONE BEFORE.
IT BELONGS TO ME!
YOURS, BUNDO?
IT'S CLOSER TO MY HOUSE THAN TO ANYBODY ELSE'S!
WHENEVER ONE OF THESE THINGS POPS UP ON THE BEACH, IT'S ALWAYS GONE THE NEXT MORNING.
HOW DANGEROUS CAN IT BE?

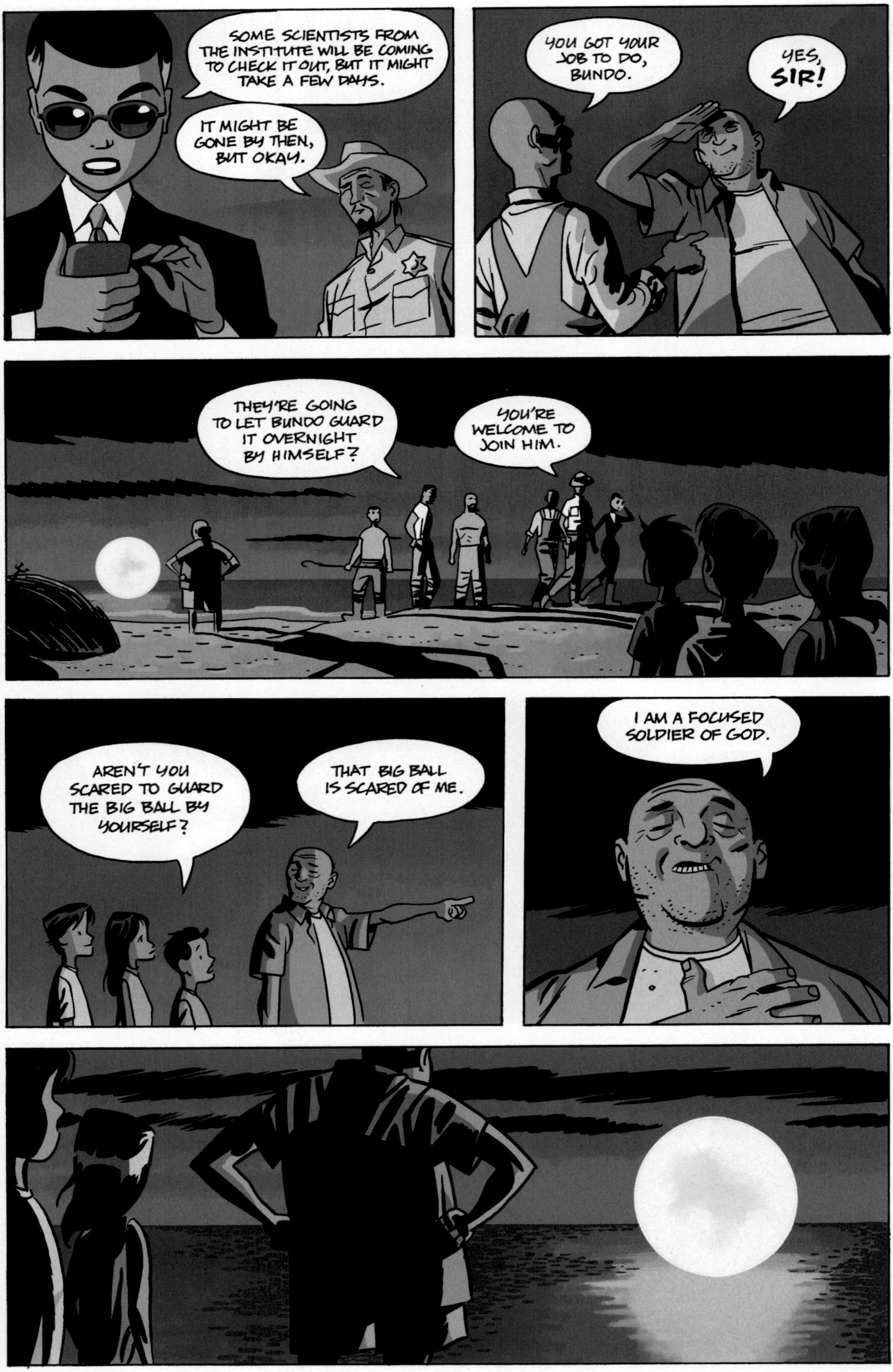

SOME SCIENTISTS FROM THE INSTITUTE WILL BE COMING TO CHECK IT OUT, BUT IT MIGHT TAKE A FEW DAYS.
IT MIGHT BE GONE BY THEN, BUT OKAY.
YOU GOT YOUR JOB TO DO, BUNDO.
YES, SIR!
THEY'RE GOING TO LET BUNDO GUARD IT OVERNIGHT BY HIMSELF?
YOU'RE WELCOME TO JOIN HIM.
AREN'T YOU SCARED TO GUARD THE BIG BALL BY YOURSELF?
THAT BIG BALL IS SCARED OF ME.
I AM A FOCUSED SOLDIER OF GOD.

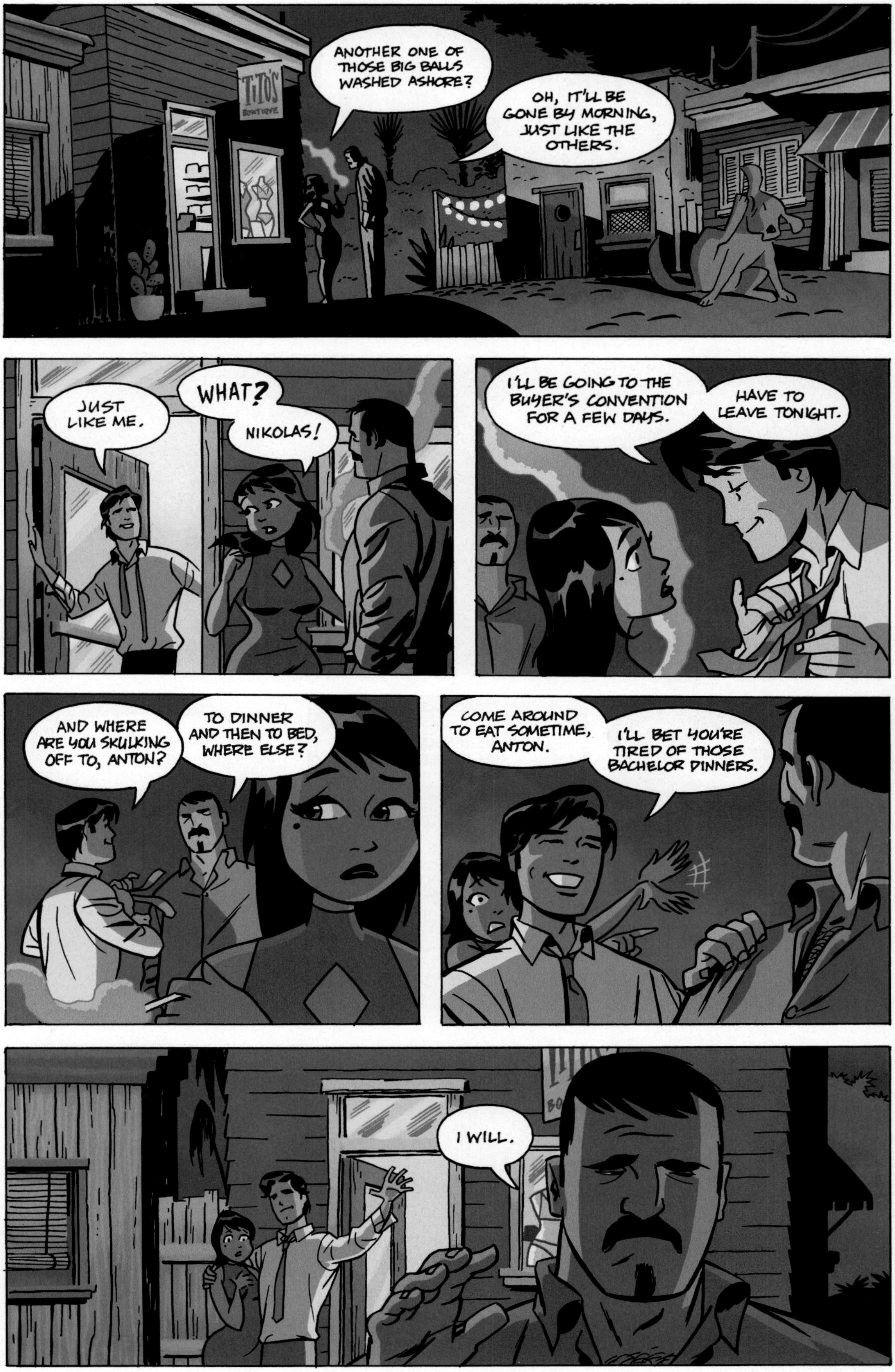
TITO'S
BOUTIQUE
ANOTHER ONE OF THOSE BIG BALLS WASHED ASHORE?
OH, IT'LL BE GONE BY MORNING, JUST LIKE THE OTHERS.
JUST LIKE ME.
WHAT?
NIKOLAS!
I'LL BE GOING TO THE BUYER'S CONVENTION FOR A FEW DAYS.
HAVE TO LEAVE TONIGHT.
AND WHERE ARE YOU SKULKING OFF TO, ANTON?
TO DINNER AND THEN TO BED, WHERE ELSE?
COME AROUND TO EAT SOMETIME, ANTON.
I'LL BET YOU'RE TIRED OF THOSE BACHELOR DINNERS.
I WILL.

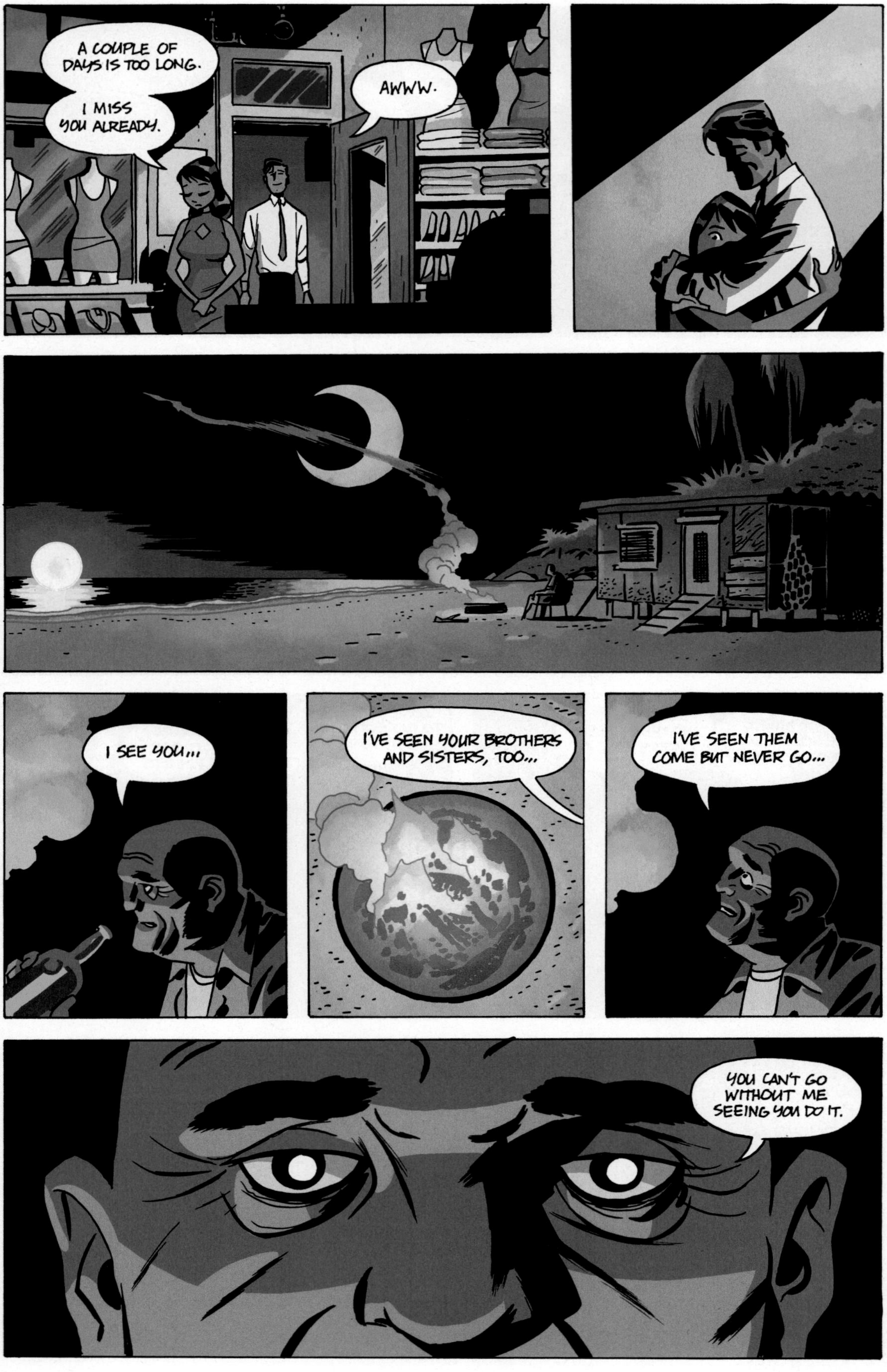
A COUPLE OF DAYS IS TOO LONG.
I MISS YOU ALREADY.
AWWW.
I SEE YOU...
I'VE SEEN YOUR BROTHERS AND SISTERS, TOO...
I'VE SEEN THEM COME BUT NEVER GO...
YOU CAN'T GO WITHOUT ME SEEING YOU DO IT.

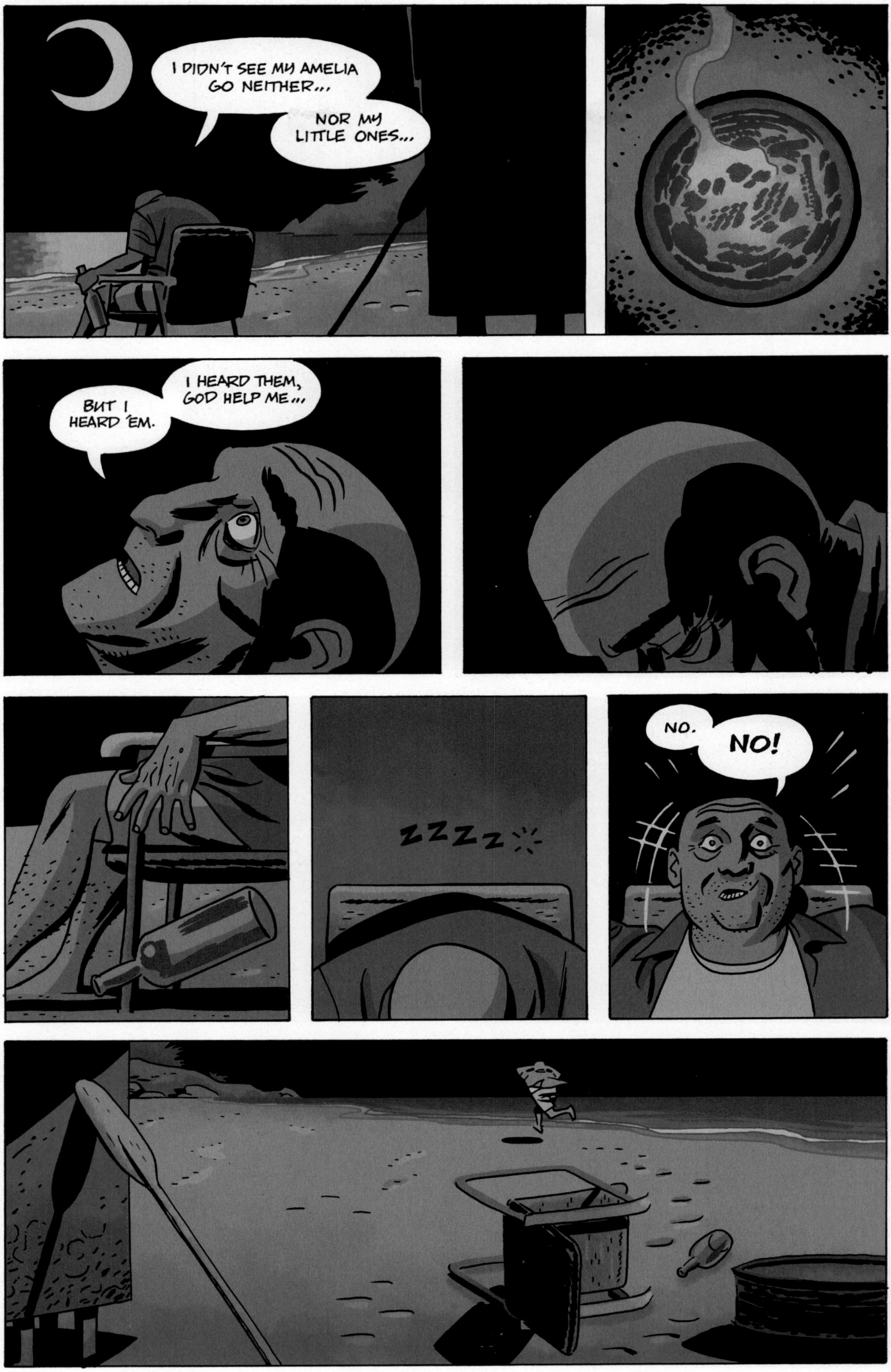
I DIDN'T SEE MY AMELIA GO NEITHER...
NOR MY LITTLE ONES...
BUT I HEARD 'EM.
I HEARD THEM, GOD HELP ME...
ZZZZ
NO.
NO!

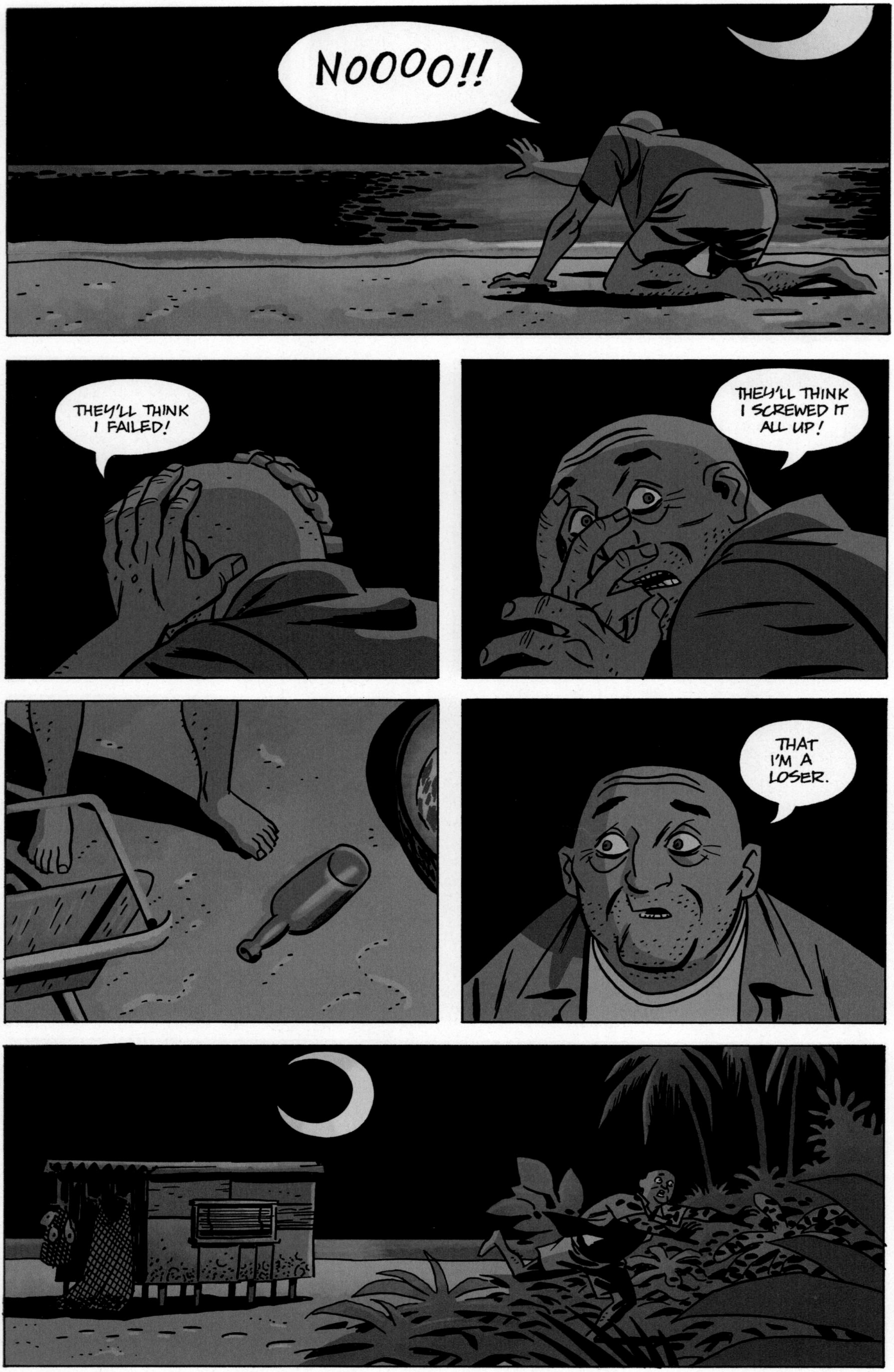
NOOOO!!
THEY'LL THINK I FAILED!
THEY'LL THINK I SCREWED IT ALL UP!
THAT I'M A LOSER.

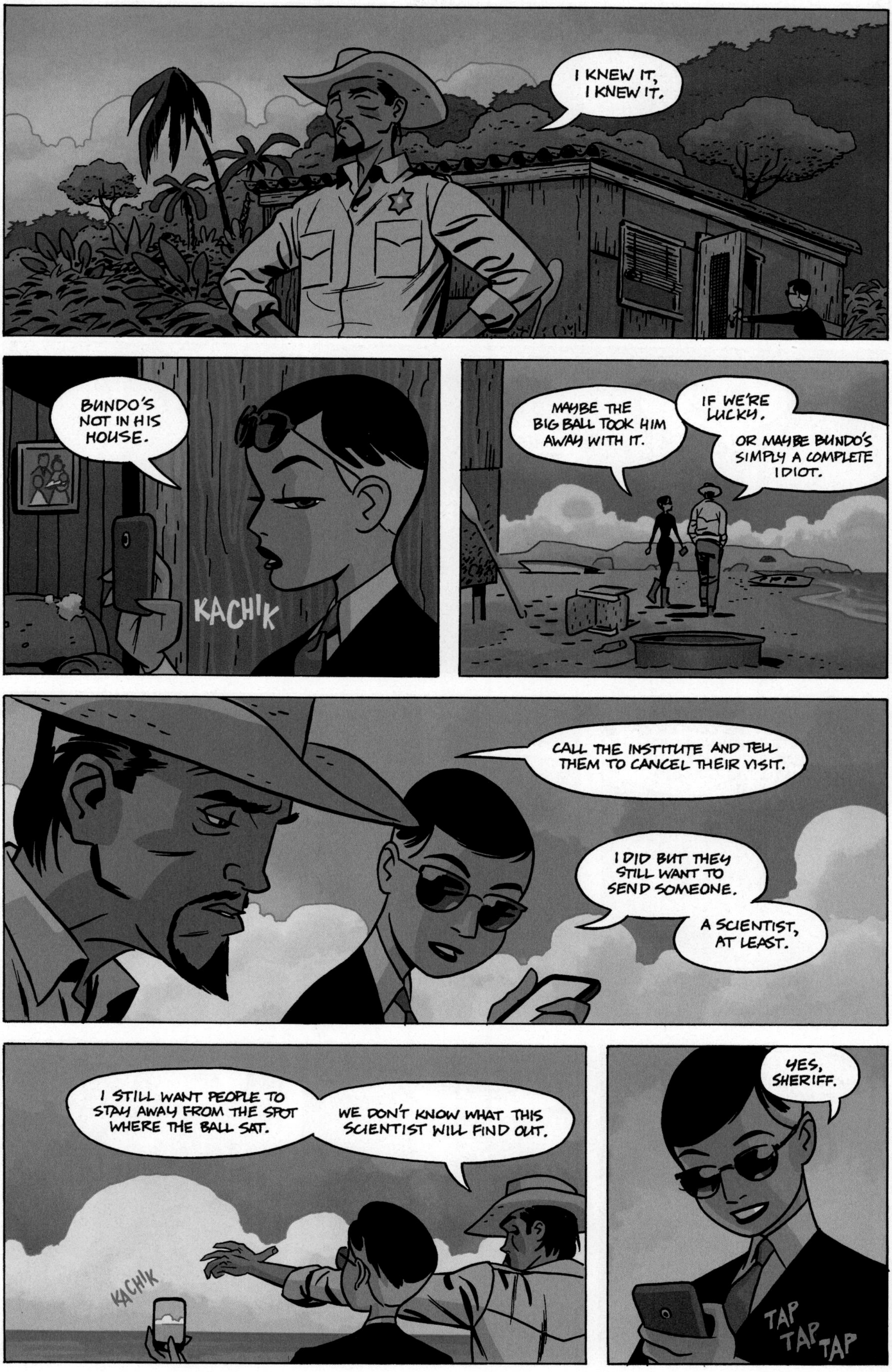
I KNEW IT, I KNEW IT.
BUNDO'S NOT IN HIS HOUSE.
KACHIK
MAYBE THE BIG BALL TOOK HIM AWAY WITH IT.
IF WE'RE LUCKY.
OR MAYBE BUNDO'S SIMPLY A COMPLETE IDIOT.
CALL THE INSTITUTE AND TELL THEM TO CANCEL THEIR VISIT.
I DID BUT THEY STILL WANT TO SEND SOMEONE.
A SCIENTIST, AT LEAST.
I STILL WANT PEOPLE TO STAY AWAY FROM THE SPOT WHERE THE BALL SAT.
WE DON'T KNOW WHAT THIS SCIENTIST WILL FIND OUT.
KACHIK
YES, SHERIFF.
TAP TAP TAP

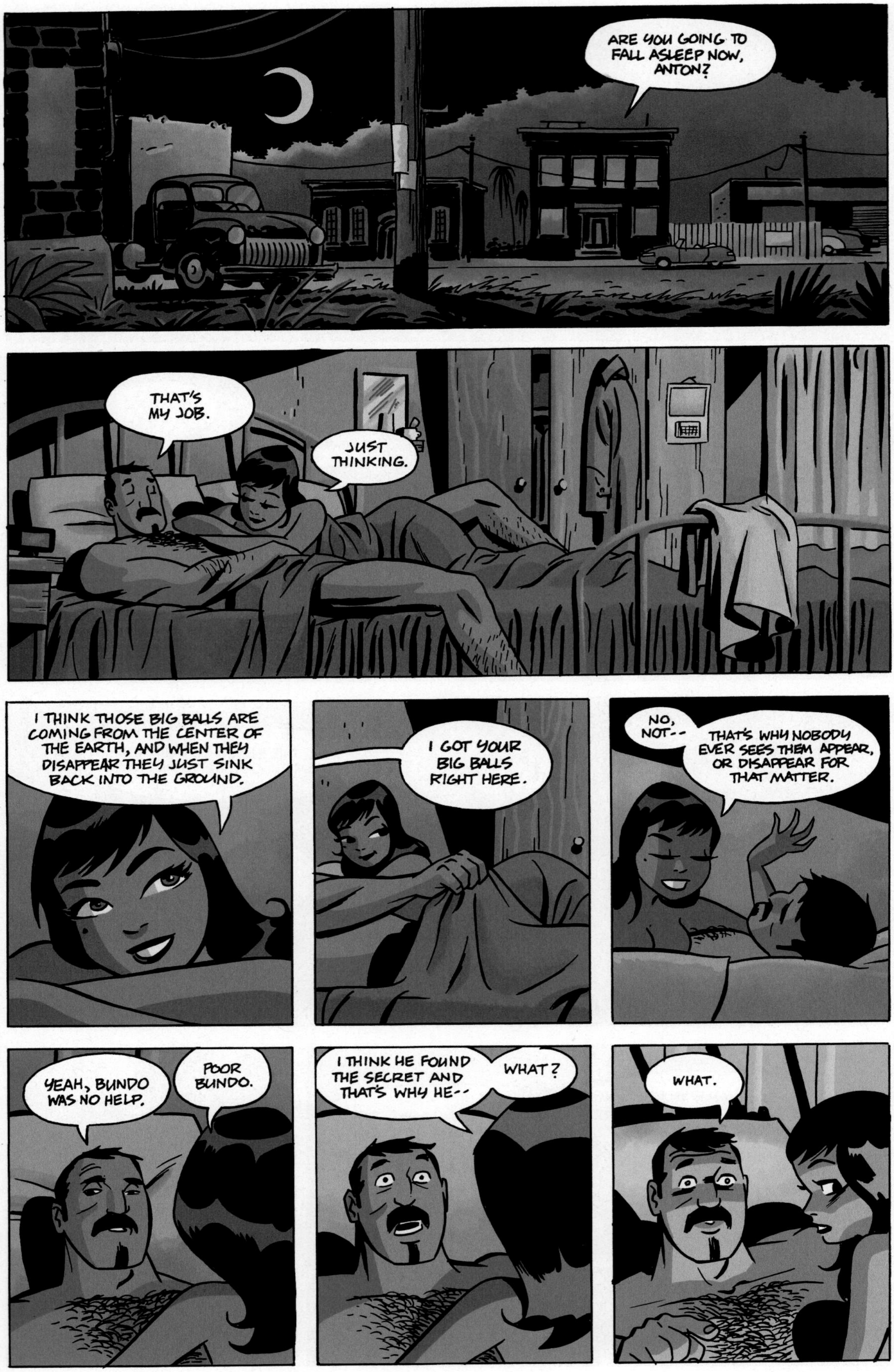
ARE YOU GOING TO FALL ASLEEP NOW, ANTON?
THAT'S MY JOB.
JUST THINKING.
I THINK THOSE BIG BALLS ARE COMING FROM THE CENTER OF THE EARTH, AND WHEN THEY DISAPPEAR THEY JUST SINK BACK INTO THE GROUND.
I GOT YOUR BIG BALLS RIGHT HERE.
NO, NOT--
THAT'S WHY NOBODY EVER SEES THEM APPEAR, OR DISAPPEAR FOR THAT MATTER.
YEAH, BUNDO WAS NO HELP.
POOR BUNDO.
I THINK HE FOUND THE SECRET AND THAT'S WHY HE--
WHAT?
WHAT.

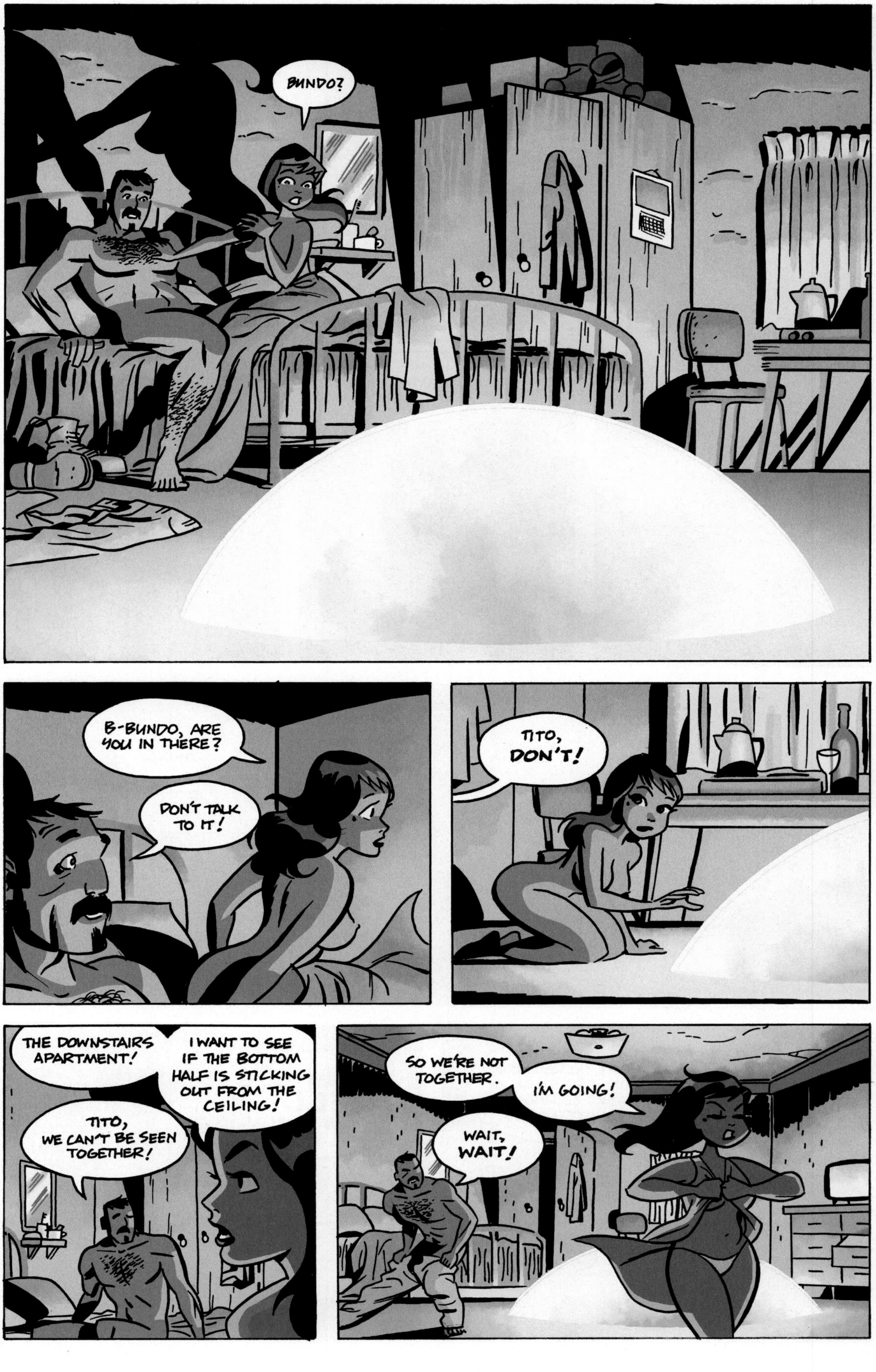
BUNDO?
B-BUNDO, ARE YOU IN THERE?
DON'T TALK TO IT!
TITO, DON'T!
THE DOWNSTAIRS APARTMENT!
I WANT TO SEE IF THE BOTTOM HALF IS STICKING OUT FROM THE CEILING!
TITO, WE CAN'T BE SEEN TOGETHER!
SO WE'RE NOT TOGETHER.
I'M GOING!
WAIT, WAIT!

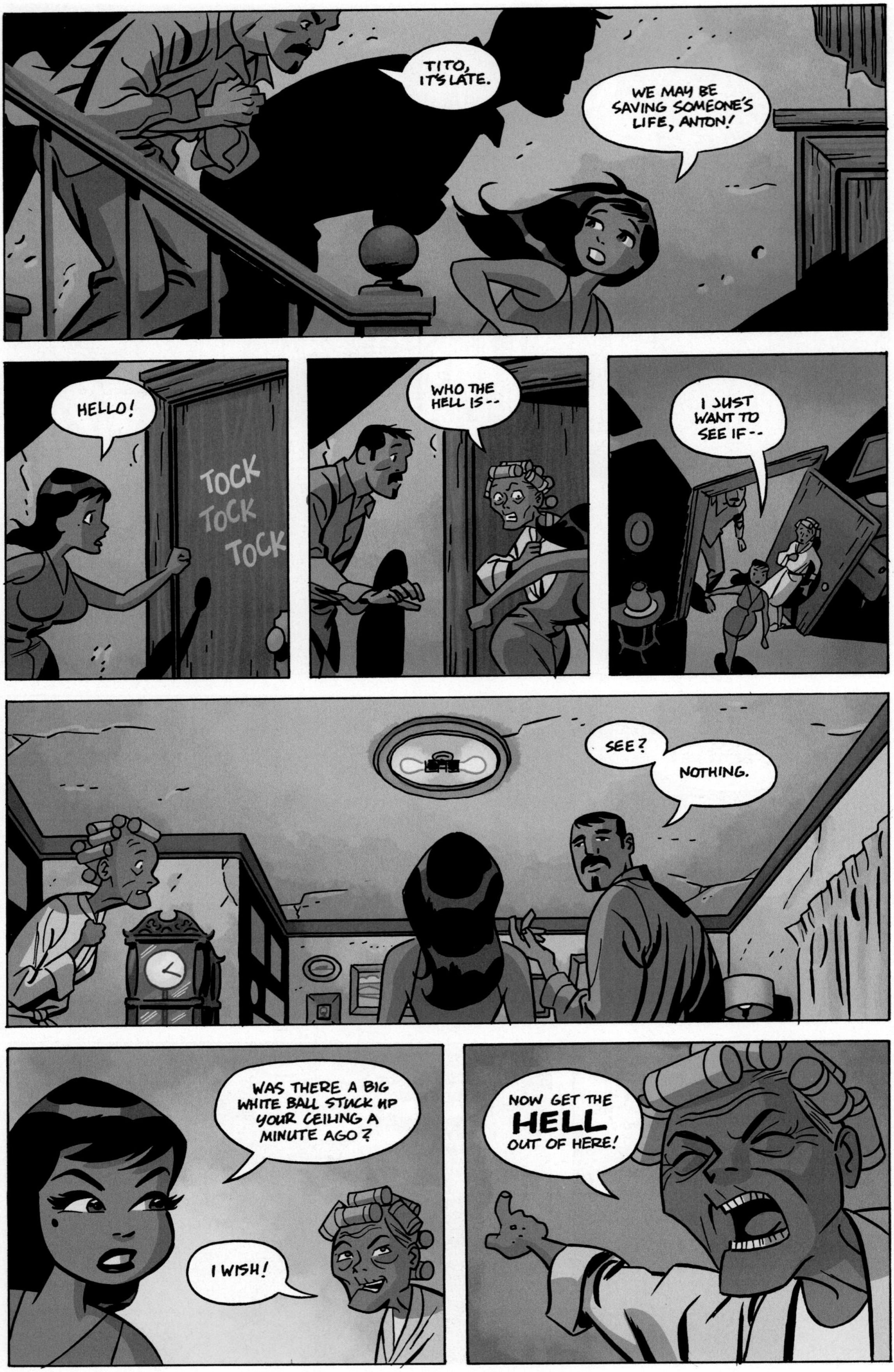
TITO, IT'S LATE.
WE MAY BE SAVING SOMEONE'S LIFE, ANTON!
HELLO!
TOCK TOCK TOCK
WHO THE HELL IS--
I JUST WANT TO SEE IF--
SEE?
NOTHING.
WAS THERE A BIG WHITE BALL STUCK UP YOUR CEILING A MINUTE AGO?
I WISH!
NOW GET THE HELL OUT OF HERE!

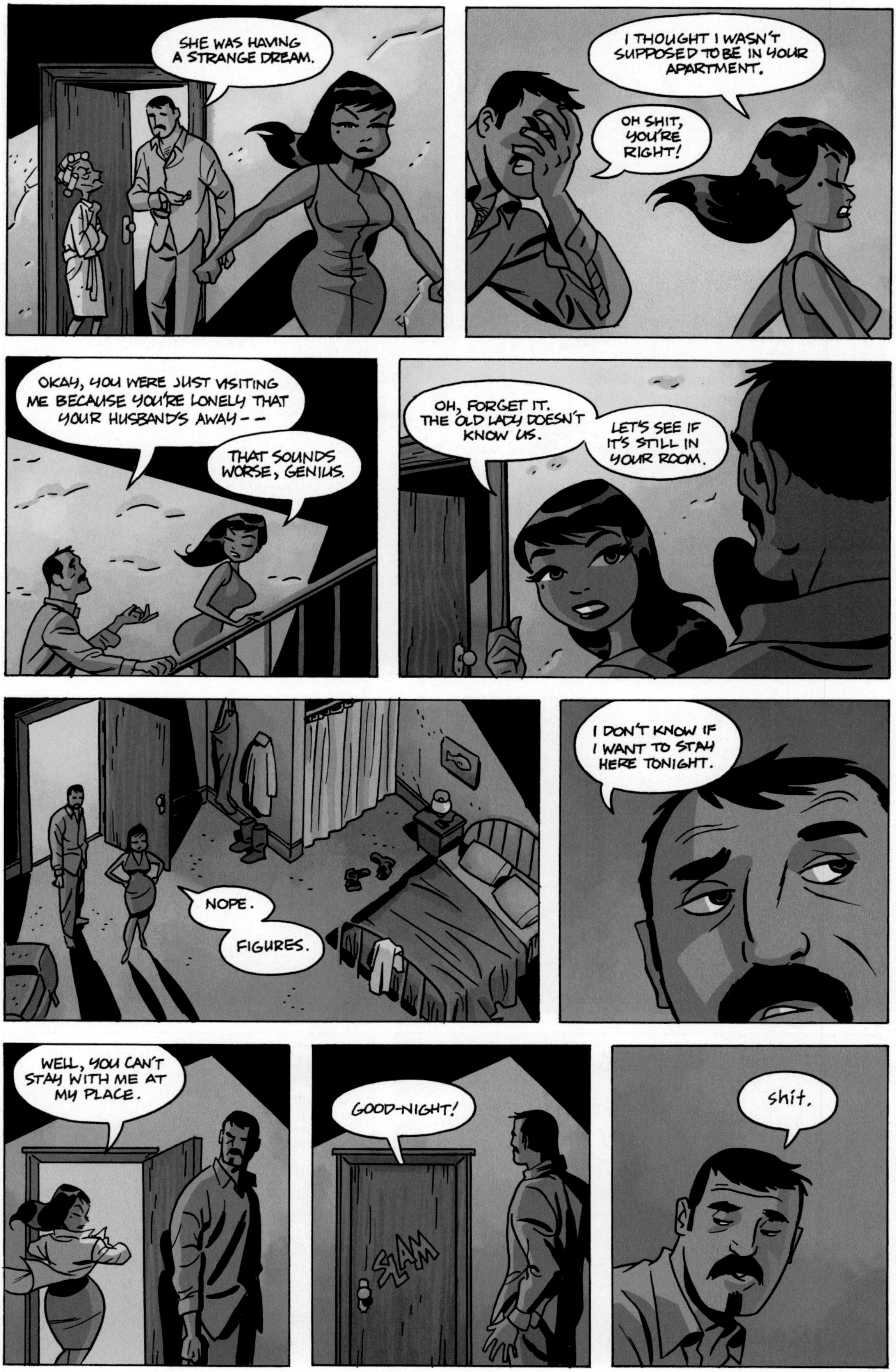
SHE WAS HAVING A STRANGE DREAM.
I THOUGHT I WASN'T SUPPOSED TO BE IN YOUR APARTMENT.
OH SHIT, YOU'RE RIGHT!
OKAY, YOU WERE JUST VISITING ME BECAUSE YOU'RE LONELY THAT YOUR HUSBAND'S AWAY--
THAT SOUNDS WORSE, GENIUS.
OH, FORGET IT. THE OLD LADY DOESN'T KNOW US.
LET'S SEE IF IT'S STILL IN YOUR ROOM.
NOPE.
FIGURES.
I DON'T KNOW IF I WANT TO STAY HERE TONIGHT.
WELL, YOU CAN'T STAY WITH ME AT MY PLACE.
GOOD-NIGHT!
SLAM
shit.

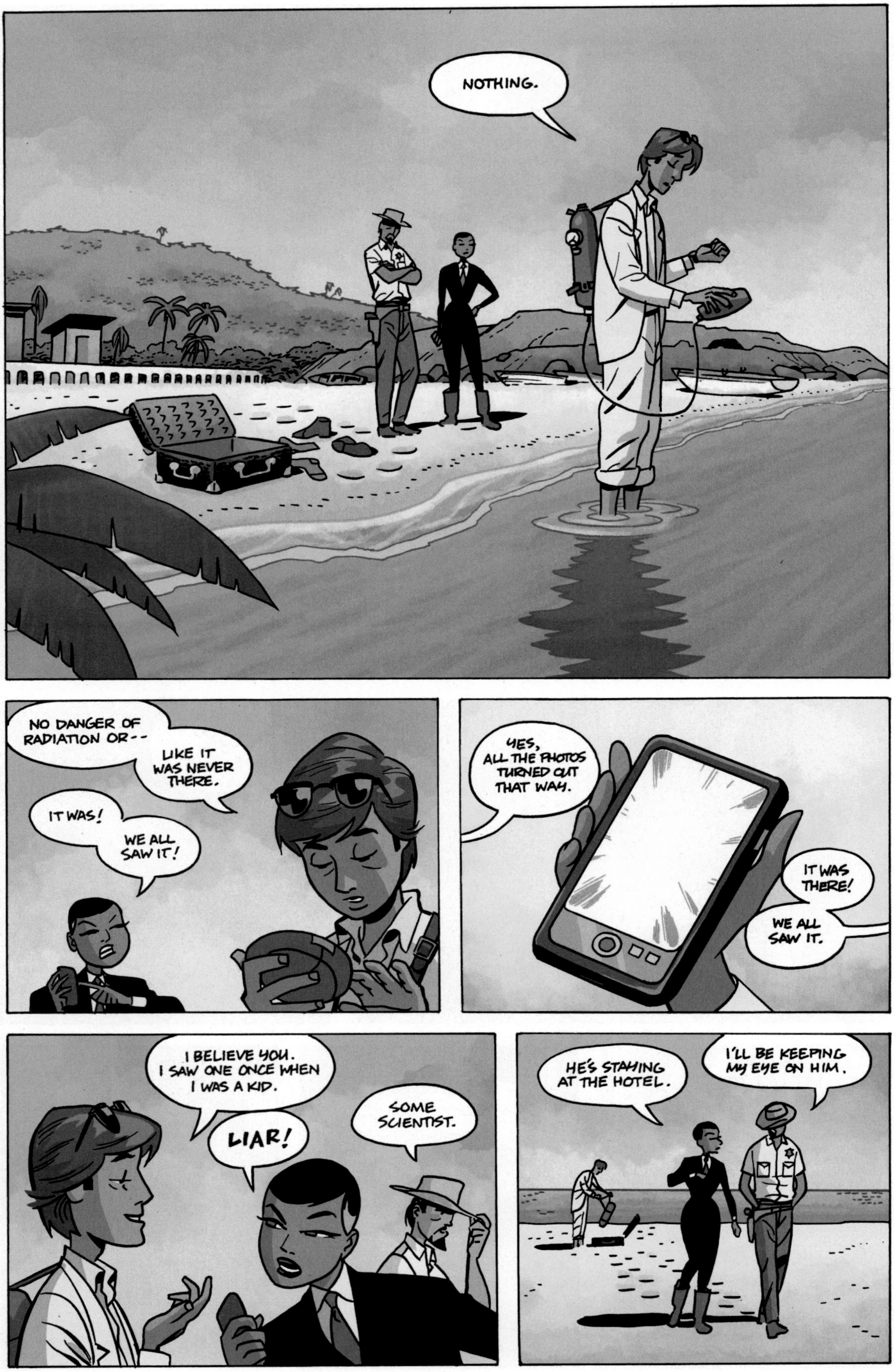
NOTHING.
NO DANGER OF RADIATION OR--
LIKE IT WAS NEVER THERE.
IT WAS!
WE ALL SAW IT!
YES, ALL THE PHOTOS TURNED OUT THAT WAY.
IT WAS THERE!
WE ALL SAW IT.
I BELIEVE YOU. I SAW ONE ONCE WHEN I WAS A KID.
LIAR!
SOME SCIENTIST.
HE'S STAYING AT THE HOTEL.
I'LL BE KEEPING MY EYE ON HIM.

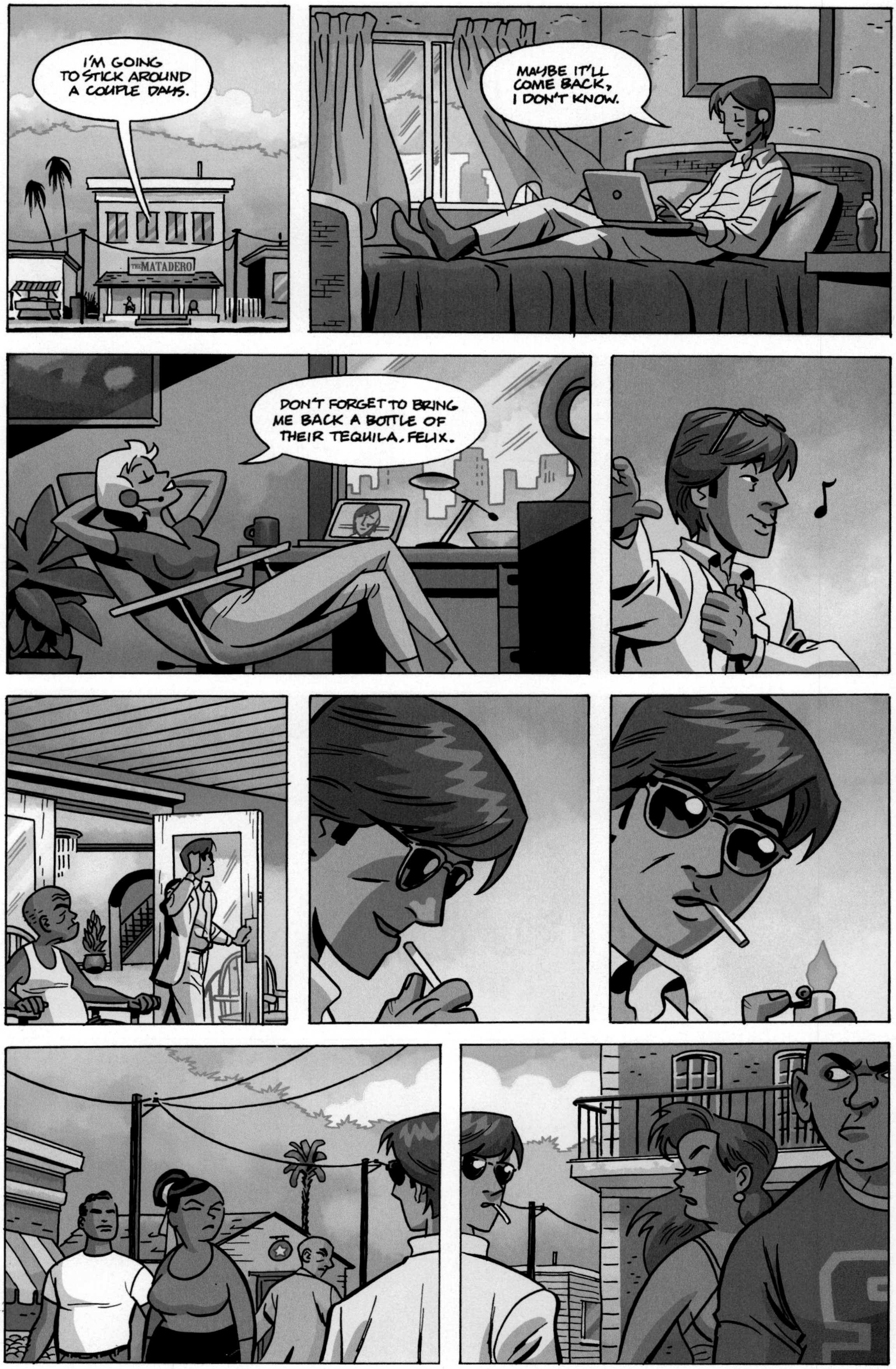
I'M GOING TO STICK AROUND A COUPLE DAYS.
THE MATADERO
MAYBE IT'LL COME BACK, I DON'T KNOW.
DON'T FORGET TO BRING ME BACK A BOTTLE OF THEIR TEQUILA, FELIX.

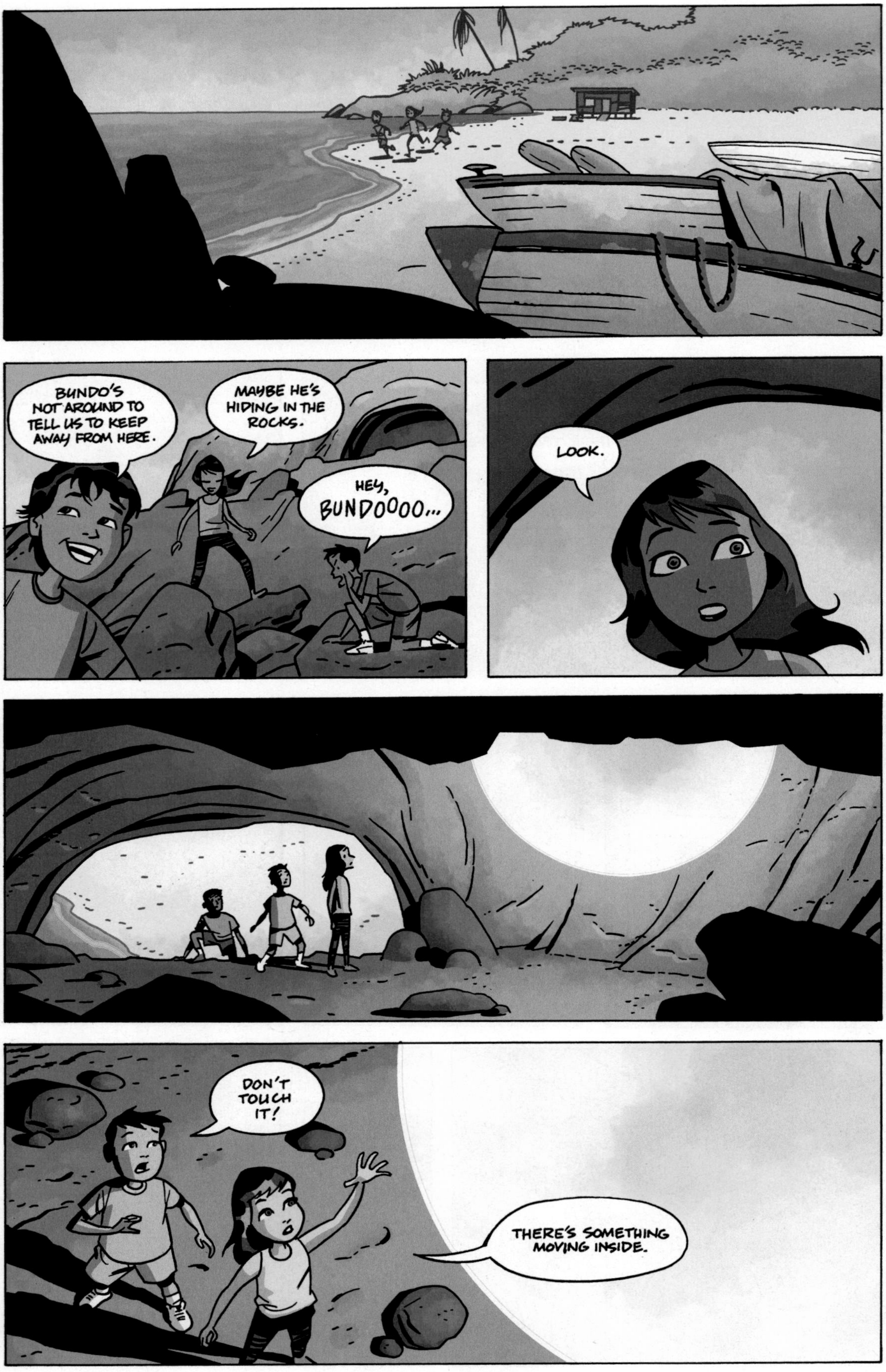
BUNDO'S NOT AROUND TO TELL US TO KEEP AWAY FROM HERE.
MAYBE HE'S HIDING IN THE ROCKS.
HEY, BUNDOOOO...
LOOK.
DON'T TOUCH IT!
THERE'S SOMETHING MOVING INSIDE.

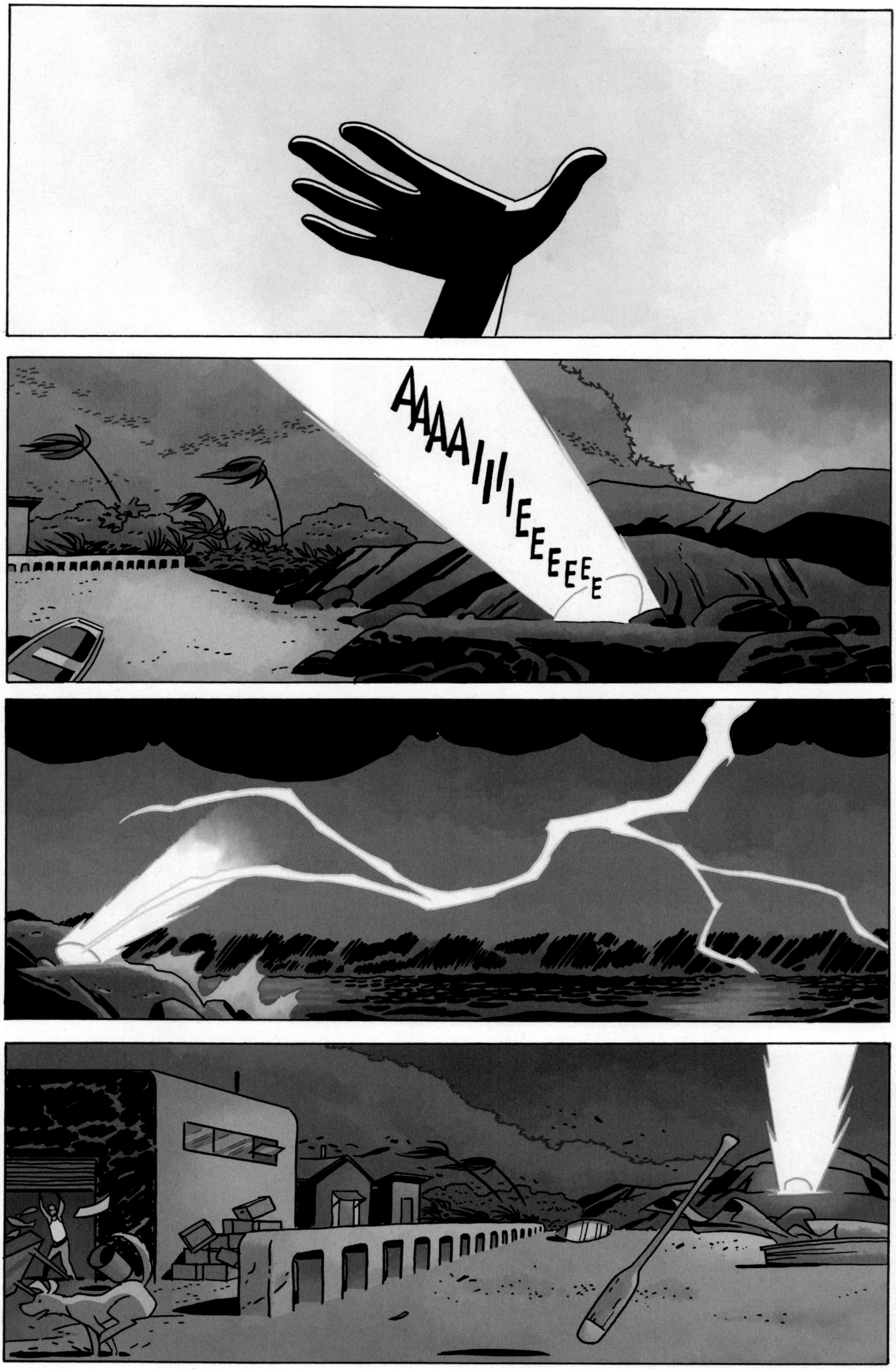
AAAAIIIIEEEEEEE

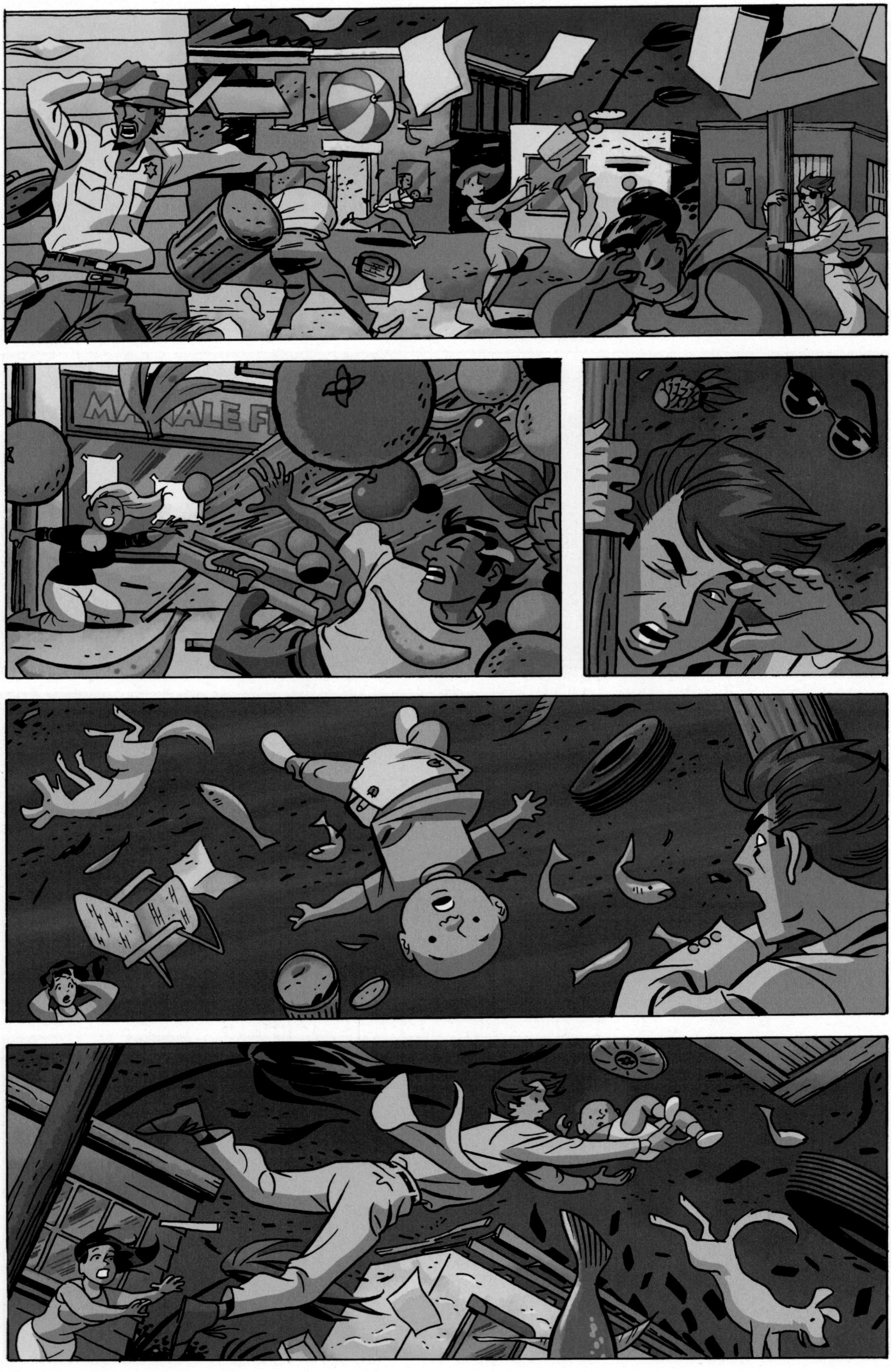

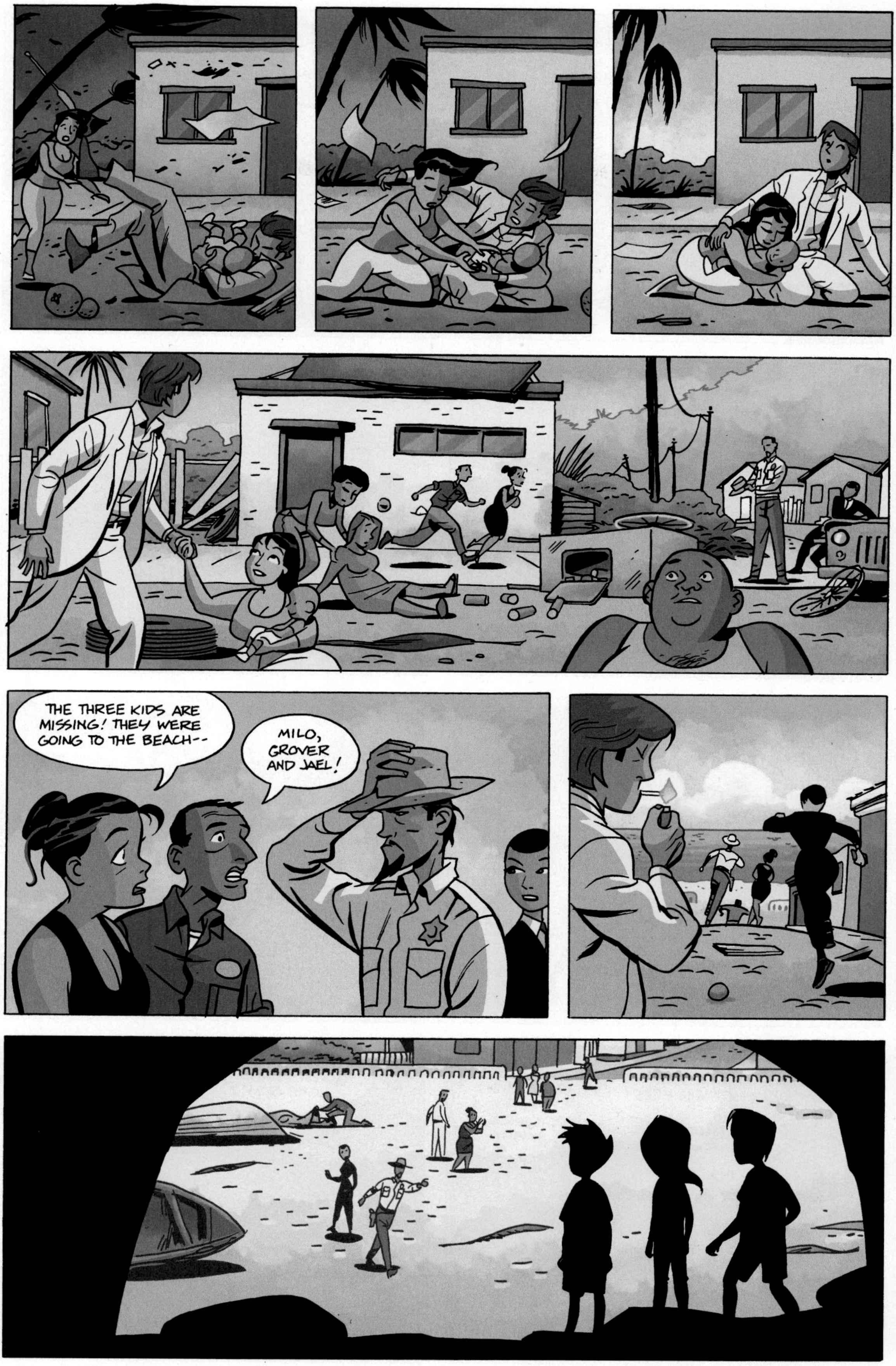
THE THREE KIDS ARE MISSING! THEY WERE GOING TO THE BEACH--
MILO, GROVER AND JAEL!

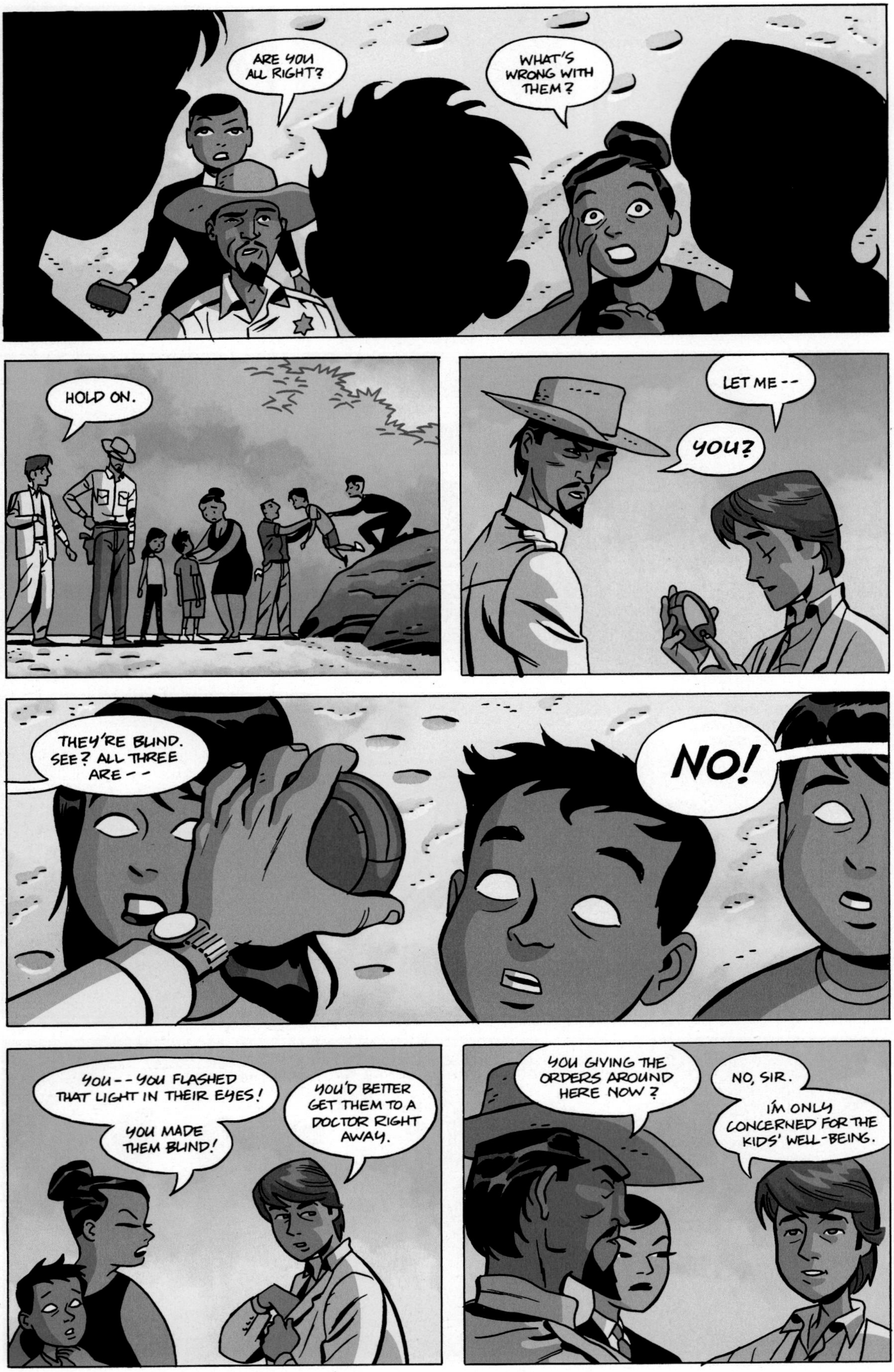
ARE YOU ALL RIGHT?
WHAT'S WRONG WITH THEM?
HOLD ON.
LET ME --
YOU?
THEY'RE BLIND. SEE? ALL THREE ARE --
NO!
YOU -- YOU FLASHED THAT LIGHT IN THEIR EYES!
YOU MADE THEM BLIND!
YOU'D BETTER GET THEM TO A DOCTOR RIGHT AWAY.
YOU GIVING THE ORDERS AROUND HERE NOW?
NO, SIR.
I'M ONLY CONCERNED FOR THE KIDS' WELL-BEING.

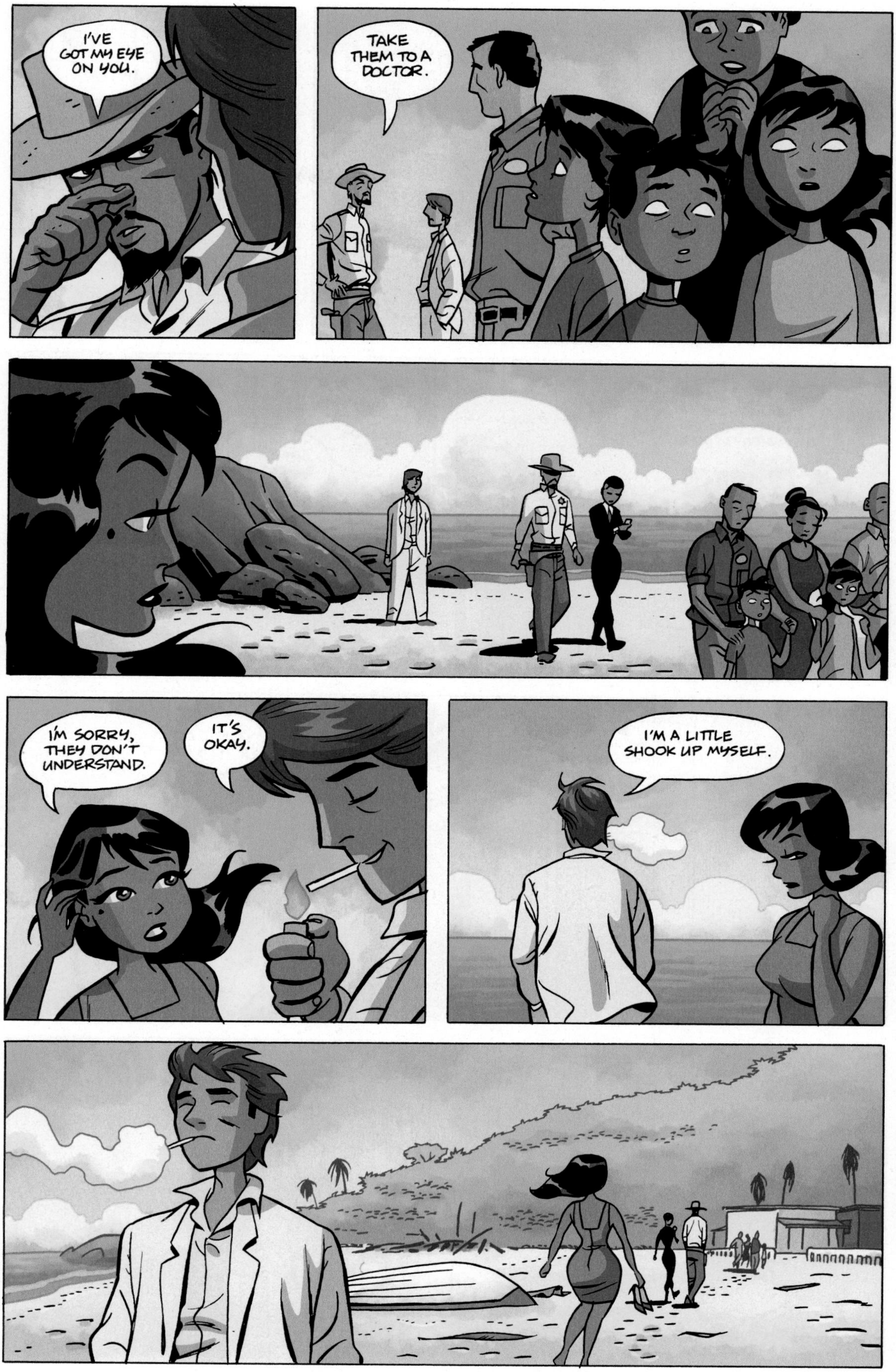
I'VE GOT MY EYE ON YOU.
TAKE THEM TO A DOCTOR.
I'M SORRY, THEY DON'T UNDERSTAND.
IT'S OKAY.
I'M A LITTLE SHOOK UP MYSELF.

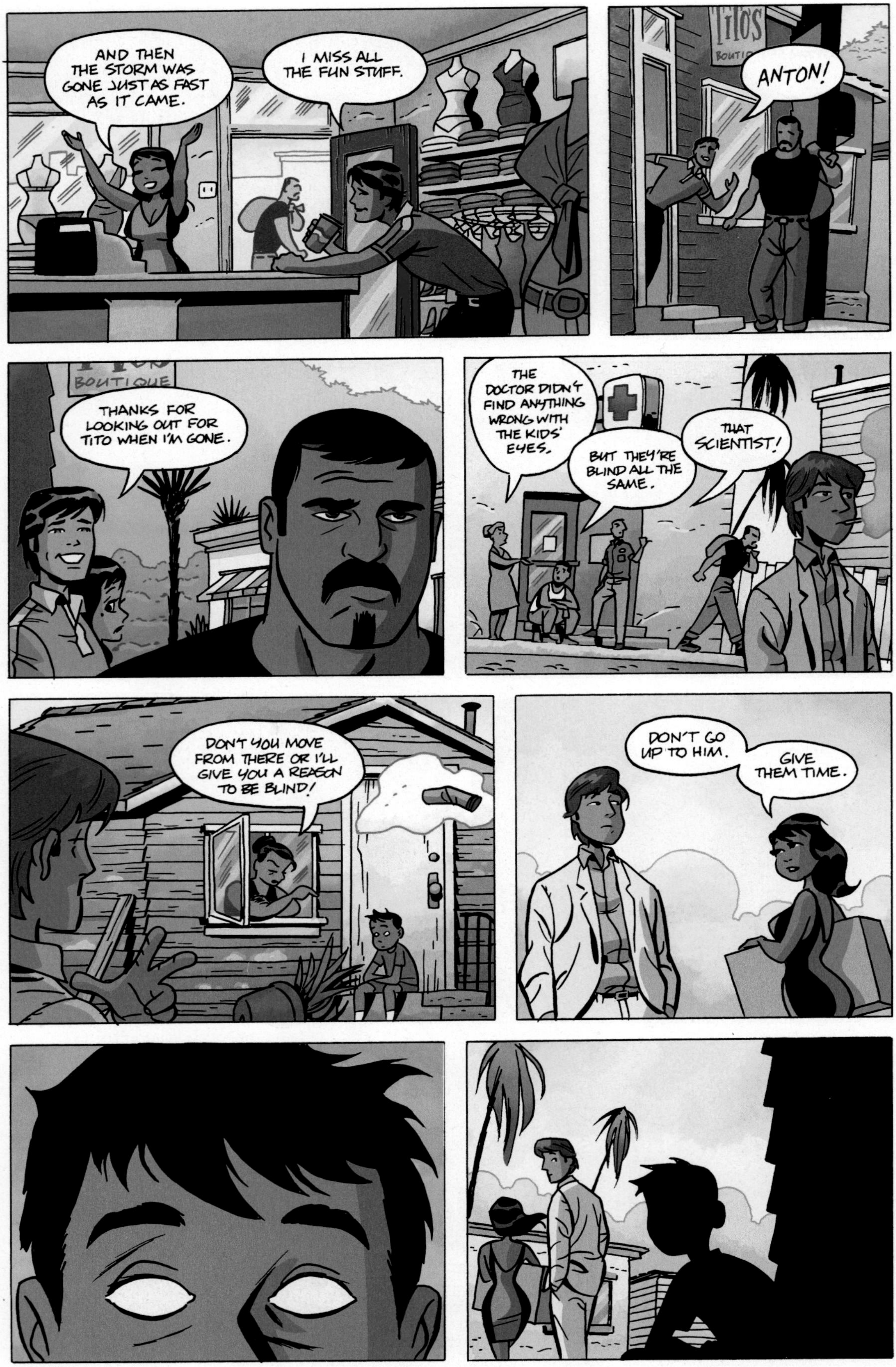
AND THEN THE STORM WAS GONE JUST AS FAST AS IT CAME.
I MISS ALL THE FUN STUFF.
TITO'S BOUTIQUE
ANTON!
BOUTIQUE
THANKS FOR LOOKING OUT FOR TITO WHEN I'M GONE.
THE DOCTOR DIDN'T FIND ANYTHING WRONG WITH THE KIDS' EYES.
BUT THEY'RE BLIND ALL THE SAME.
THAT SCIENTIST!
DON'T YOU MOVE FROM THERE OR I'LL GIVE YOU A REASON TO BE BLIND!
DON'T GO UP TO HIM.
GIVE THEM TIME.

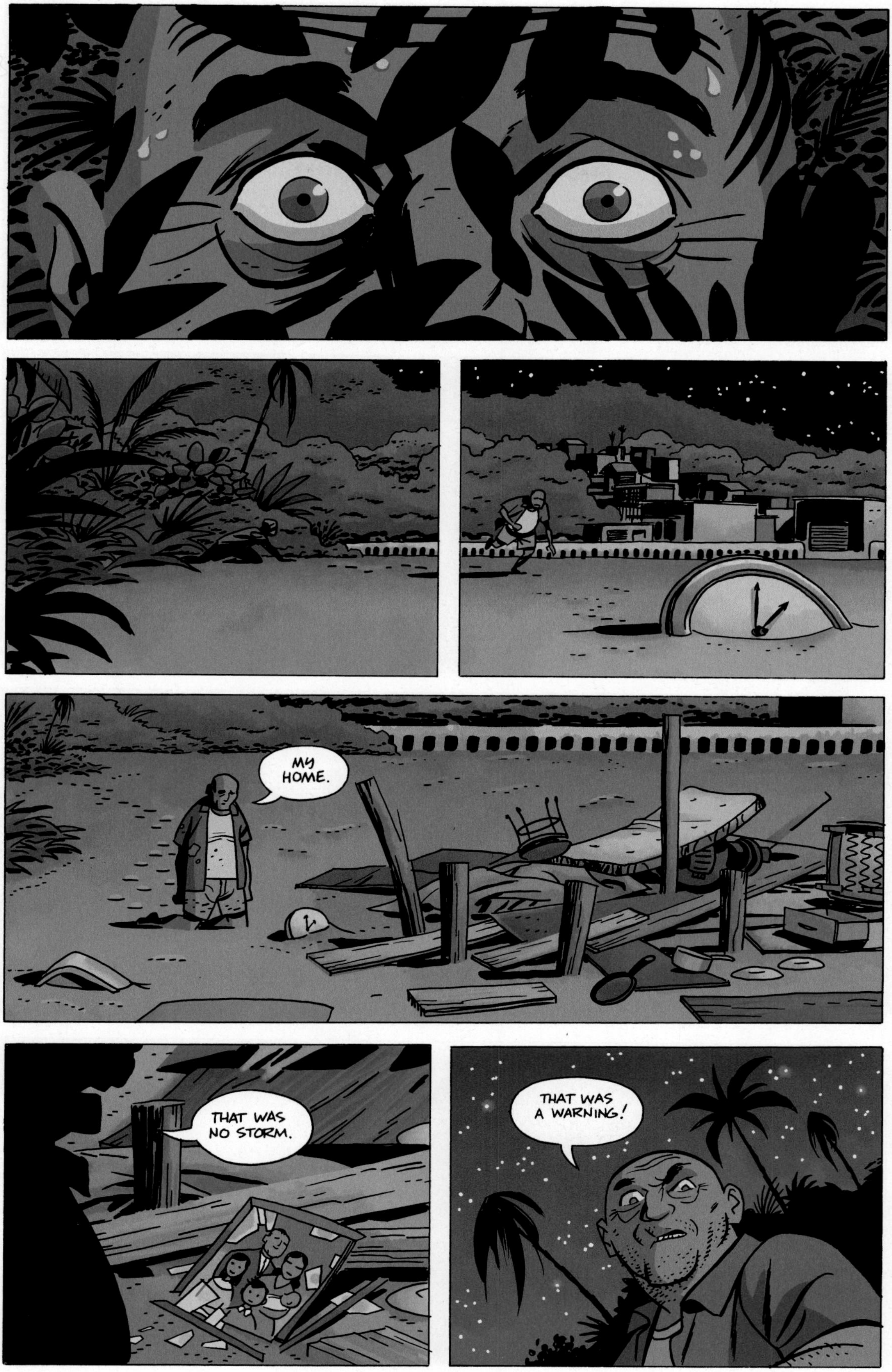
MY HOME.
THAT WAS NO STORM.
THAT WAS A WARNING!

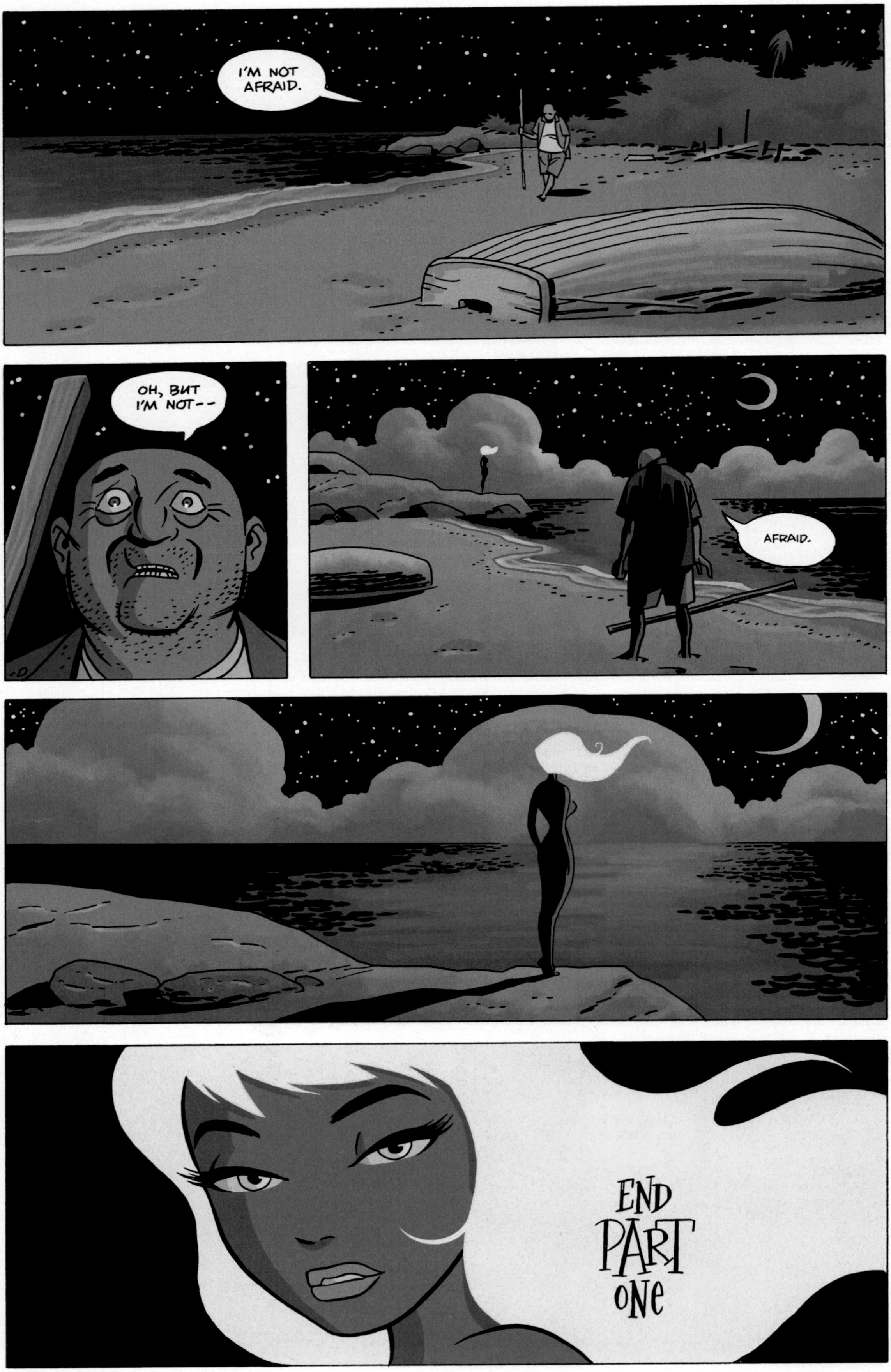
I'M NOT AFRAID.
OH, BUT I'M NOT--
AFRAID.
END PART ONE

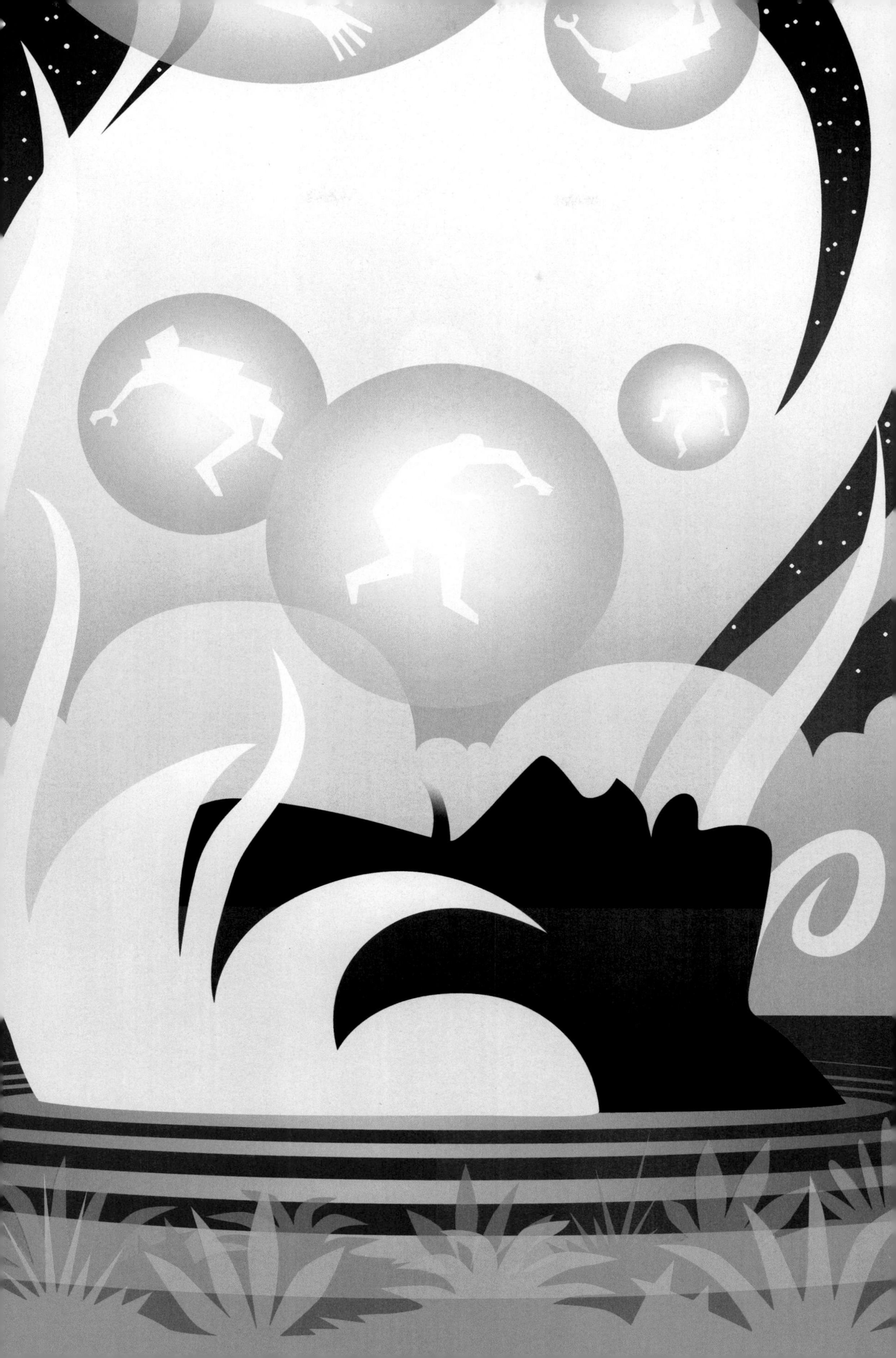

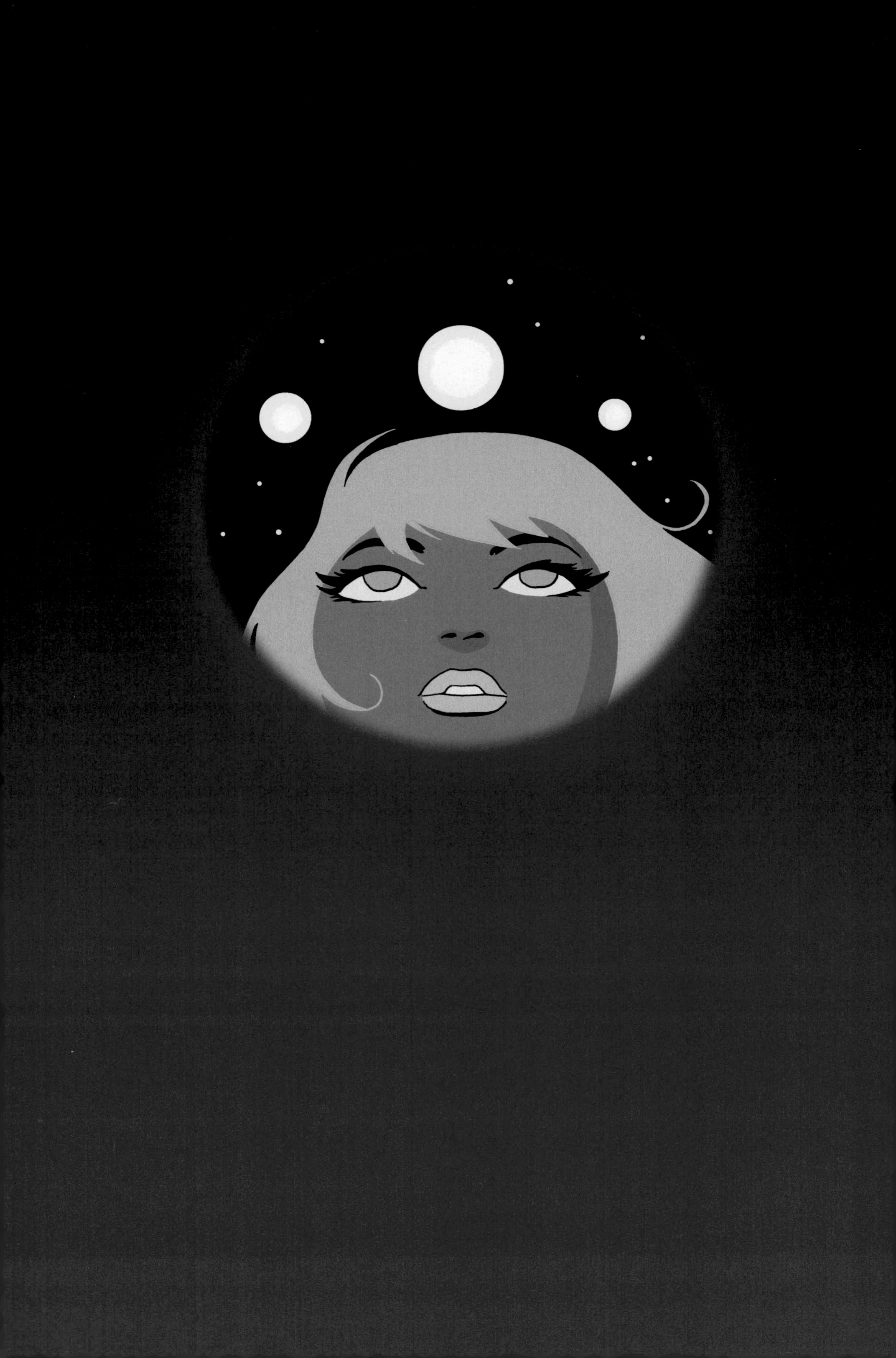

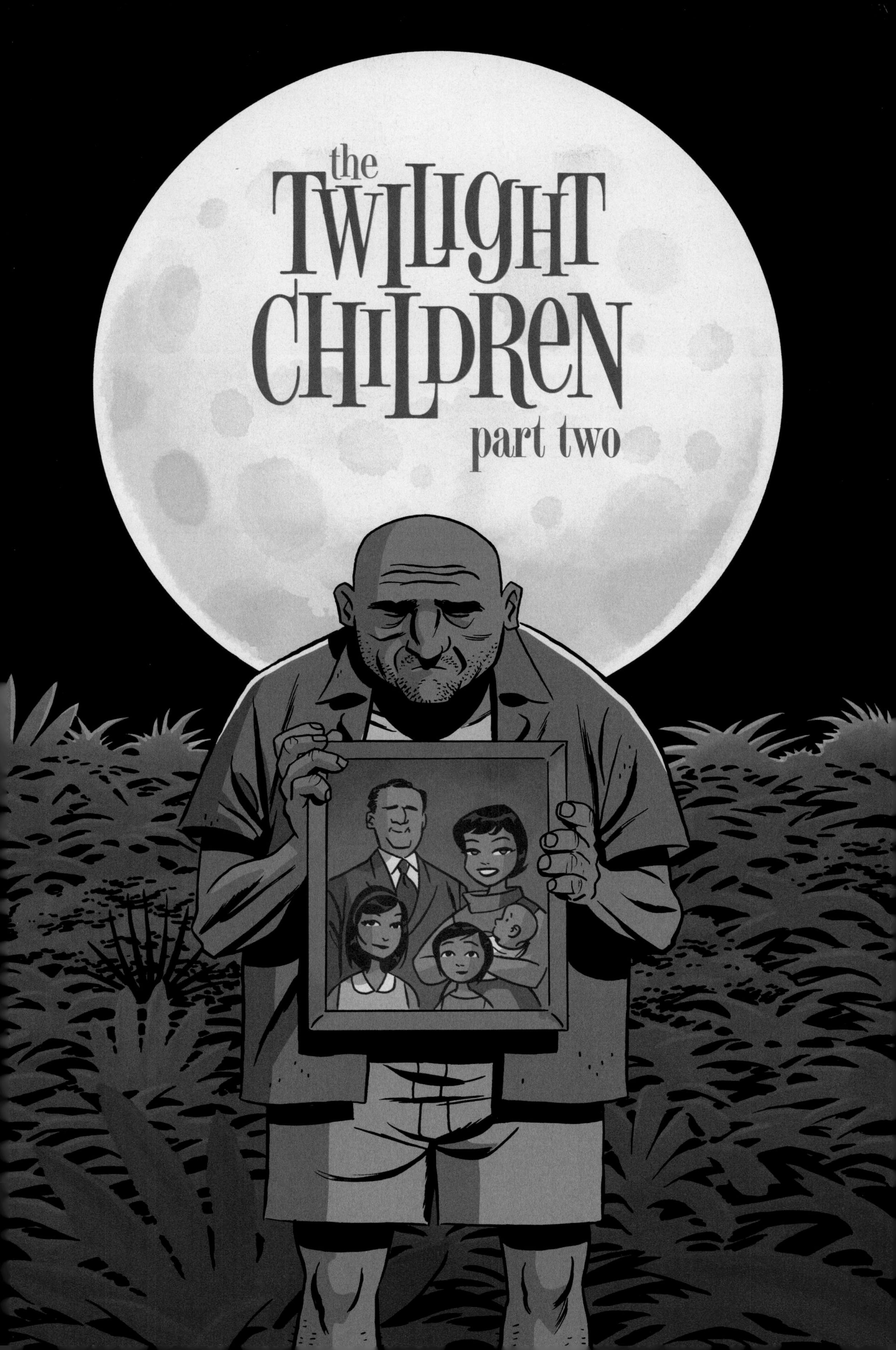
the TWILIGHT CHILDREN
part two

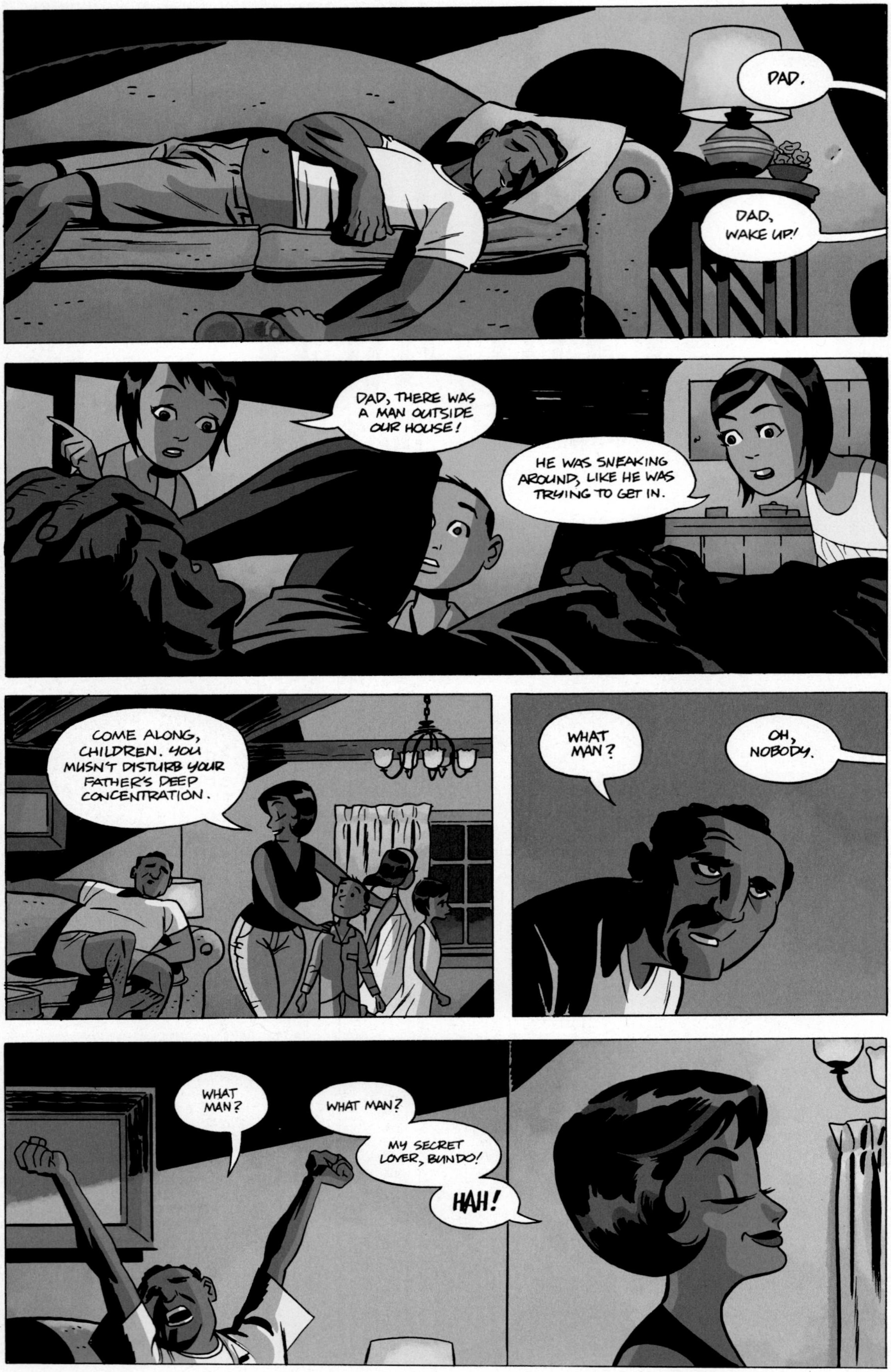
DAD.
DAD, WAKE UP!
DAD, THERE WAS A MAN OUTSIDE OUR HOUSE!
HE WAS SNEAKING AROUND, LIKE HE WAS TRYING TO GET IN.
COME ALONG, CHILDREN. YOU MUSN'T DISTURB YOUR FATHER'S DEEP CONCENTRATION.
WHAT MAN?
OH, NOBODY.
WHAT MAN?
WHAT MAN?
MY SECRET LOVER, BUNDO!
HAH!

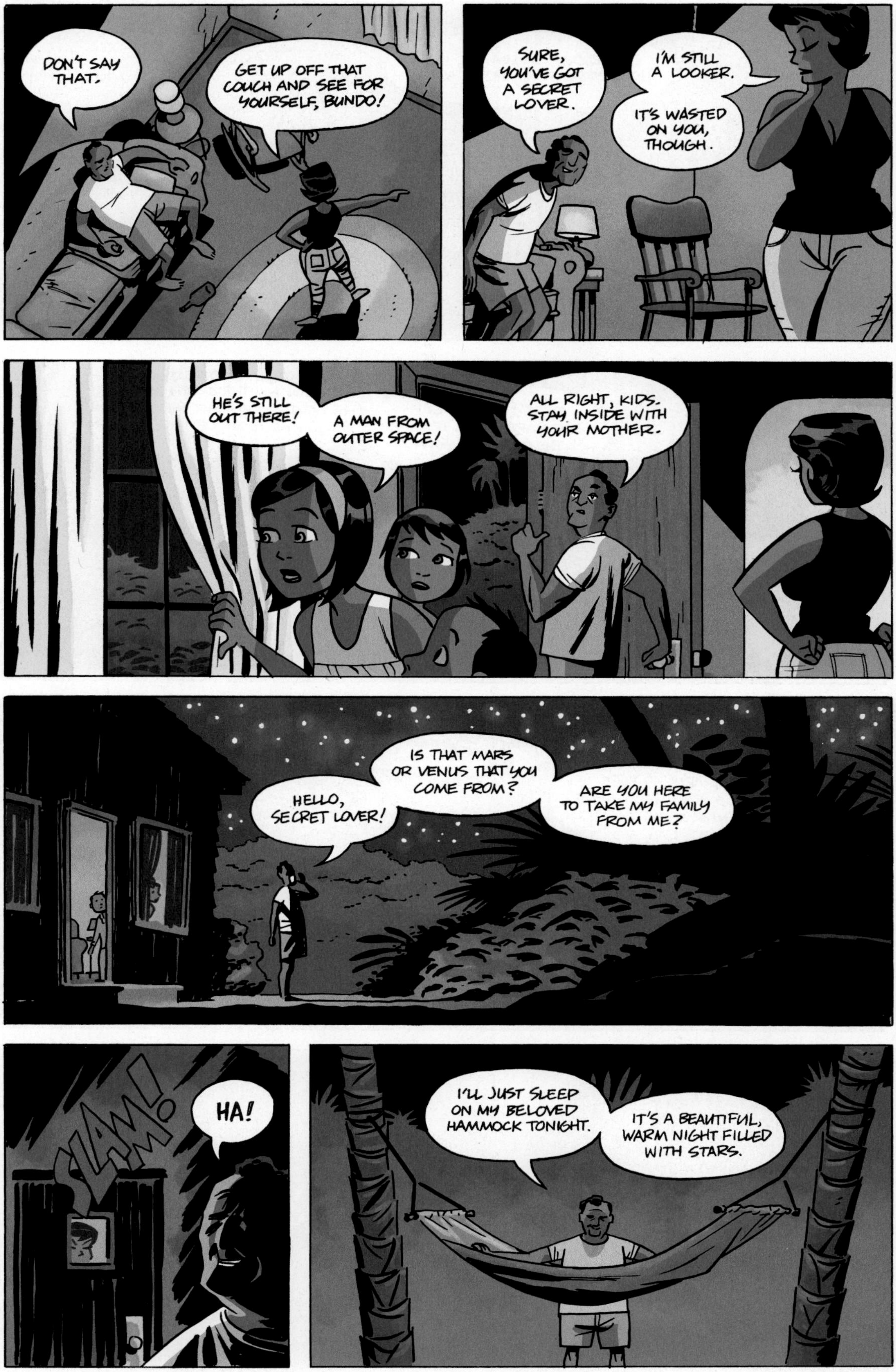
DON'T SAY THAT.
GET UP OFF THAT COUCH AND SEE FOR YOURSELF, BUNDO!
SURE, YOU'VE GOT A SECRET LOVER.
I'M STILL A LOOKER.
IT'S WASTED ON YOU, THOUGH.
HE'S STILL OUT THERE!
A MAN FROM OUTER SPACE!
ALL RIGHT, KIDS. STAY INSIDE WITH YOUR MOTHER.
HELLO, SECRET LOVER!
IS THAT MARS OR VENUS THAT YOU COME FROM?
ARE YOU HERE TO TAKE MY FAMILY FROM ME?
SLAM!
HA!
I'LL JUST SLEEP ON MY BELOVED HAMMOCK TONIGHT.
IT'S A BEAUTIFUL, WARM NIGHT FILLED WITH STARS.

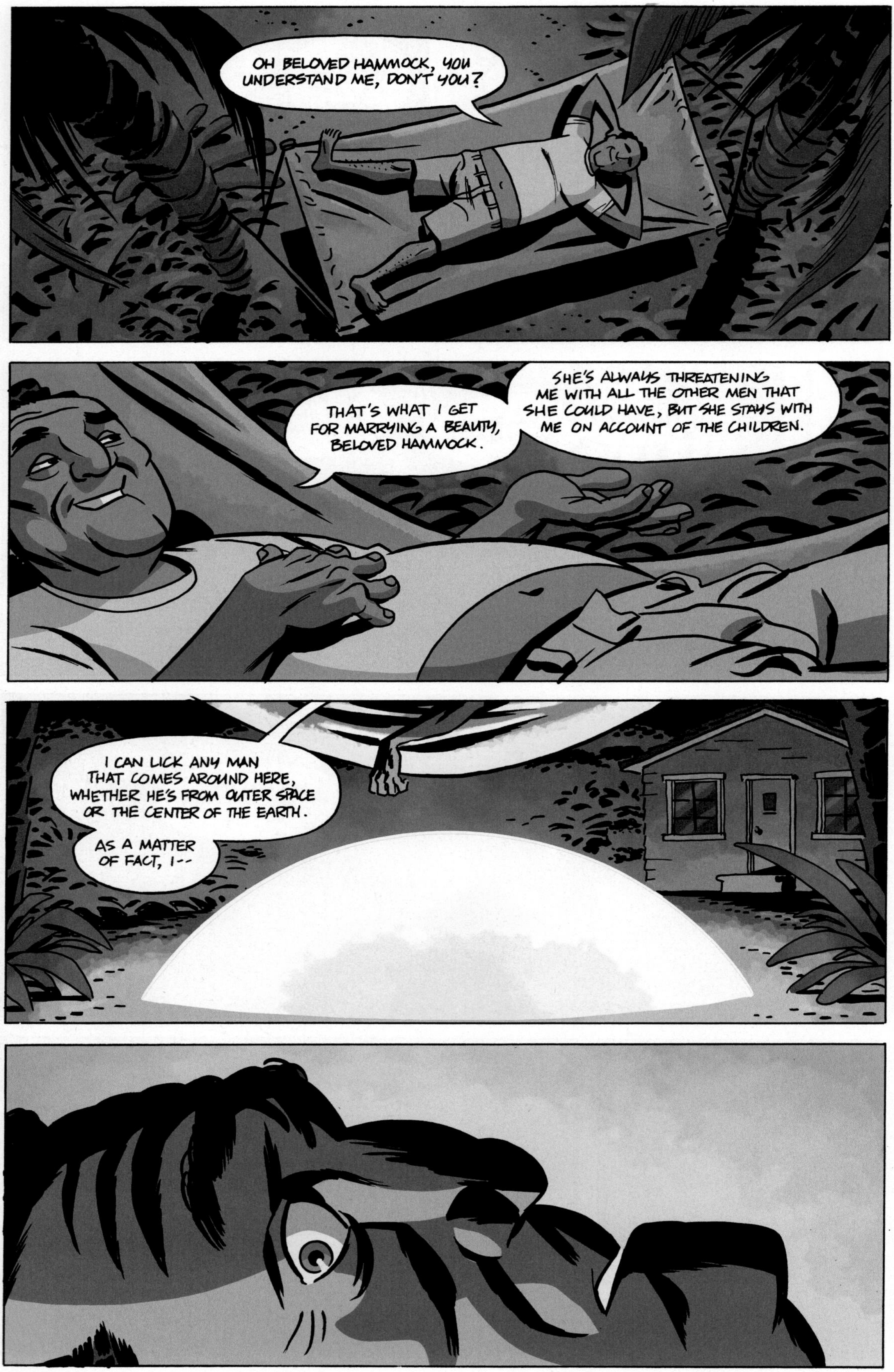
OH BELOVED HAMMOCK, YOU UNDERSTAND ME, DON'T YOU?
THAT'S WHAT I GET FOR MARRYING A BEAUTY, BELOVED HAMMOCK.
SHE'S ALWAYS THREATENING ME WITH ALL THE OTHER MEN THAT SHE COULD HAVE, BUT SHE STAYS WITH ME ON ACCOUNT OF THE CHILDREN.
I CAN LICK ANY MAN THAT COMES AROUND HERE, WHETHER HE'S FROM OUTER SPACE OR THE CENTER OF THE EARTH.
AS A MATTER OF FACT, I--

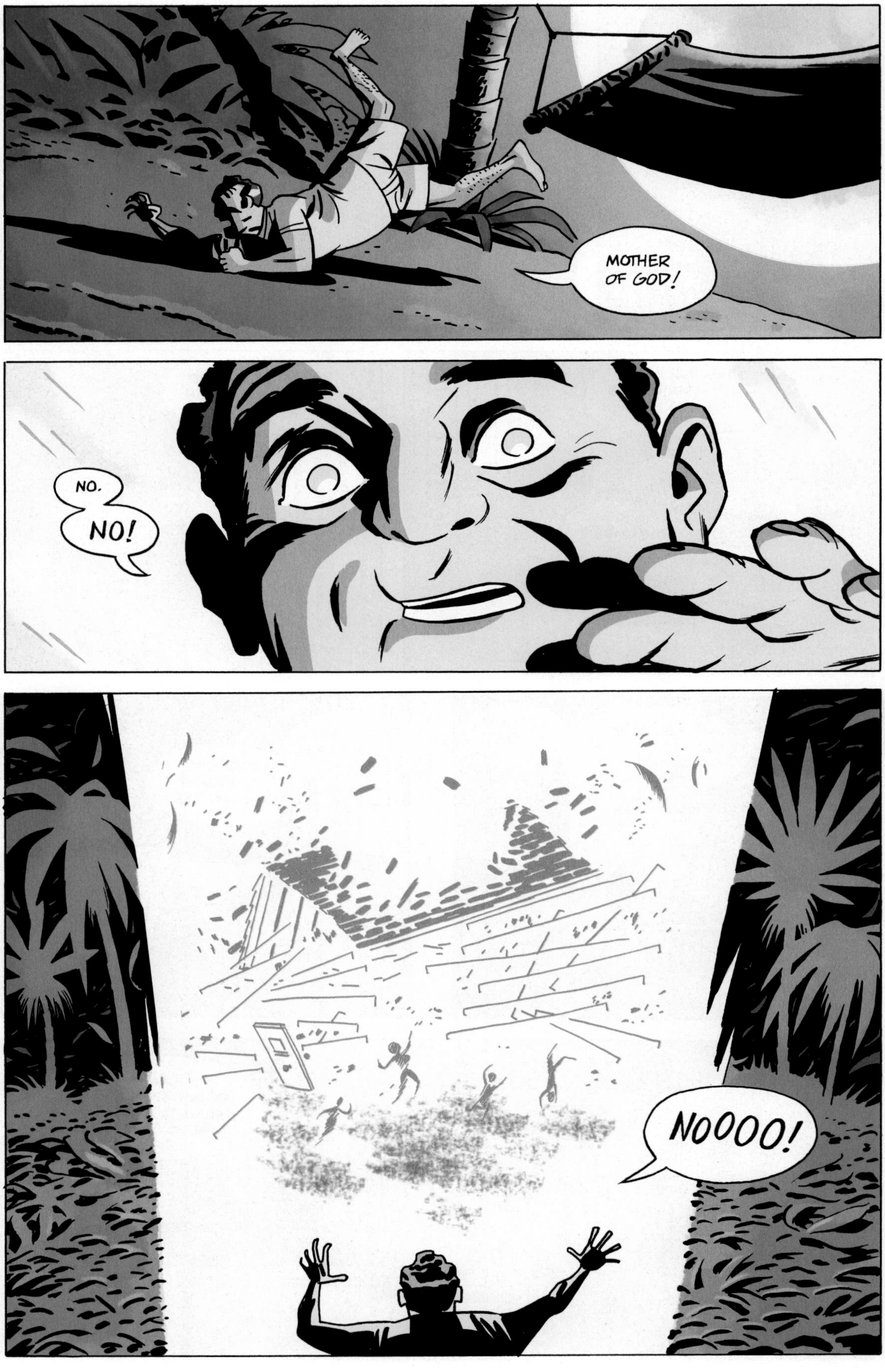
MOTHER OF GOD!
NO.
NO!
NOOOO!

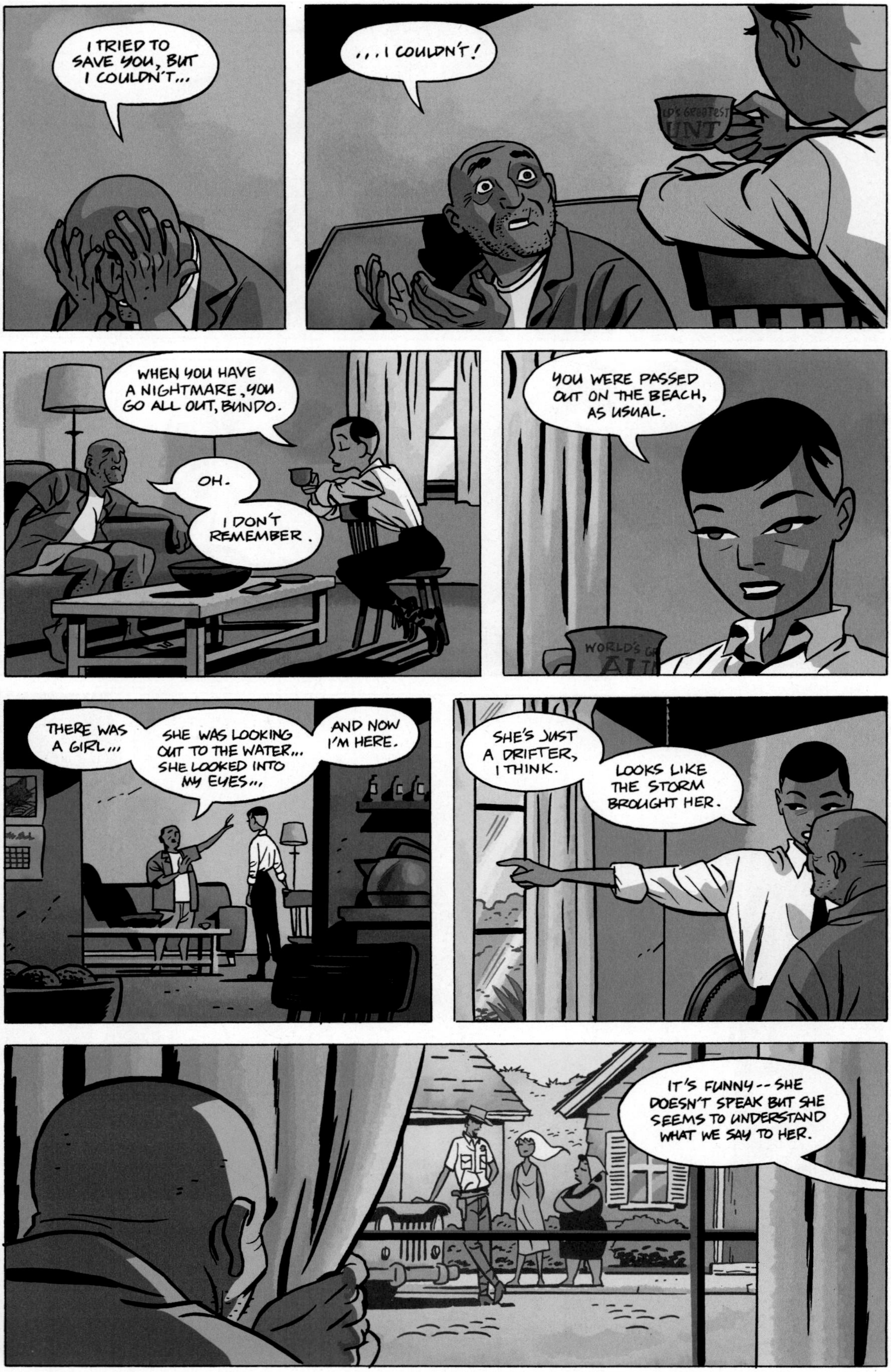
I TRIED TO SAVE YOU, BUT I COULDN'T...
...I COULDN'T!
WHEN YOU HAVE A NIGHTMARE, YOU GO ALL OUT, BUNDO.
OH.
I DON'T REMEMBER.
YOU WERE PASSED OUT ON THE BEACH, AS USUAL.
THERE WAS A GIRL...
SHE WAS LOOKING OUT TO THE WATER... SHE LOOKED INTO MY EYES...
AND NOW I'M HERE.
SHE'S JUST A DRIFTER, I THINK.
LOOKS LIKE THE STORM BROUGHT HER.
IT'S FUNNY-- SHE DOESN'T SPEAK BUT SHE SEEMS TO UNDERSTAND WHAT WE SAY TO HER.

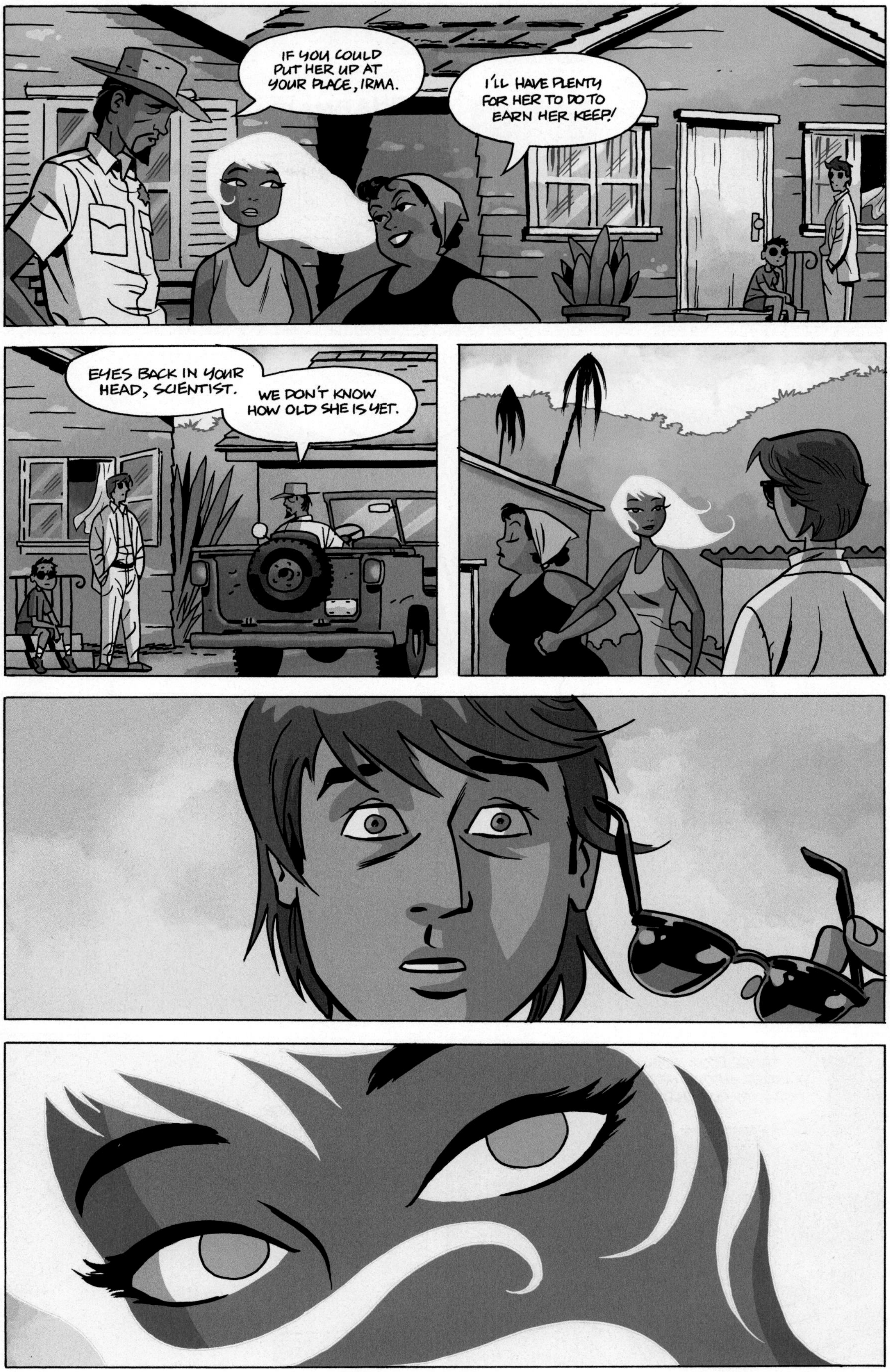
IF YOU COULD PUT HER UP AT YOUR PLACE, IRMA.
I'LL HAVE PLENTY FOR HER TO DO TO EARN HER KEEP!
EYES BACK IN YOUR HEAD, SCIENTIST.
WE DON'T KNOW HOW OLD SHE IS YET.

WHAT'S KEEPING YOU IN TOWN, BOY?

PHARMACIA

I'M STAYING FOR A WHILE TO SEE IF ANOTHER OF THOSE ORBS SHOWS UP, DOCTOR.

MR. SCIENTIST, WHAT ARE THOSE ORTS?

ORBS!

WELL...

ARE THEY FROM HELL?

WHEN I FIND OUT, YOU'LL BE THE FIRST TO KNOW, HONEY.

THEY'RE FROM OUTER SPACE, I'LL BET.

THOSE POOR KIDS. BLINDED BY ONE OF THOSE ORBS, AS YOU CALL THEM.

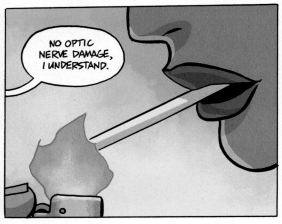

NO OPTIC NERVE DAMAGE, I UNDERSTAND.

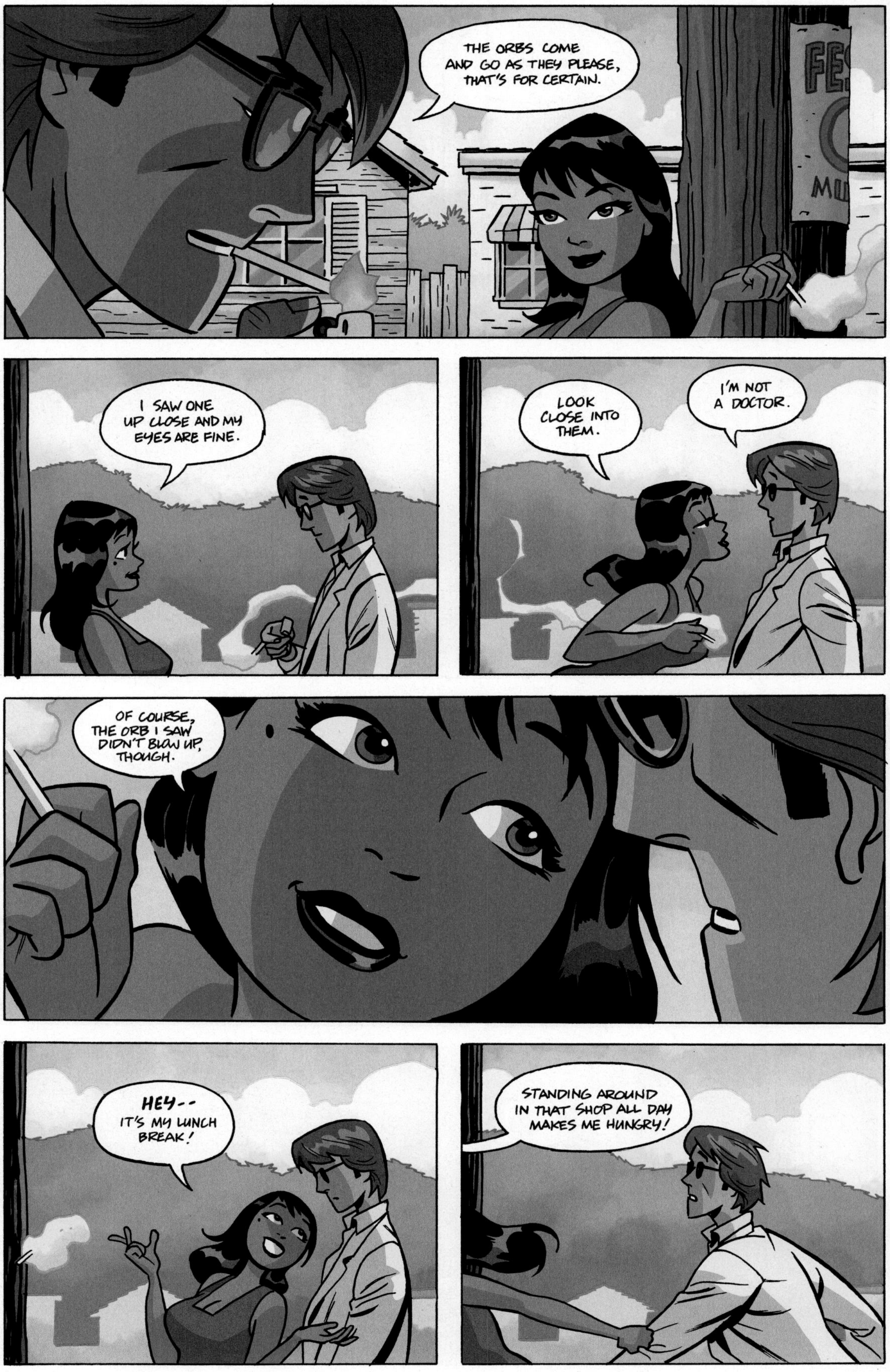
THE ORBS COME AND GO AS THEY PLEASE, THAT'S FOR CERTAIN.
I SAW ONE UP CLOSE AND MY EYES ARE FINE.
LOOK CLOSE INTO THEM.
I'M NOT A DOCTOR.
OF COURSE, THE ORB I SAW DIDN'T BLOW UP, THOUGH.
HEY-- IT'S MY LUNCH BREAK!
STANDING AROUND IN THAT SHOP ALL DAY MAKES ME HUNGRY!

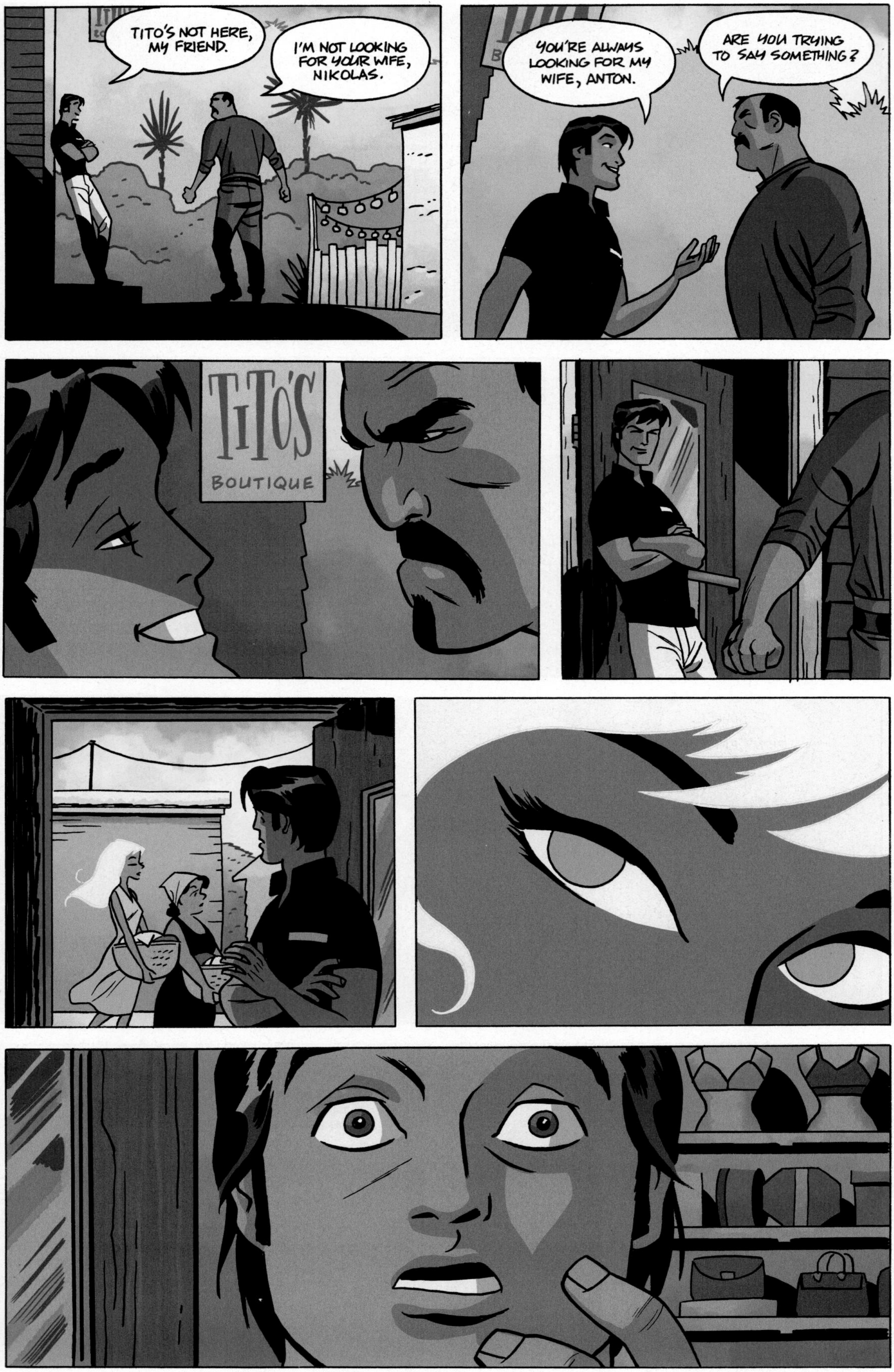
TITO'S NOT HERE, MY FRIEND.
I'M NOT LOOKING FOR YOUR WIFE, NIKOLAS.
YOU'RE ALWAYS LOOKING FOR MY WIFE, ANTON.
ARE YOU TRYING TO SAY SOMETHING?
TITO'S
BOUTIQUE

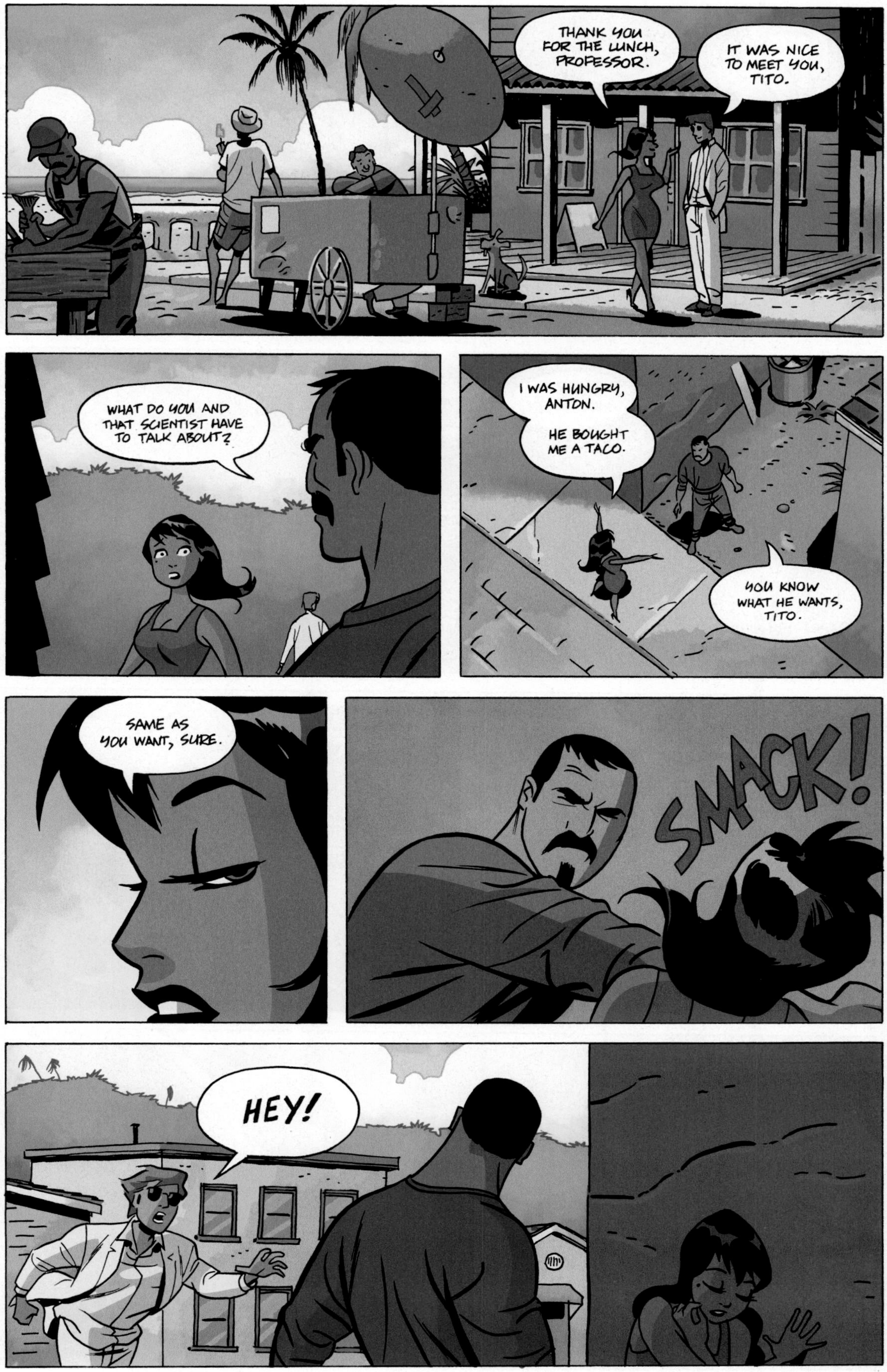
THANK YOU FOR THE LUNCH, PROFESSOR.
IT WAS NICE TO MEET YOU, TITO.
WHAT DO YOU AND THAT SCIENTIST HAVE TO TALK ABOUT?
I WAS HUNGRY, ANTON.
HE BOUGHT ME A TACO.
YOU KNOW WHAT HE WANTS, TITO.
SAME AS YOU WANT, SURE.
SMACK!
HEY!

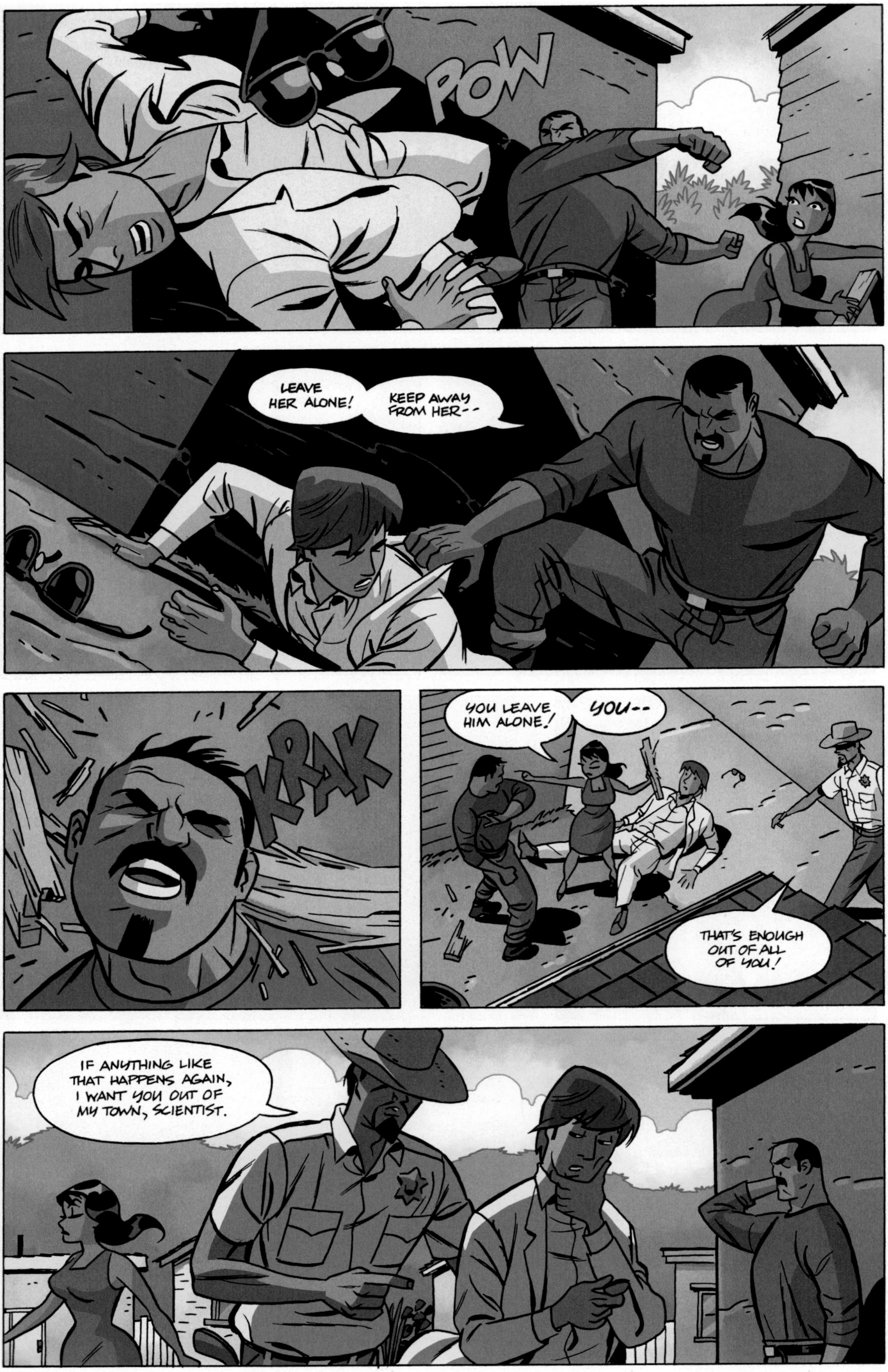
POW
LEAVE HER ALONE!
KEEP AWAY FROM HER--
KRAK
YOU LEAVE HIM ALONE!
YOU--
THAT'S ENOUGH OUT OF ALL OF YOU!
IF ANYTHING LIKE THAT HAPPENS AGAIN, I WANT YOU OUT OF MY TOWN, SCIENTIST.

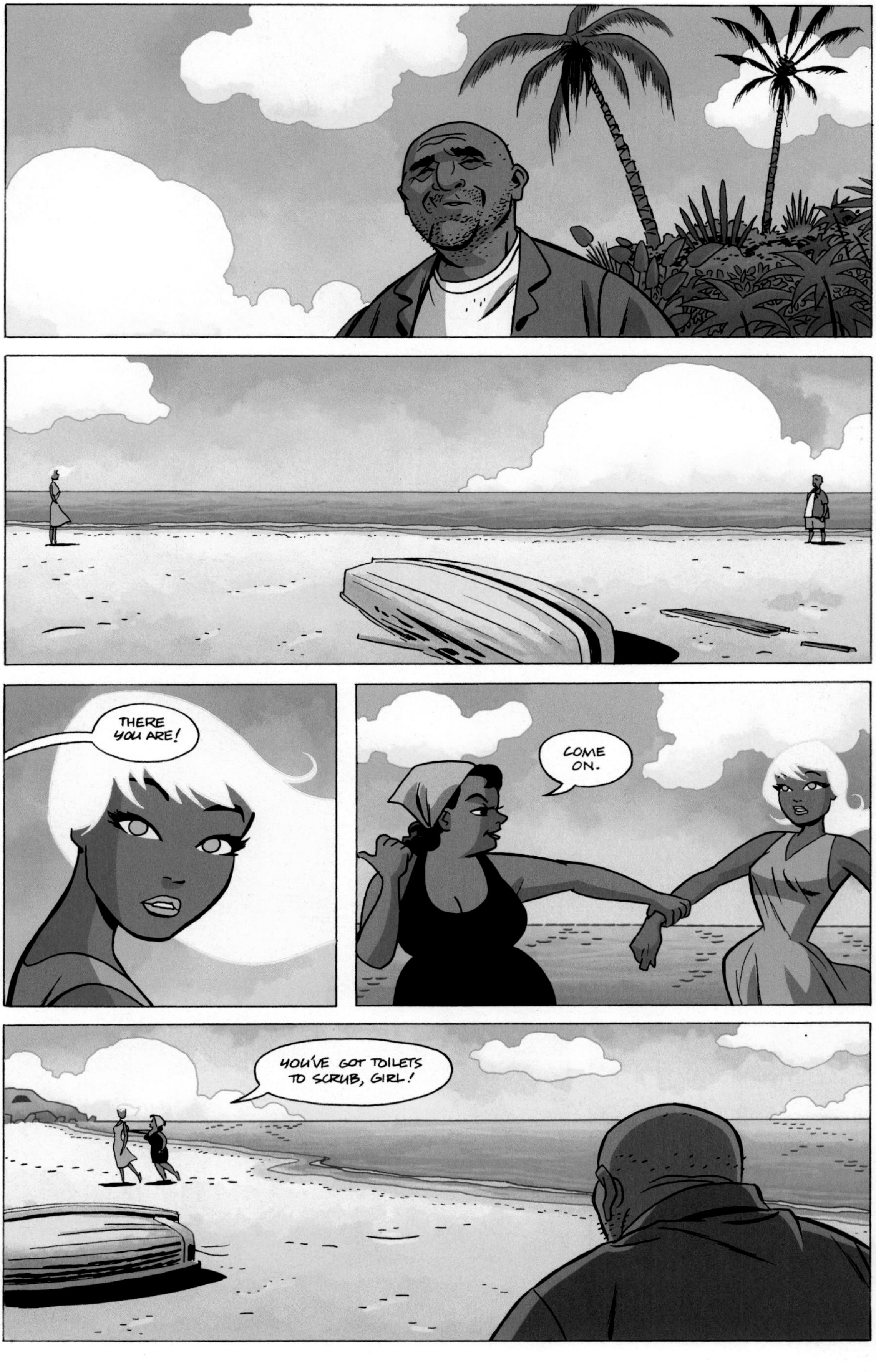
THERE YOU ARE!
COME ON.
YOU'VE GOT TOILETS TO SCRUB, GIRL!

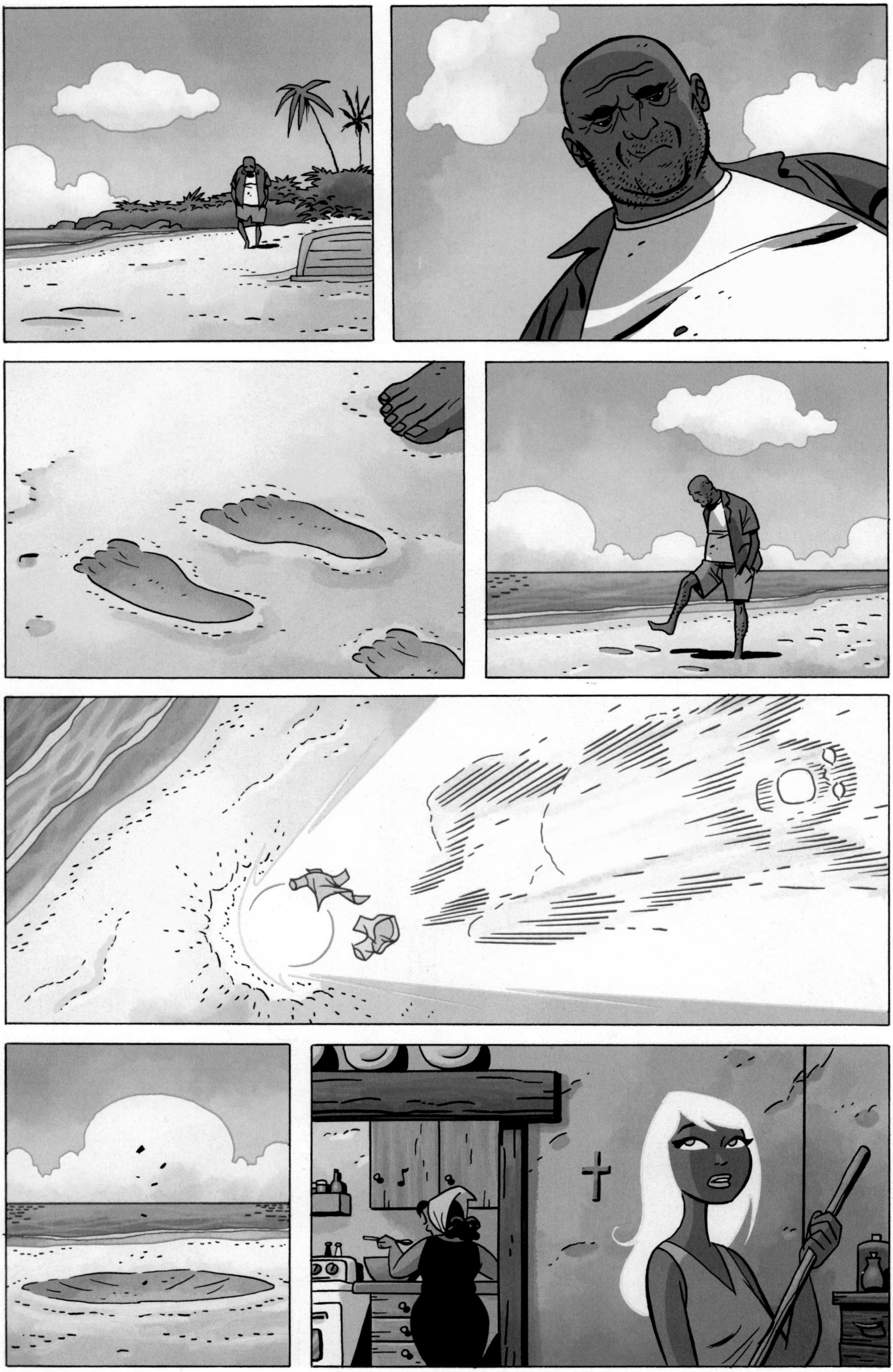

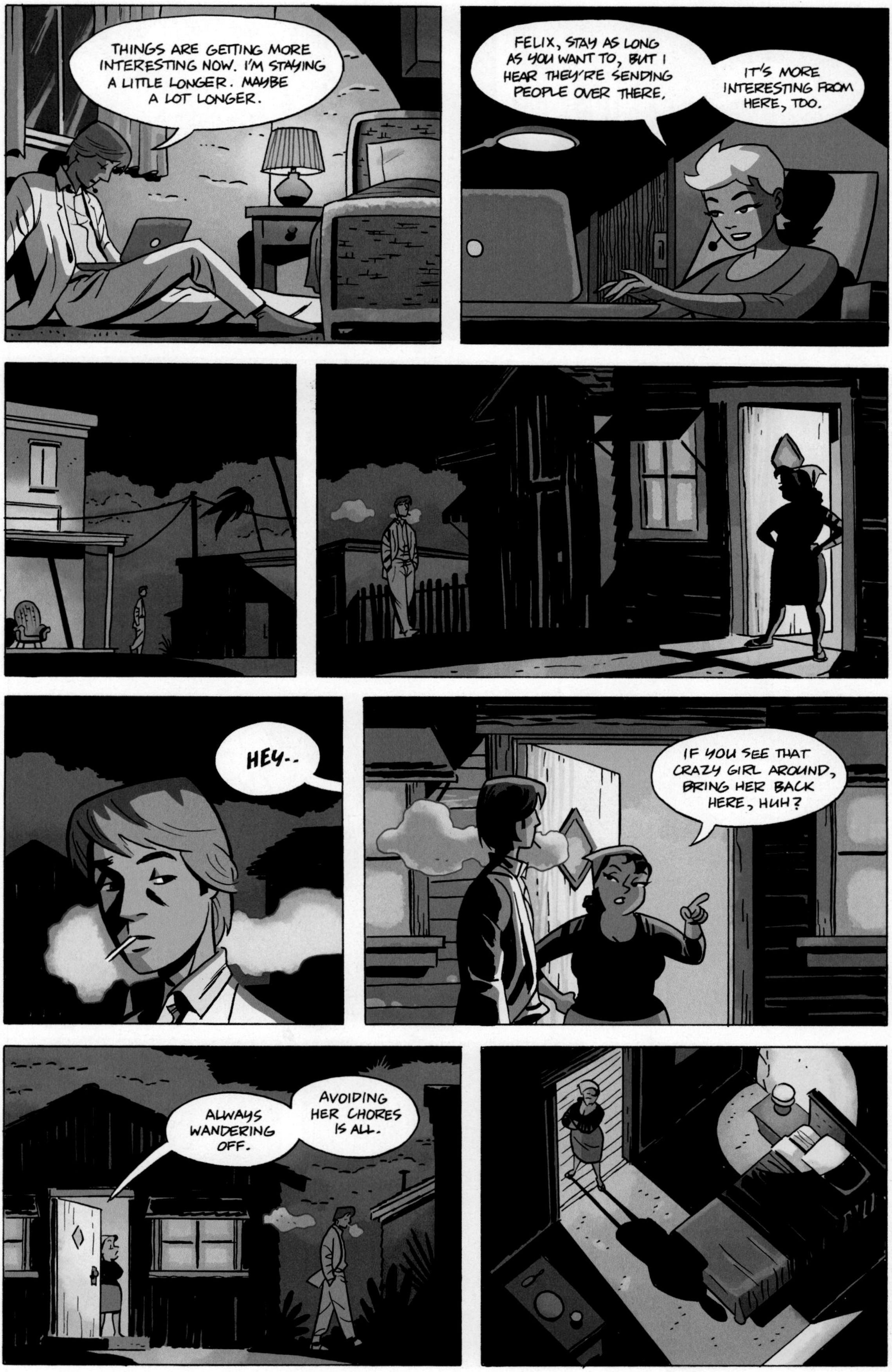

THINGS ARE GETTING MORE INTERESTING NOW. I'M STAYING A LITTLE LONGER. MAYBE A LOT LONGER.
FELIX, STAY AS LONG AS YOU WANT TO, BUT I HEAR THEY'RE SENDING PEOPLE OVER THERE.
IT'S MORE INTERESTING FROM HERE, TOO.
HEY..
IF YOU SEE THAT CRAZY GIRL AROUND, BRING HER BACK HERE, HUH?
ALWAYS WANDERING OFF.
AVOIDING HER CHORES IS ALL.

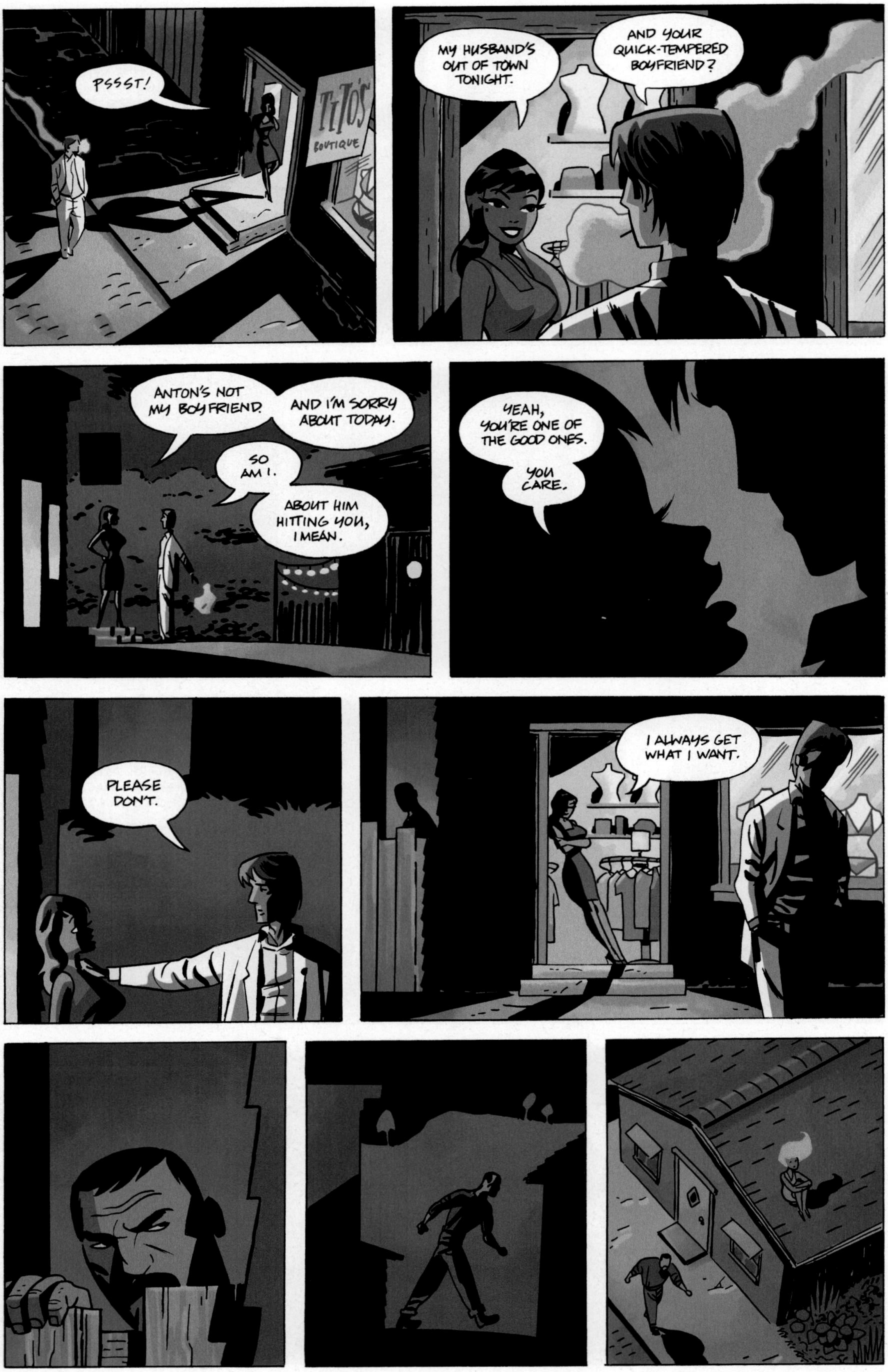
PSSST!
TITO'S BOUTIQUE
MY HUSBAND'S OUT OF TOWN TONIGHT.
AND YOUR QUICK-TEMPERED BOYFRIEND?
ANTON'S NOT MY BOYFRIEND.
AND I'M SORRY ABOUT TODAY.
SO AM I.
ABOUT HIM HITTING YOU, I MEAN.
YEAH, YOU'RE ONE OF THE GOOD ONES.
YOU CARE.
PLEASE DON'T.
I ALWAYS GET WHAT I WANT.

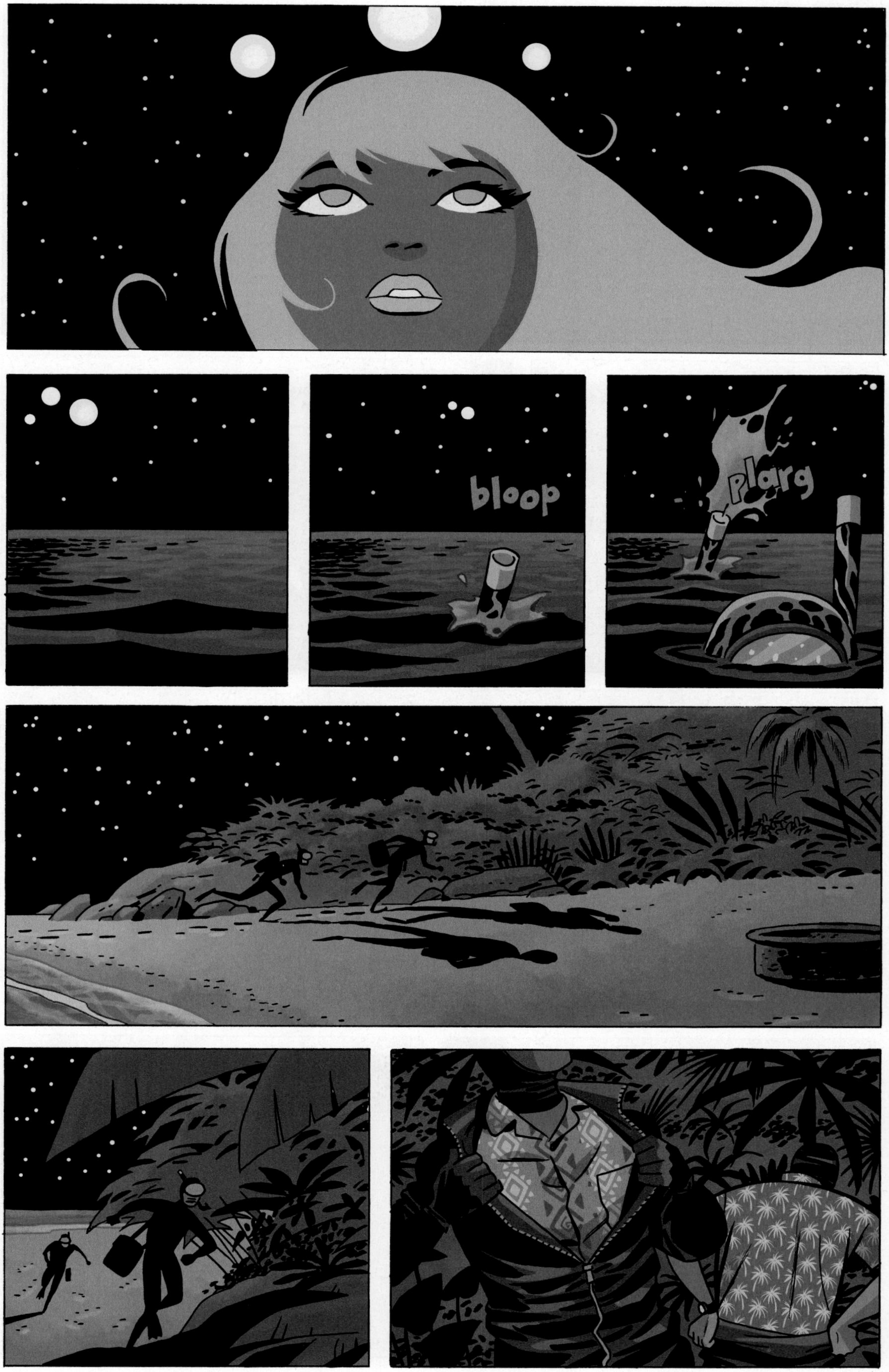
bloop
plarg

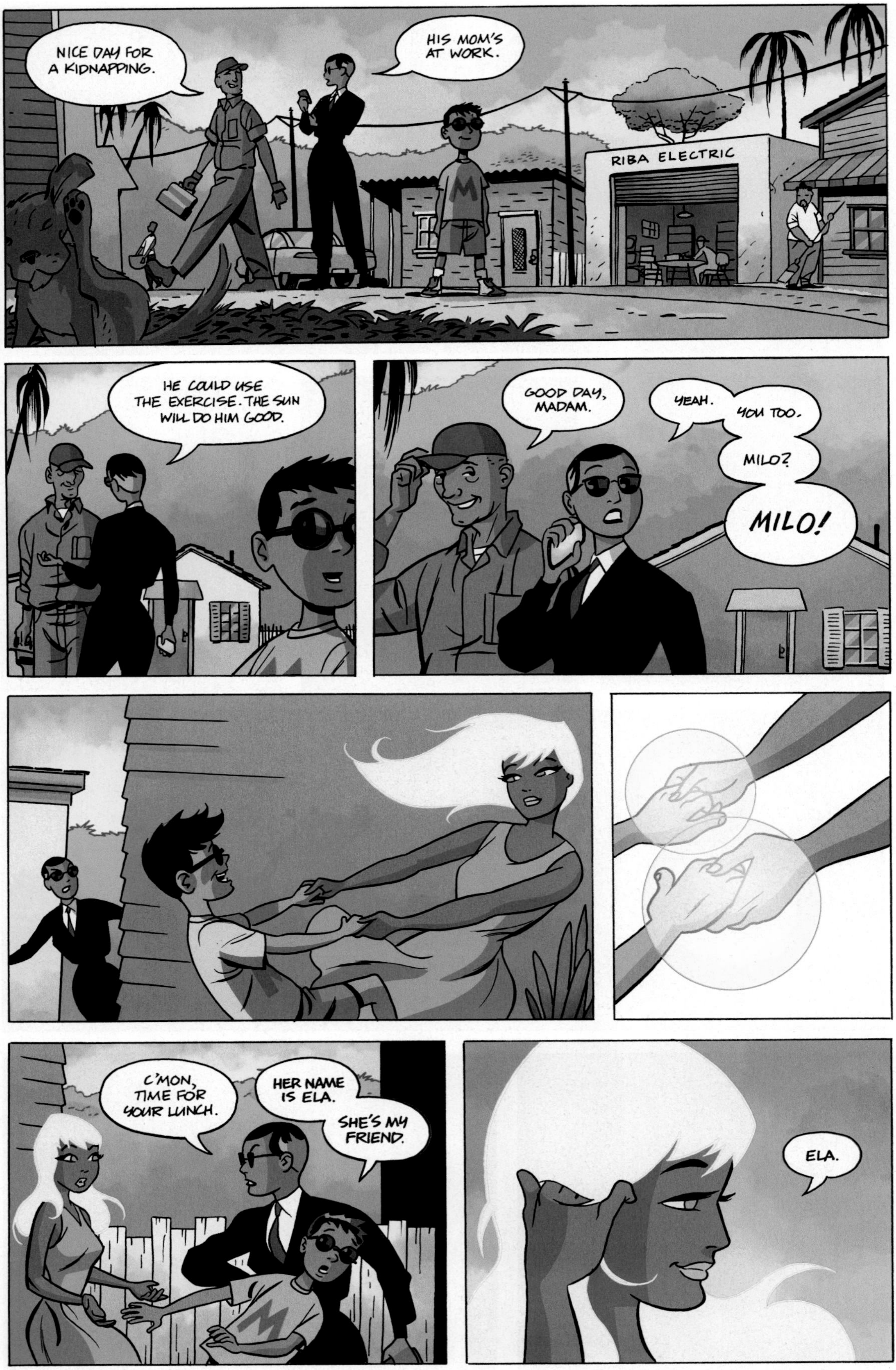
NICE DAY FOR A KIDNAPPING.
HIS MOM'S AT WORK.
RIBA ELECTRIC
HE COULD USE THE EXERCISE. THE SUN WILL DO HIM GOOD.
GOOD DAY, MADAM.
YEAH.
YOU TOO.
MILO?
MILO!
C'MON, TIME FOR YOUR LUNCH.
HER NAME IS ELA.
SHE'S MY FRIEND.
ELA.

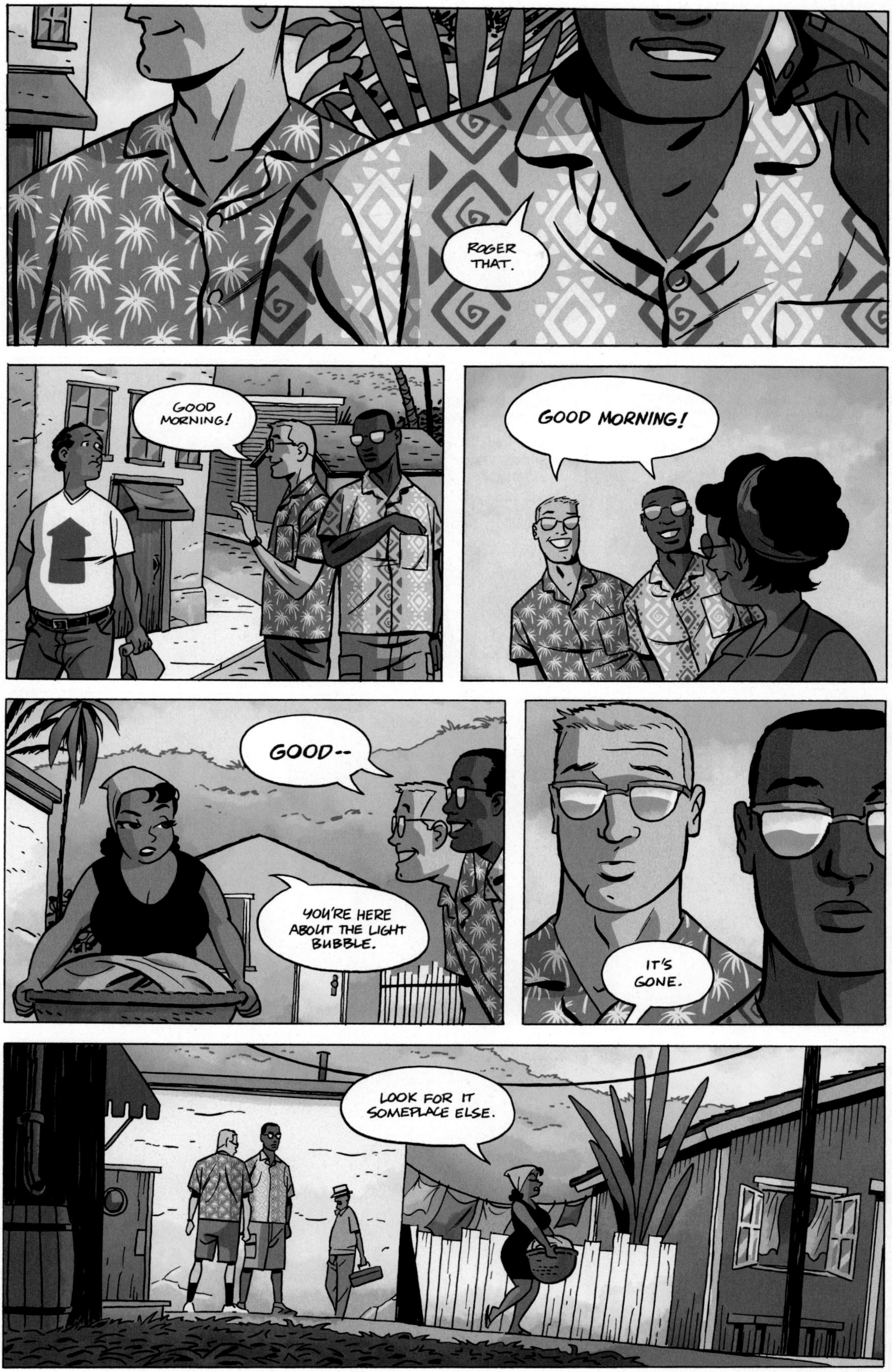
ROGER THAT.
GOOD MORNING!
GOOD MORNING!
GOOD--
YOU'RE HERE ABOUT THE LIGHT BUBBLE.
IT'S GONE.
LOOK FOR IT SOMEPLACE ELSE.

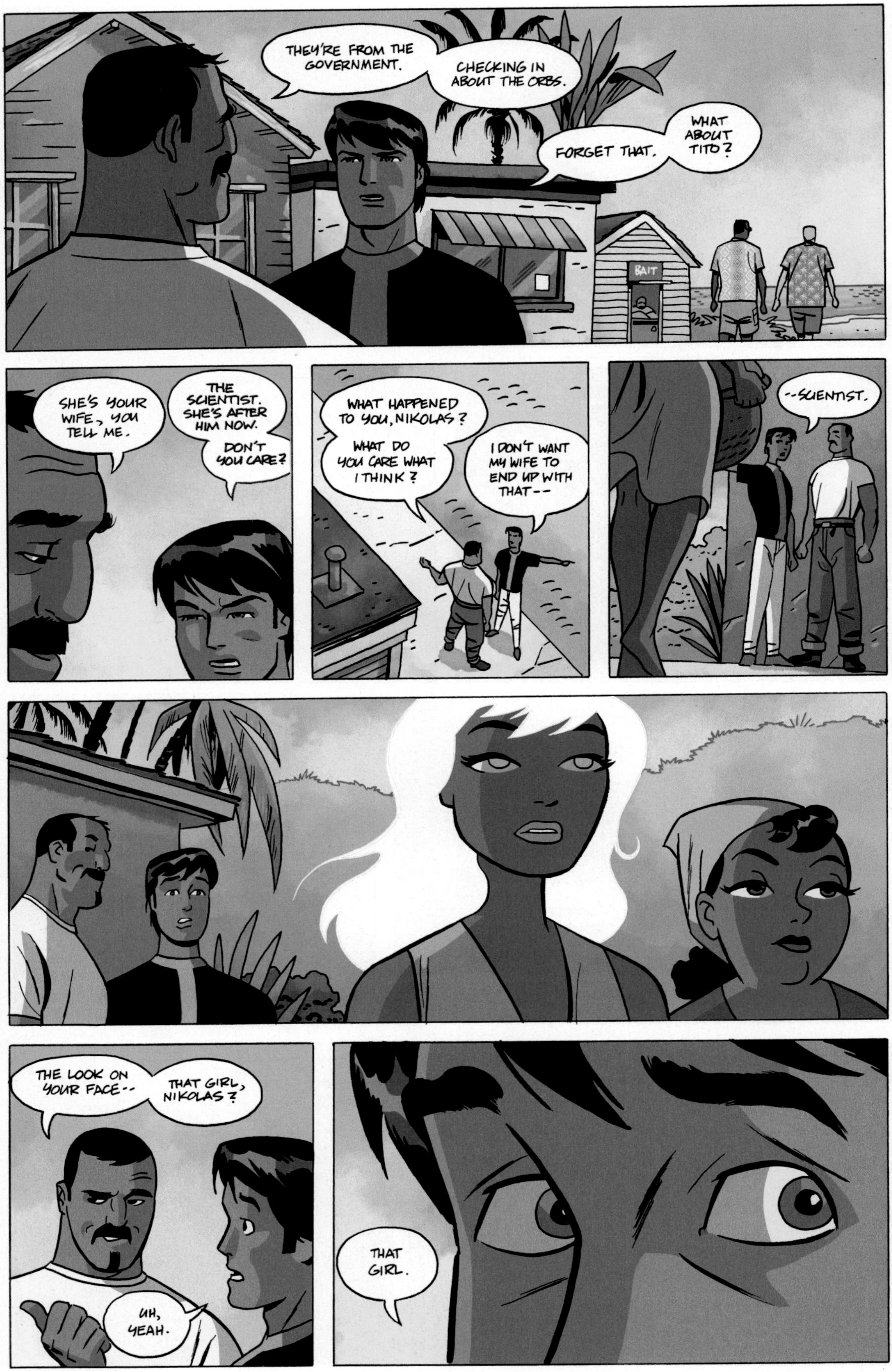
THEY'RE FROM THE GOVERNMENT.
CHECKING IN ABOUT THE ORBS.
FORGET THAT.
WHAT ABOUT TITO?
BAIT
SHE'S YOUR WIFE, YOU TELL ME.
THE SCIENTIST. SHE'S AFTER HIM NOW.
DON'T YOU CARE?
WHAT HAPPENED TO YOU, NIKOLAS?
WHAT DO YOU CARE WHAT I THINK?
I DON'T WANT MY WIFE TO END UP WITH THAT--
--SCIENTIST.
THE LOOK ON YOUR FACE--
THAT GIRL, NIKOLAS?
UH, YEAH.
THAT GIRL.

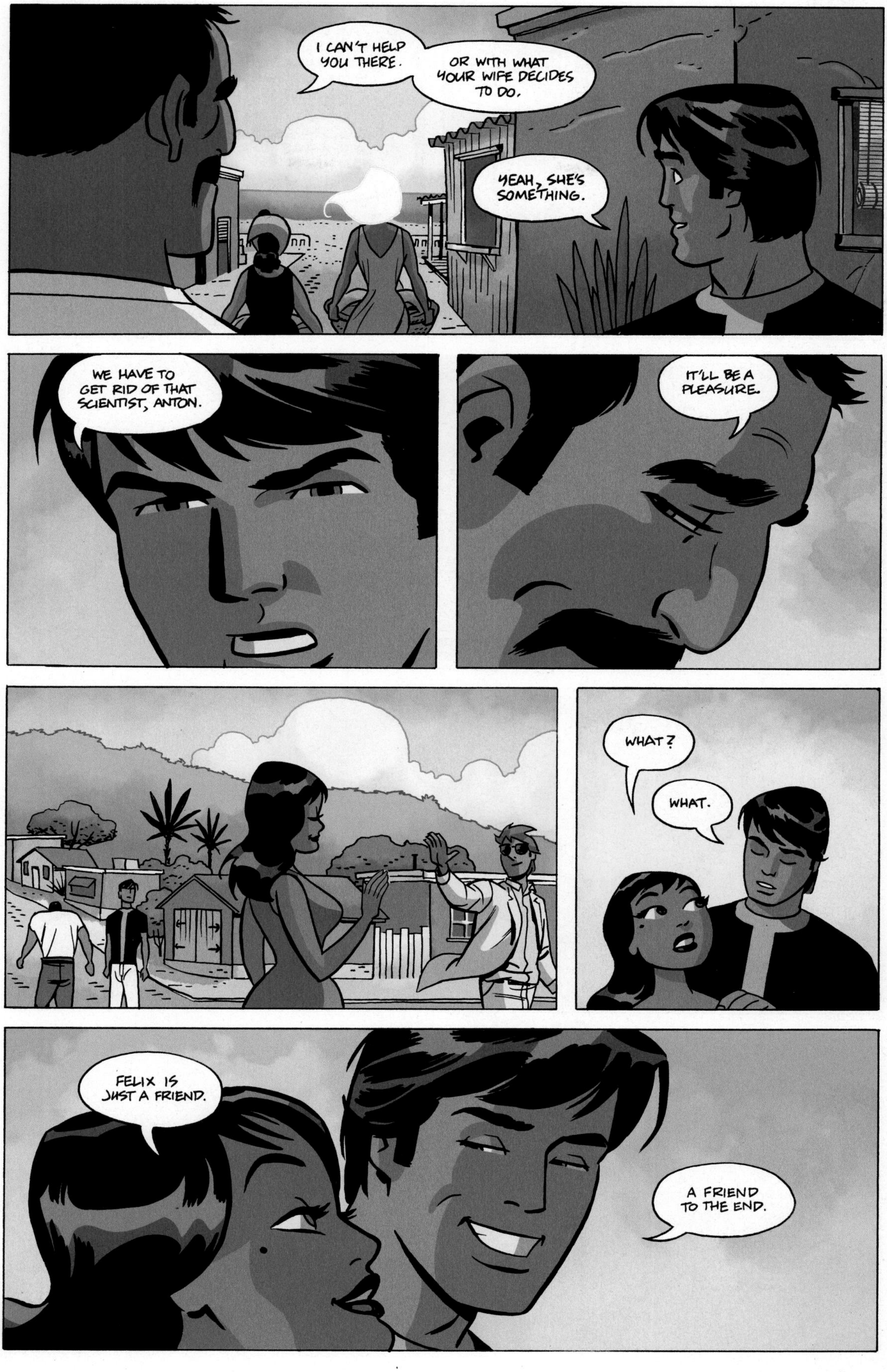
I CAN'T HELP YOU THERE.
OR WITH WHAT YOUR WIFE DECIDES TO DO.
YEAH, SHE'S SOMETHING.
WE HAVE TO GET RID OF THAT SCIENTIST, ANTON.
IT'LL BE A PLEASURE.
WHAT?
WHAT.
FELIX IS JUST A FRIEND.
A FRIEND TO THE END.

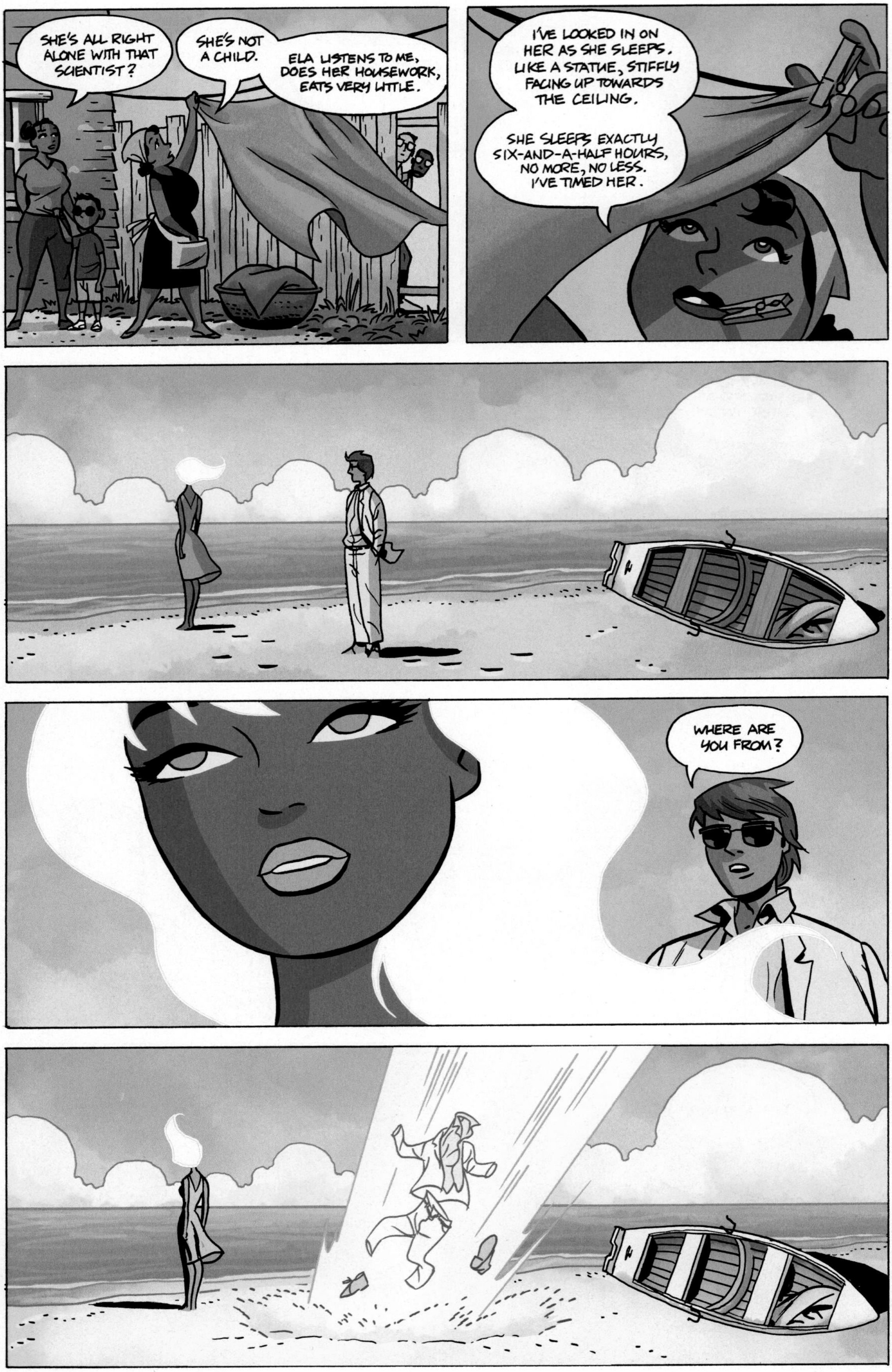
SHE'S ALL RIGHT ALONE WITH THAT SCIENTIST?
SHE'S NOT A CHILD.
ELA LISTENS TO ME, DOES HER HOUSEWORK, EATS VERY LITTLE.
I'VE LOOKED IN ON HER AS SHE SLEEPS. LIKE A STATUE, STIFFLY FACING UP TOWARDS THE CEILING.
SHE SLEEPS EXACTLY SIX-AND-A-HALF HOURS, NO MORE, NO LESS. I'VE TIMED HER.
WHERE ARE YOU FROM?

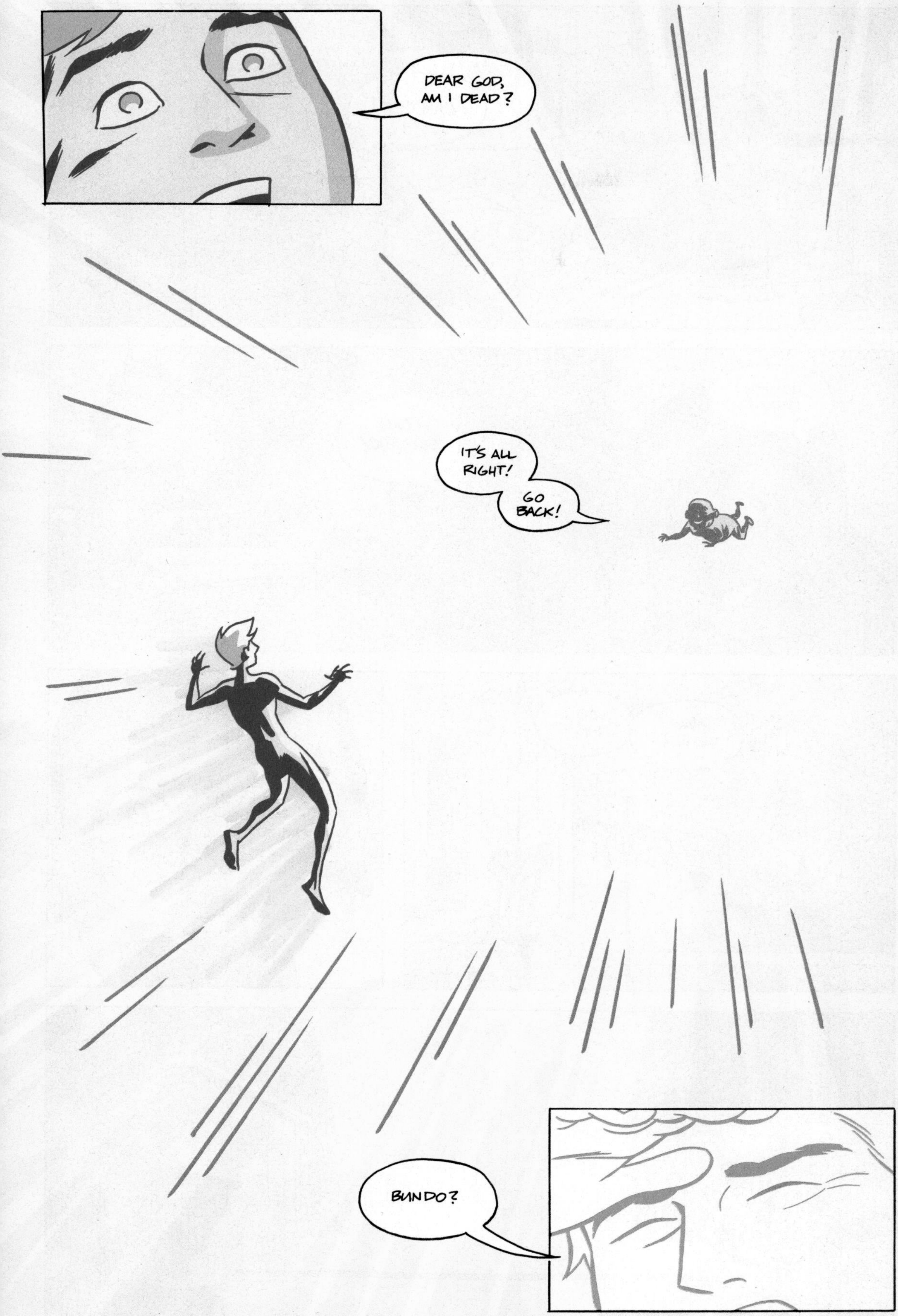
DEAR GOD, AM I DEAD?
IT'S ALL RIGHT!
GO BACK!
BUNDO?

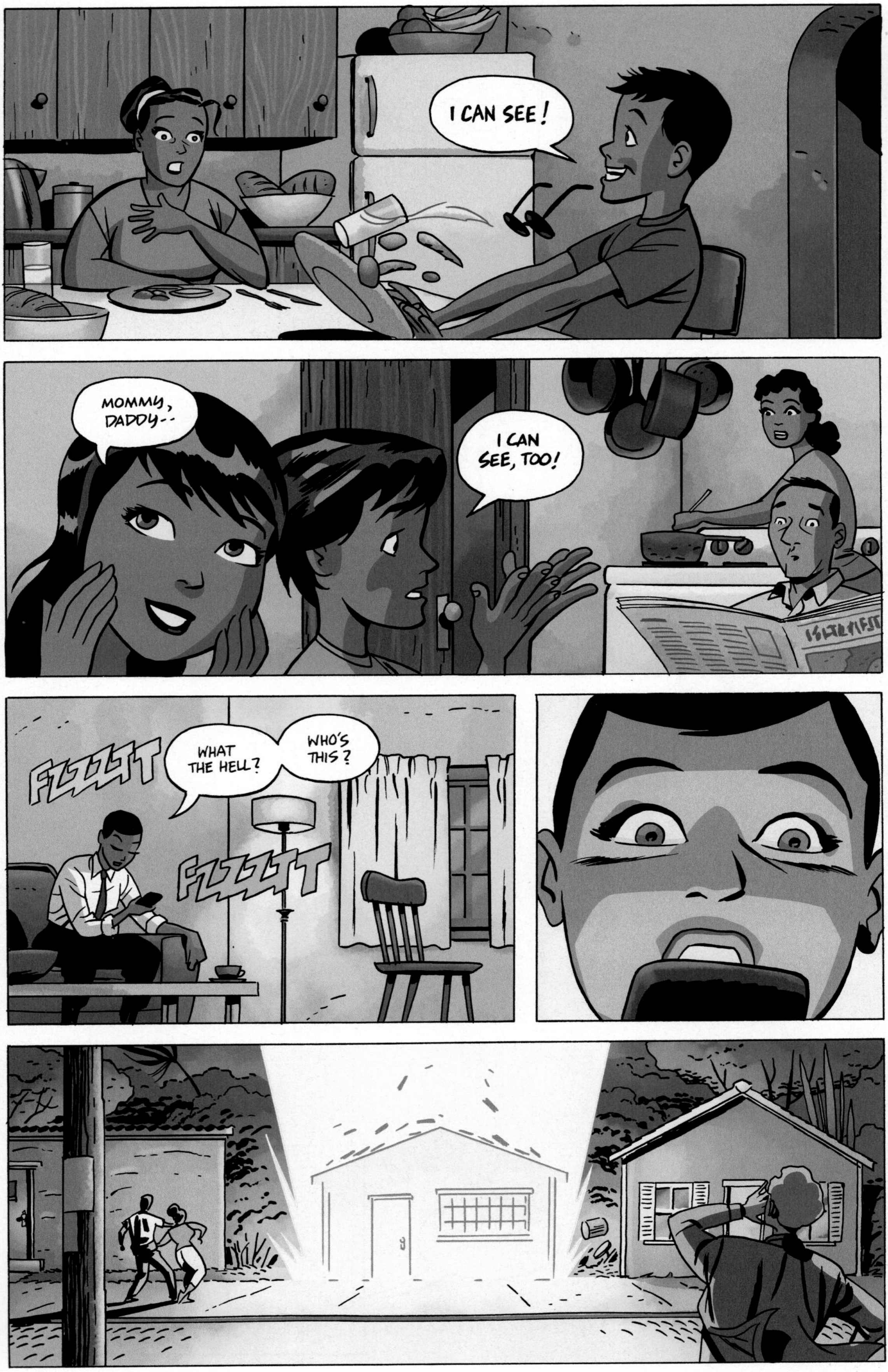
I CAN SEE!
MOMMY, DADDY--
I CAN SEE, TOO!
FZZZTT
WHAT THE HELL?
WHO'S THIS?
FZZZTT

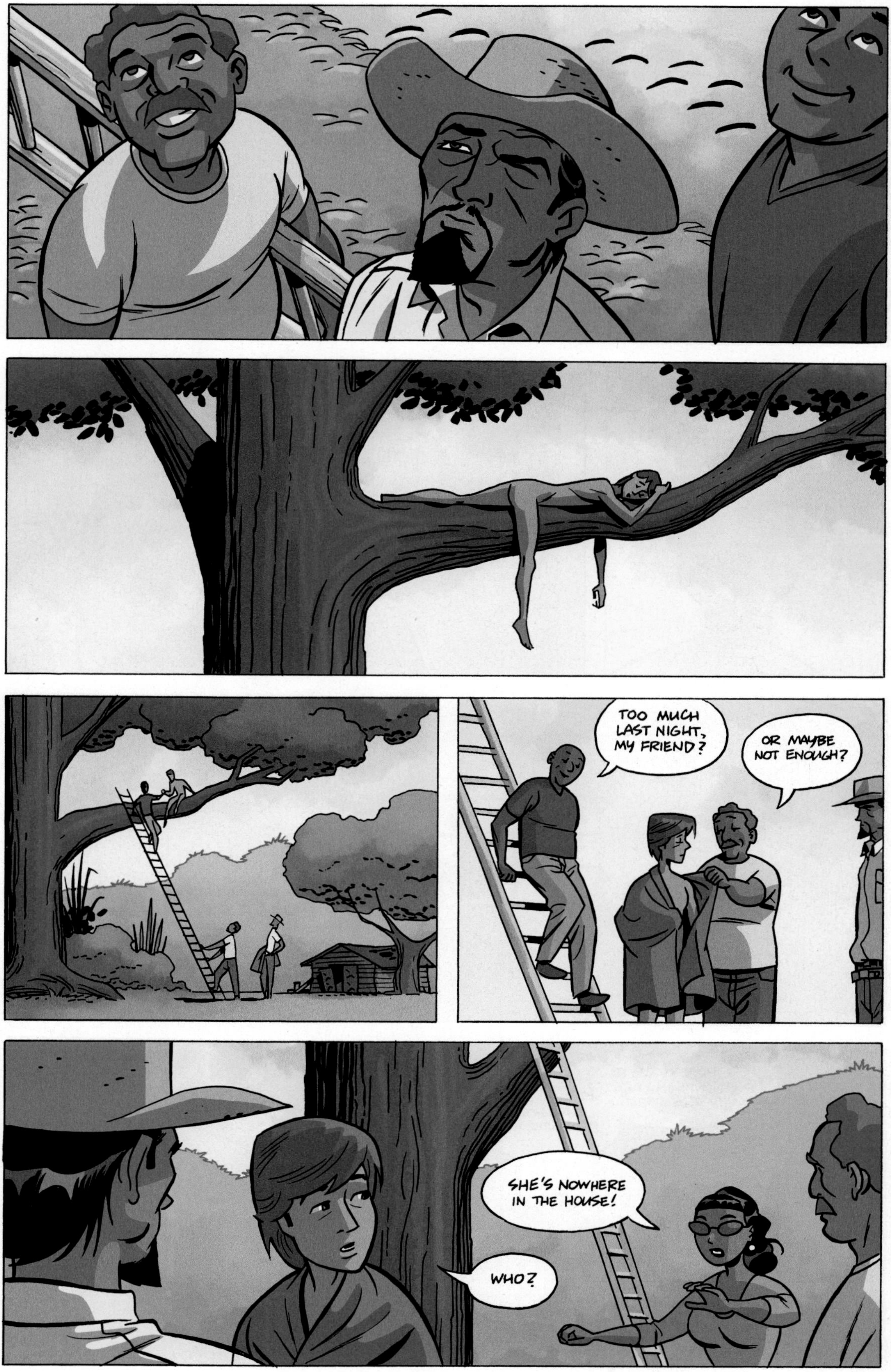
TOO MUCH LAST NIGHT, MY FRIEND?
OR MAYBE NOT ENOUGH?
SHE'S NOWHERE IN THE HOUSE!
WHO?

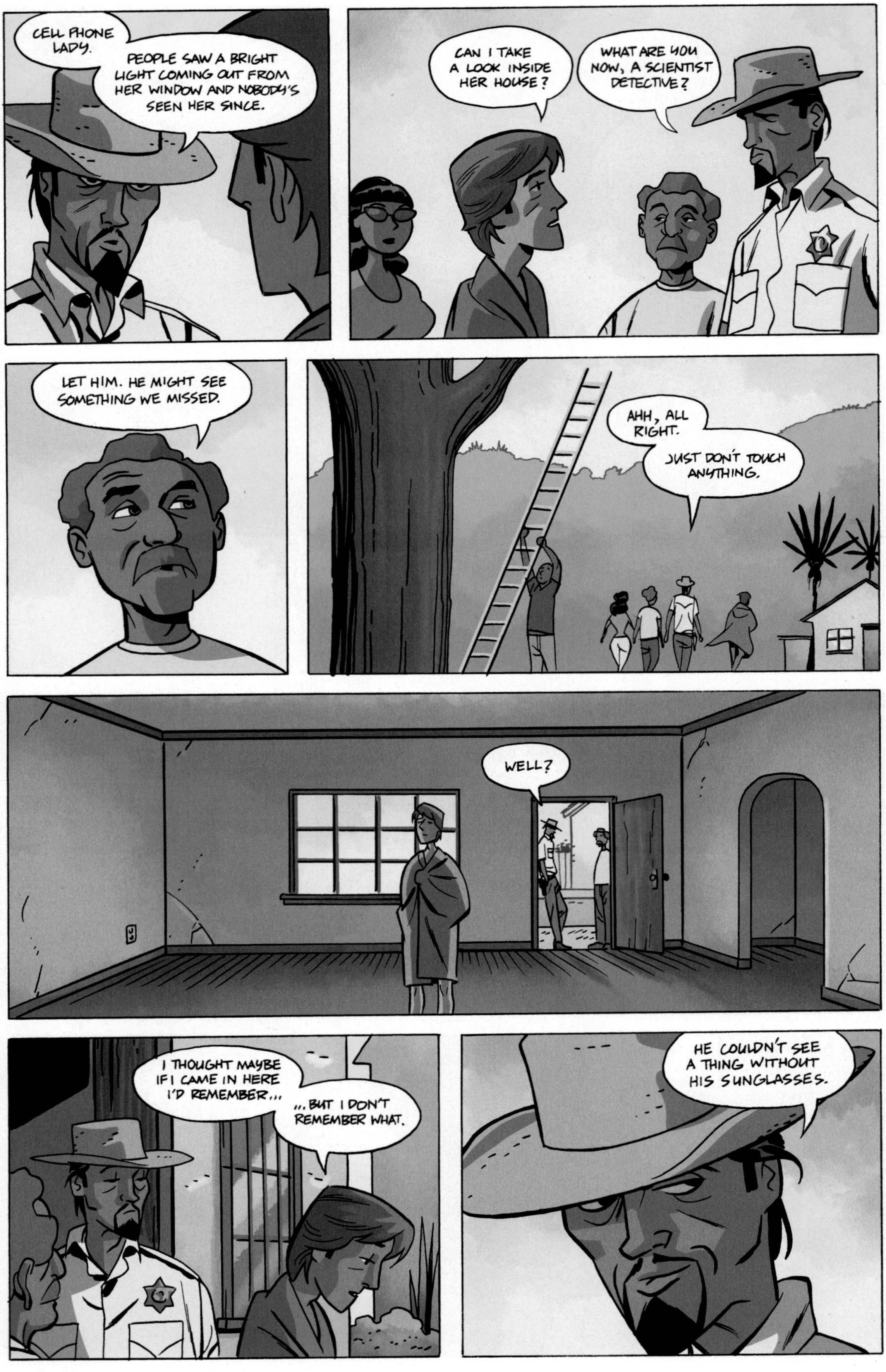
CELL PHONE LADY.
PEOPLE SAW A BRIGHT LIGHT COMING OUT FROM HER WINDOW AND NOBODY'S SEEN HER SINCE.
CAN I TAKE A LOOK INSIDE HER HOUSE?
WHAT ARE YOU NOW, A SCIENTIST DETECTIVE?
LET HIM. HE MIGHT SEE SOMETHING WE MISSED.
AHH, ALL RIGHT.
JUST DON'T TOUCH ANYTHING.
WELL?
I THOUGHT MAYBE IF I CAME IN HERE I'D REMEMBER...
...BUT I DON'T REMEMBER WHAT.
HE COULDN'T SEE A THING WITHOUT HIS SUNGLASSES.

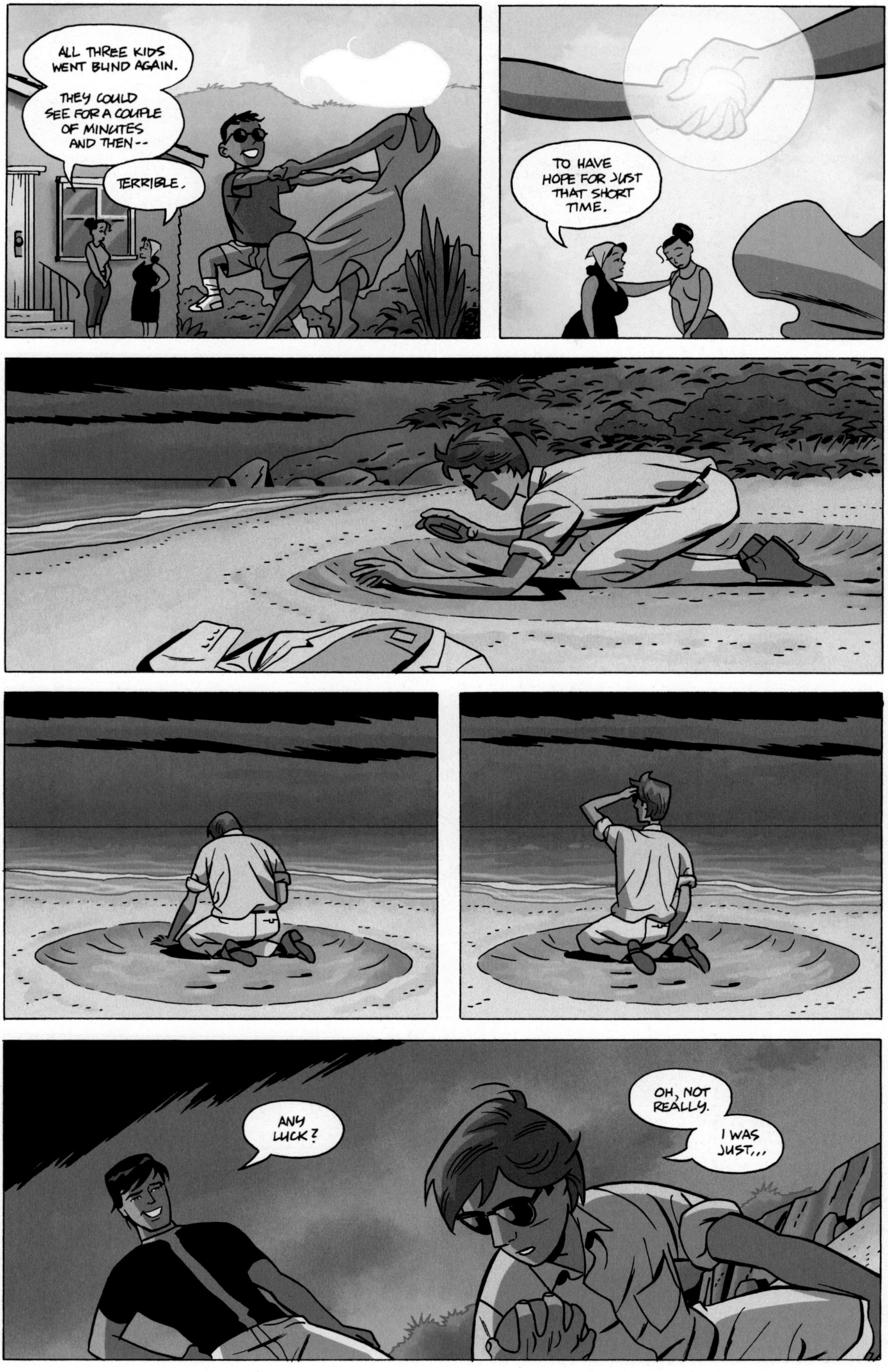
ALL THREE KIDS WENT BLIND AGAIN.
THEY COULD SEE FOR A COUPLE OF MINUTES AND THEN--
TERRIBLE.
TO HAVE HOPE FOR JUST THAT SHORT TIME.
ANY LUCK?
OH, NOT REALLY.
I WAS JUST,,,

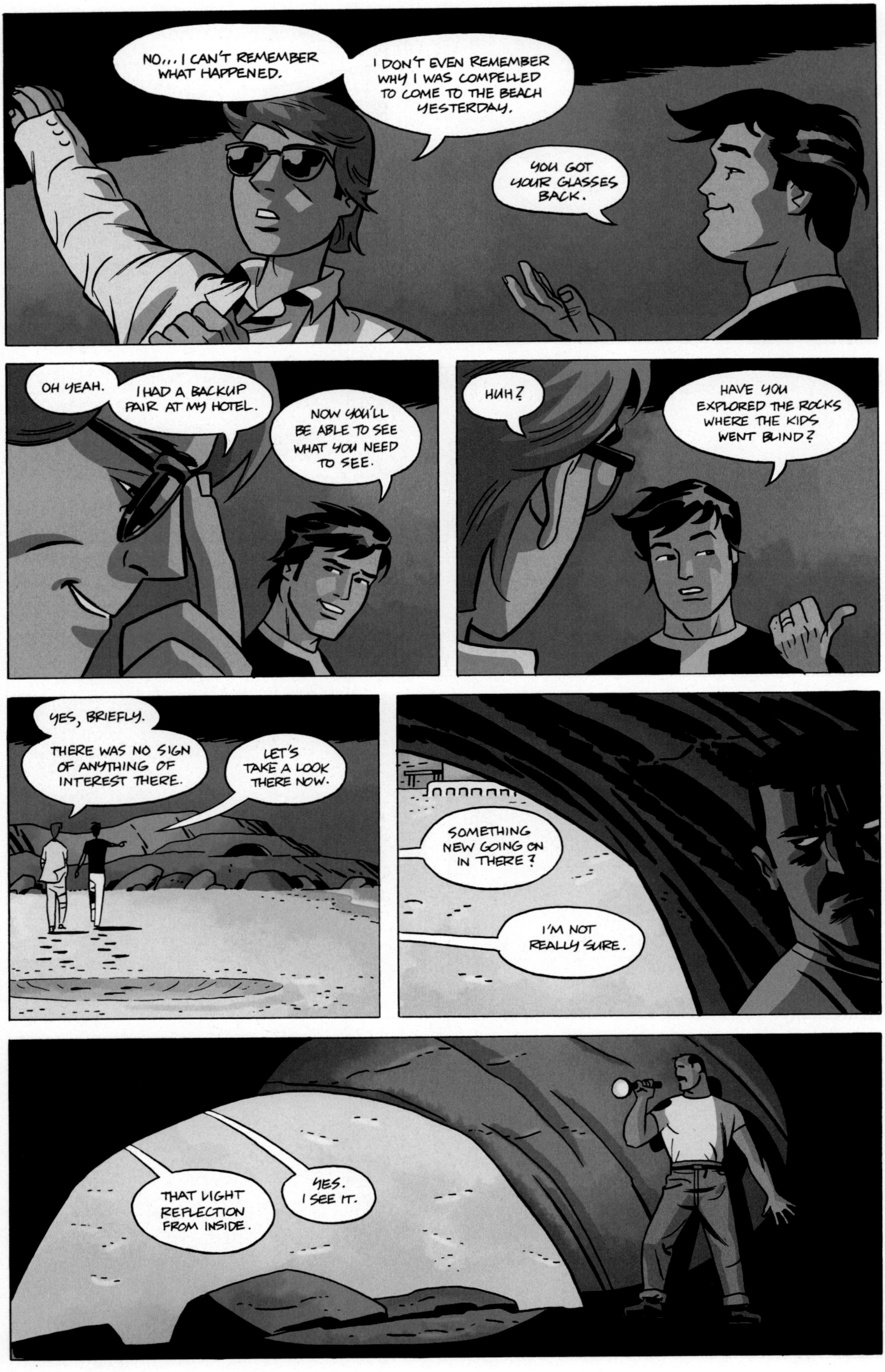
NO... I CAN'T REMEMBER WHAT HAPPENED.
I DON'T EVEN REMEMBER WHY I WAS COMPELLED TO COME TO THE BEACH YESTERDAY.
YOU GOT YOUR GLASSES BACK.
OH YEAH.
I HAD A BACKUP PAIR AT MY HOTEL.
NOW YOU'LL BE ABLE TO SEE WHAT YOU NEED TO SEE.
HUH?
HAVE YOU EXPLORED THE ROCKS WHERE THE KIDS WENT BLIND?
YES, BRIEFLY.
THERE WAS NO SIGN OF ANYTHING OF INTEREST THERE.
LET'S TAKE A LOOK THERE NOW.
SOMETHING NEW GOING ON IN THERE?
I'M NOT REALLY SURE.
THAT LIGHT REFLECTION FROM INSIDE.
YES. I SEE IT.

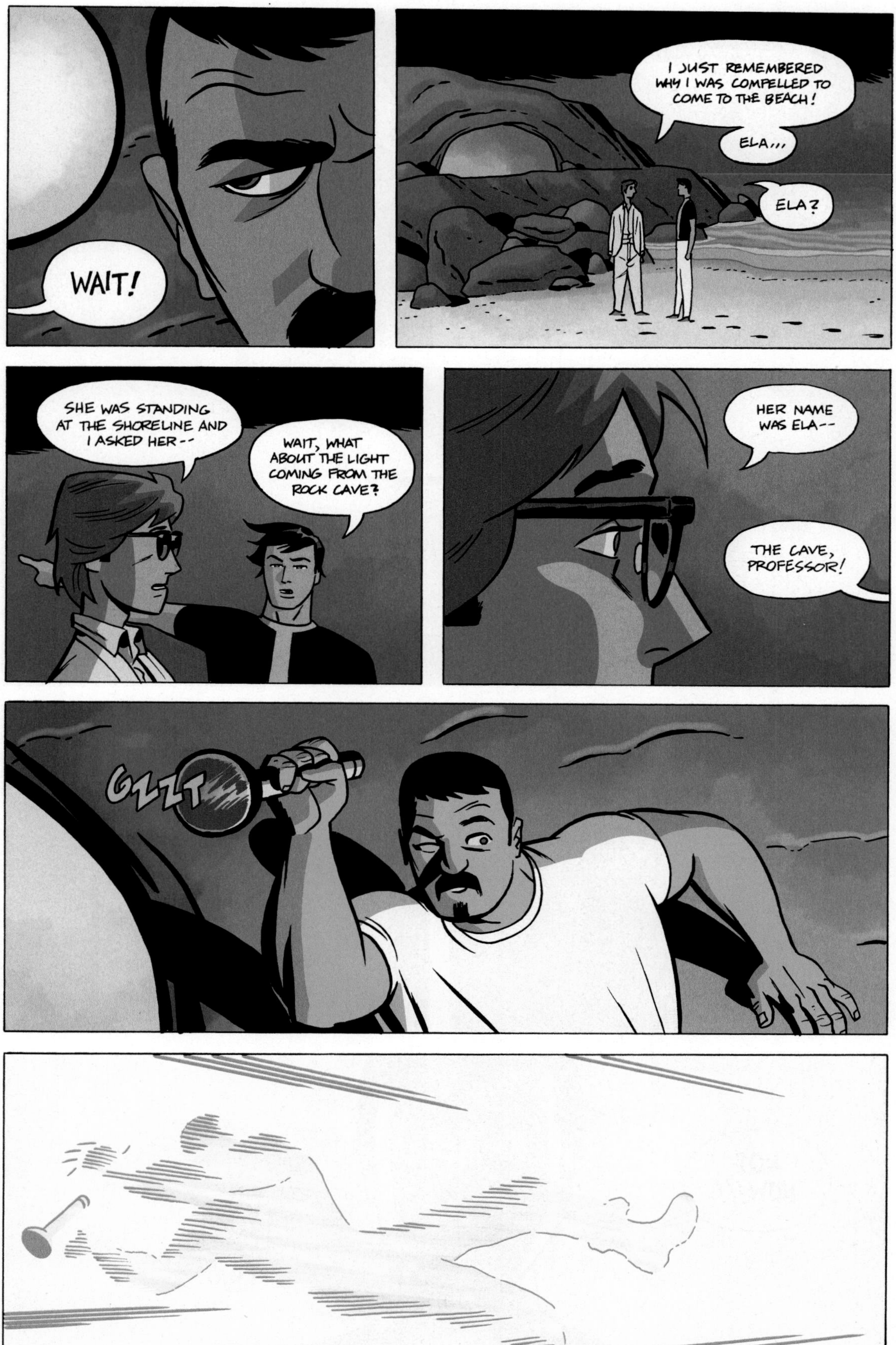
WAIT!
I JUST REMEMBERED WHY I WAS COMPELLED TO COME TO THE BEACH!
ELA,,,
ELA?
SHE WAS STANDING AT THE SHORELINE AND I ASKED HER--
WAIT, WHAT ABOUT THE LIGHT COMING FROM THE ROCK CAVE?
HER NAME WAS ELA--
THE CAVE, PROFESSOR!
GZZT

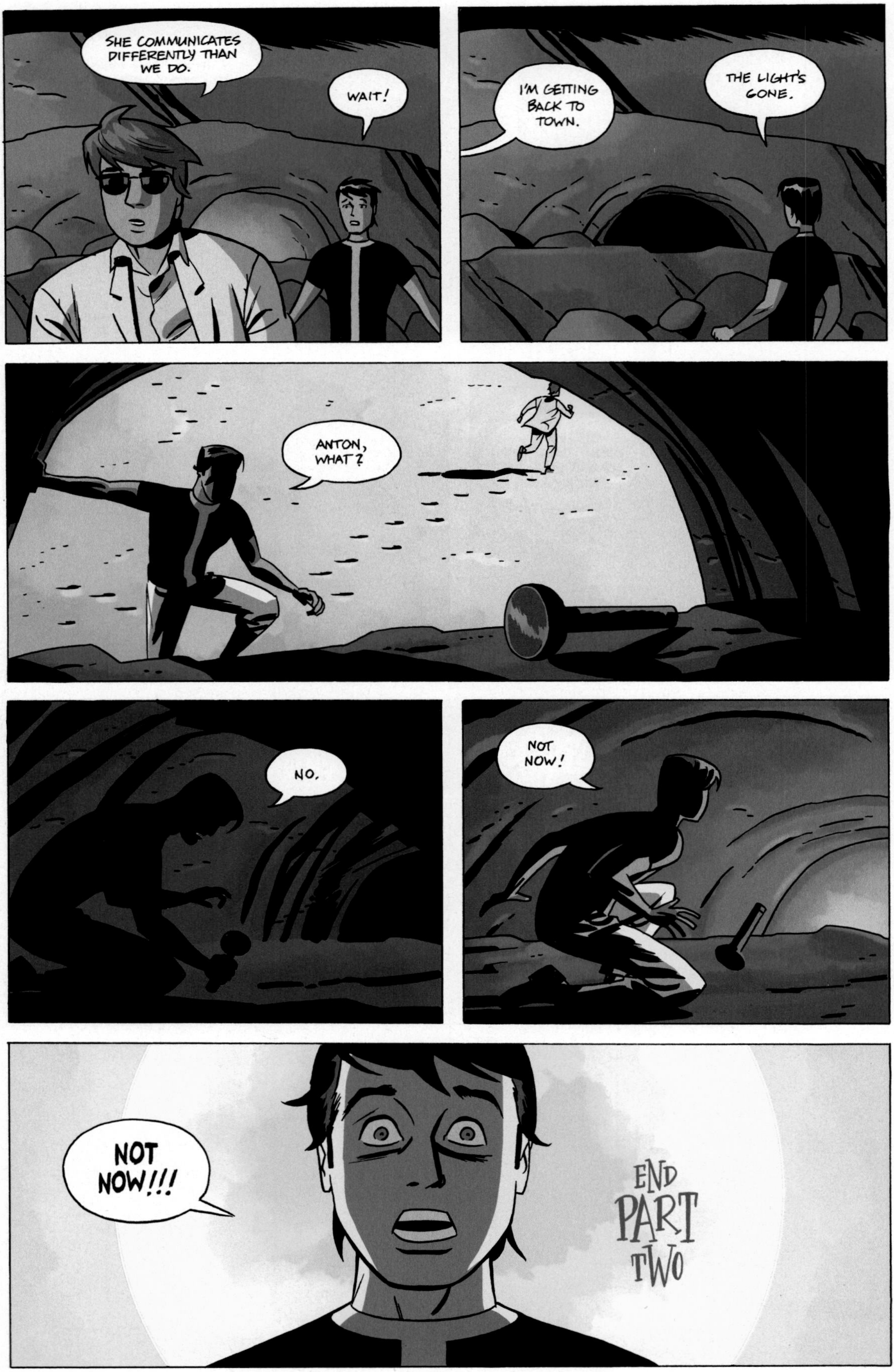
SHE COMMUNICATES DIFFERENTLY THAN WE DO.
WAIT!
I'M GETTING BACK TO TOWN.
THE LIGHT'S GONE.
ANTON, WHAT?
NO.
NOT NOW!
NOT NOW!!!
END PART TWO

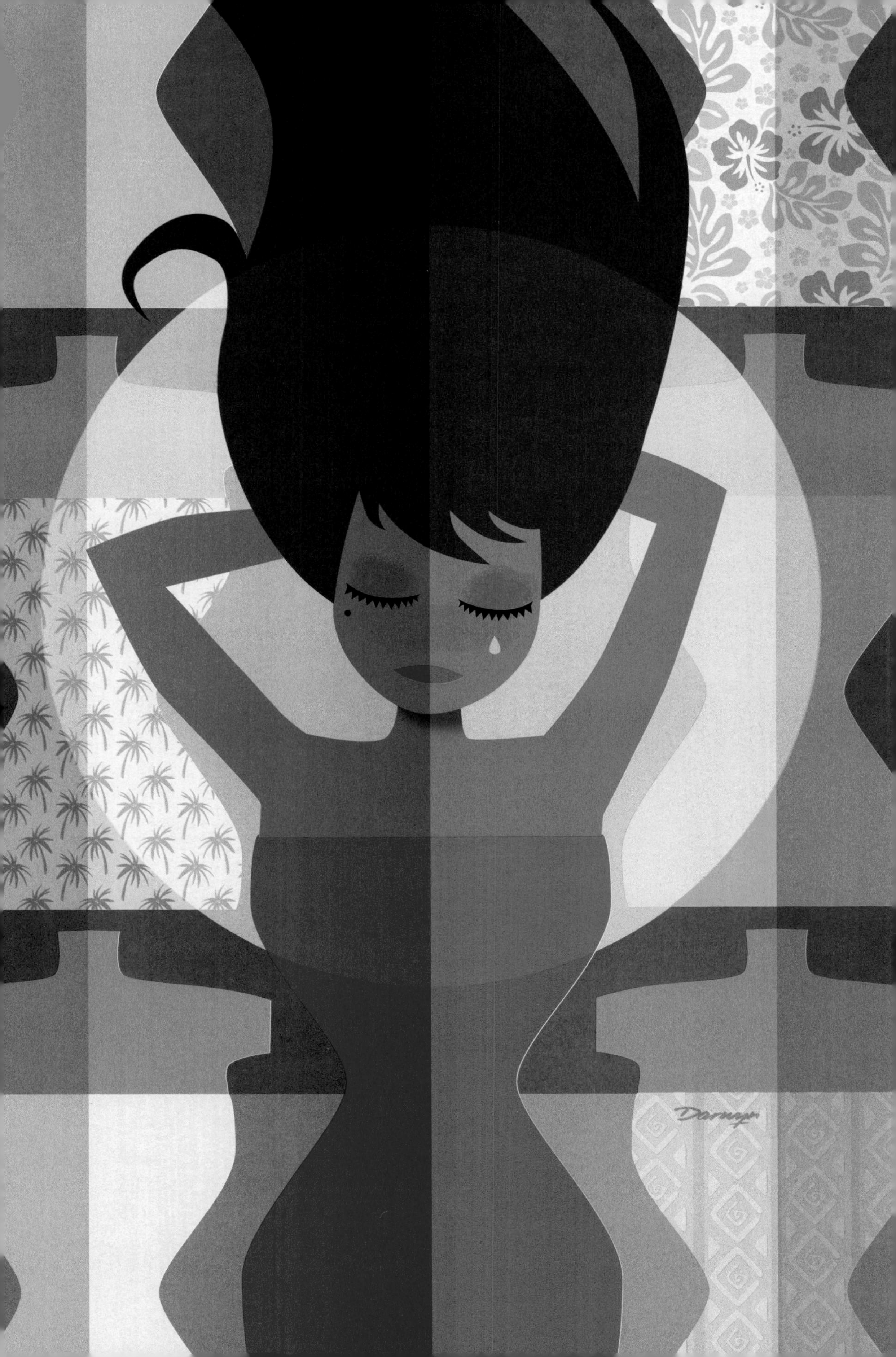

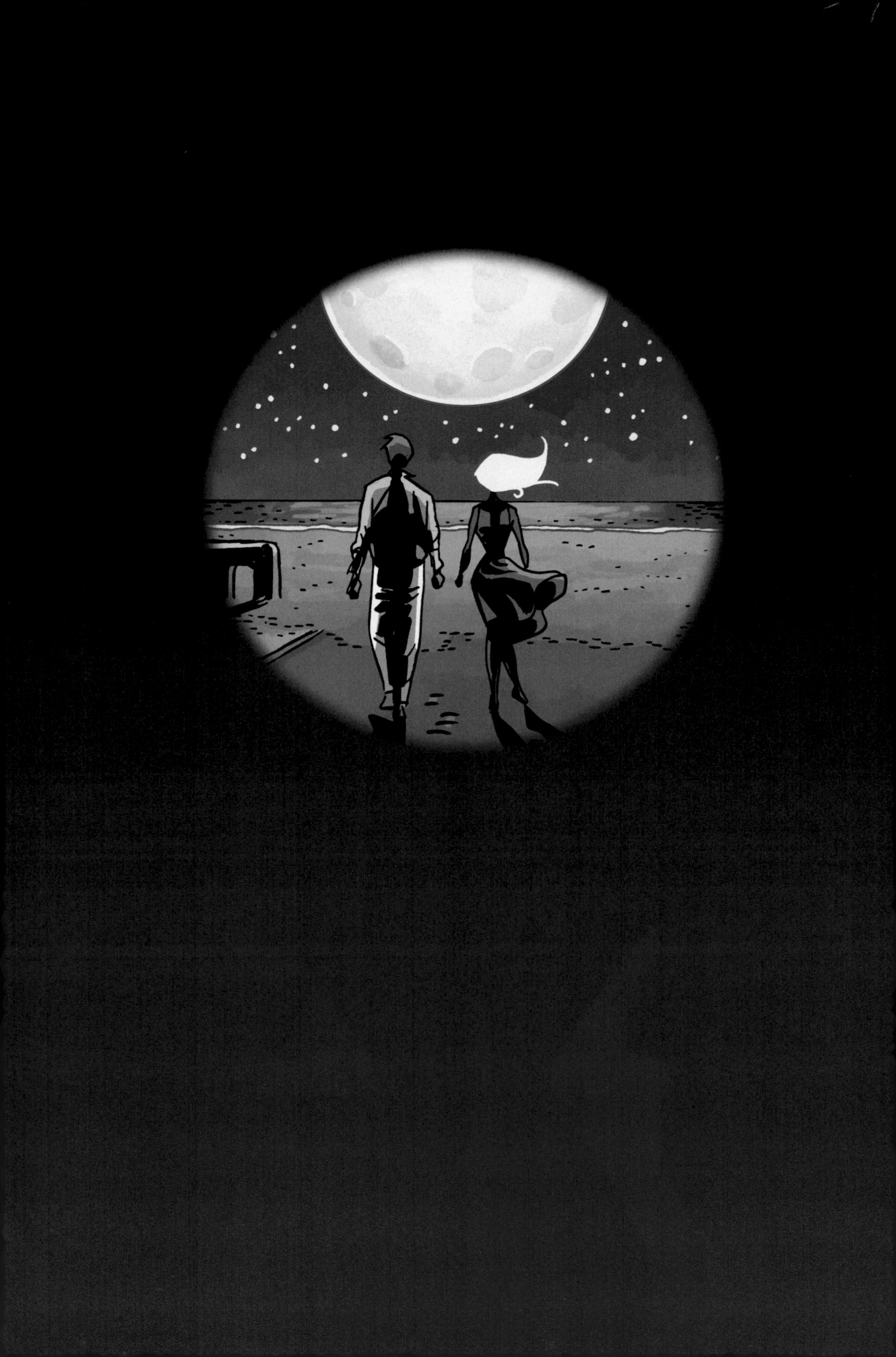

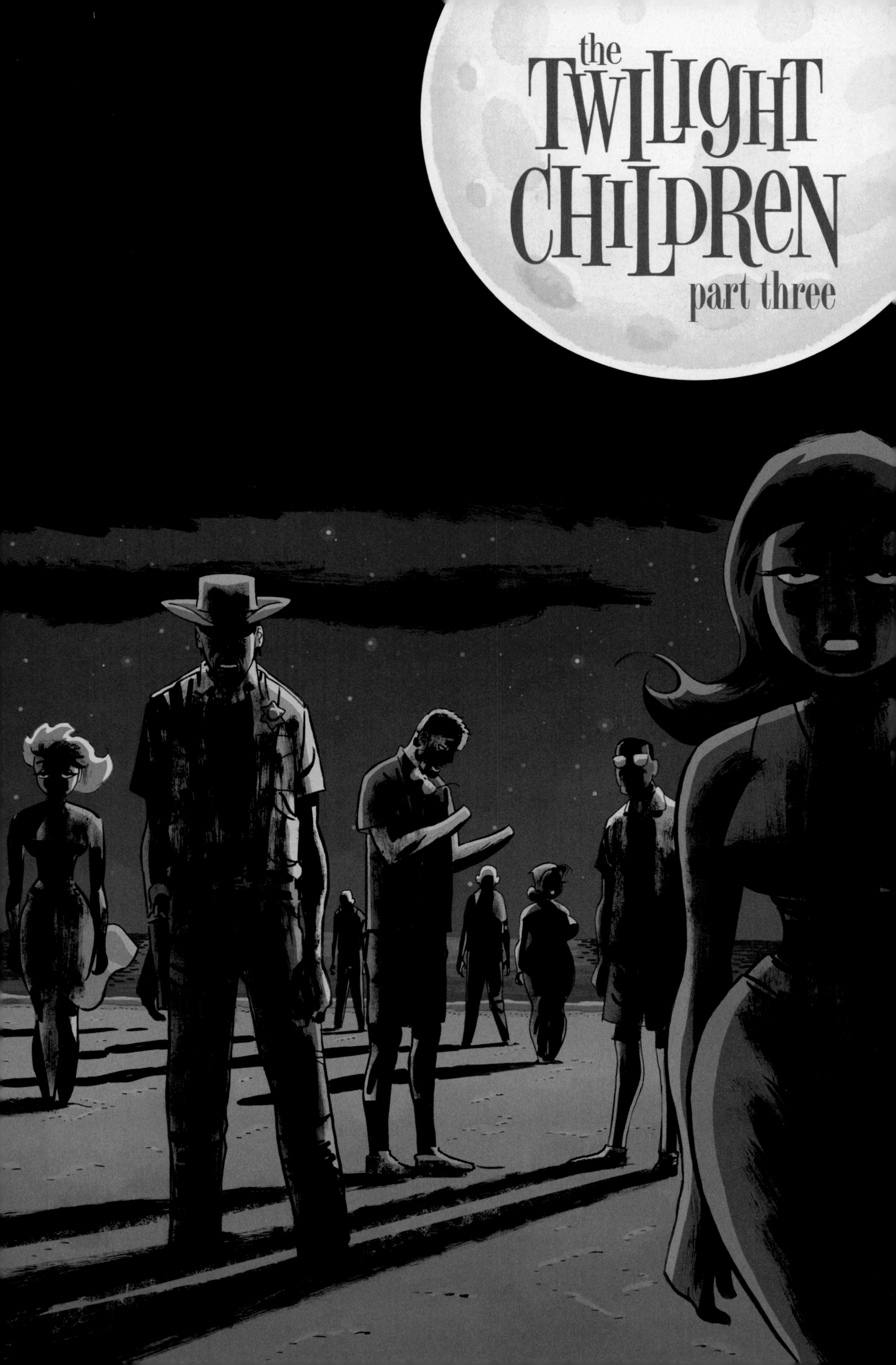
the TWILIGHT CHILDREN
part three

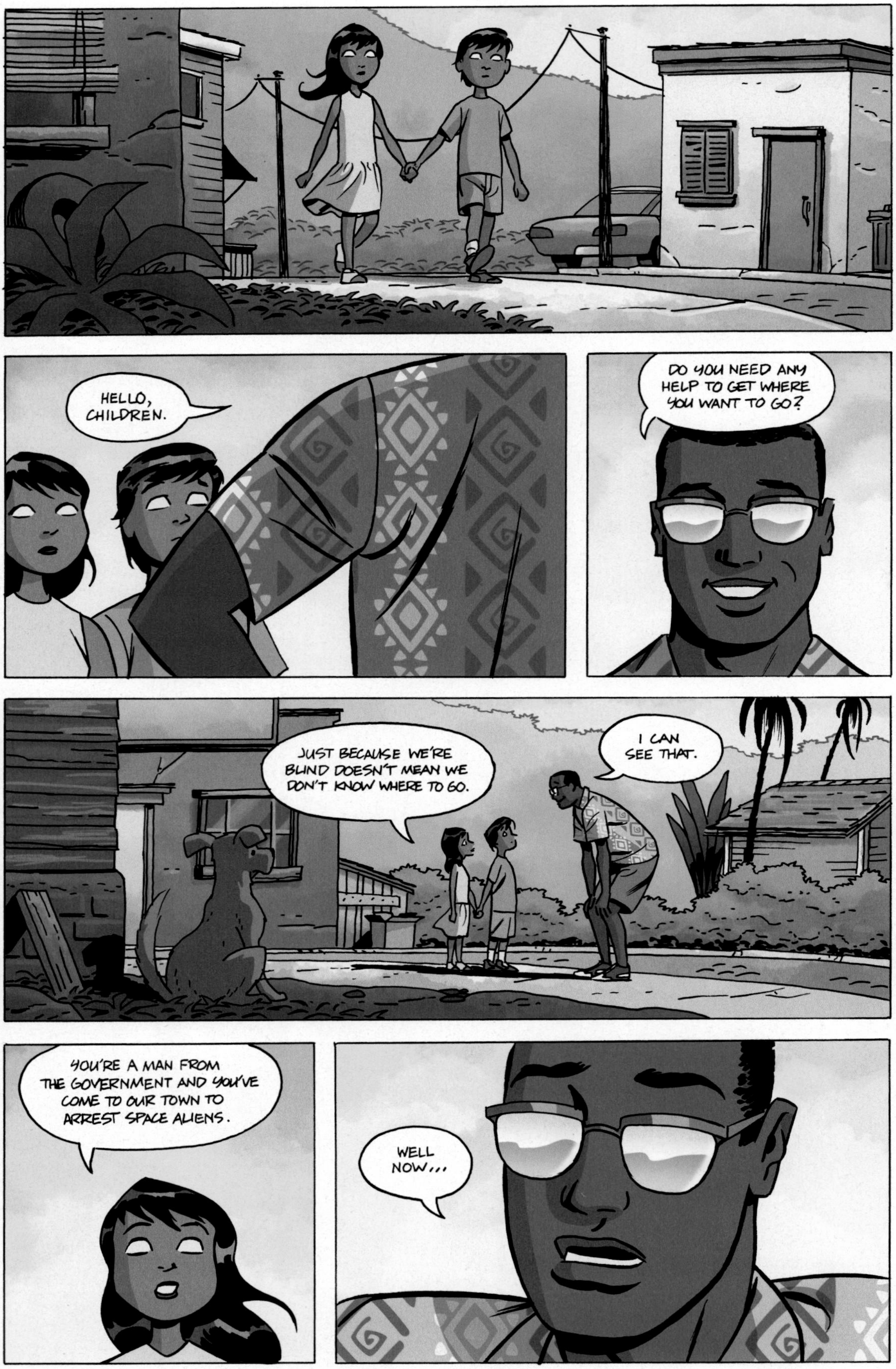
HELLO, CHILDREN.
DO YOU NEED ANY HELP TO GET WHERE YOU WANT TO GO?
JUST BECAUSE WE'RE BLIND DOESN'T MEAN WE DON'T KNOW WHERE TO GO.
I CAN SEE THAT.
YOU'RE A MAN FROM THE GOVERNMENT AND YOU'VE COME TO OUR TOWN TO ARREST SPACE ALIENS.
WELL NOW...

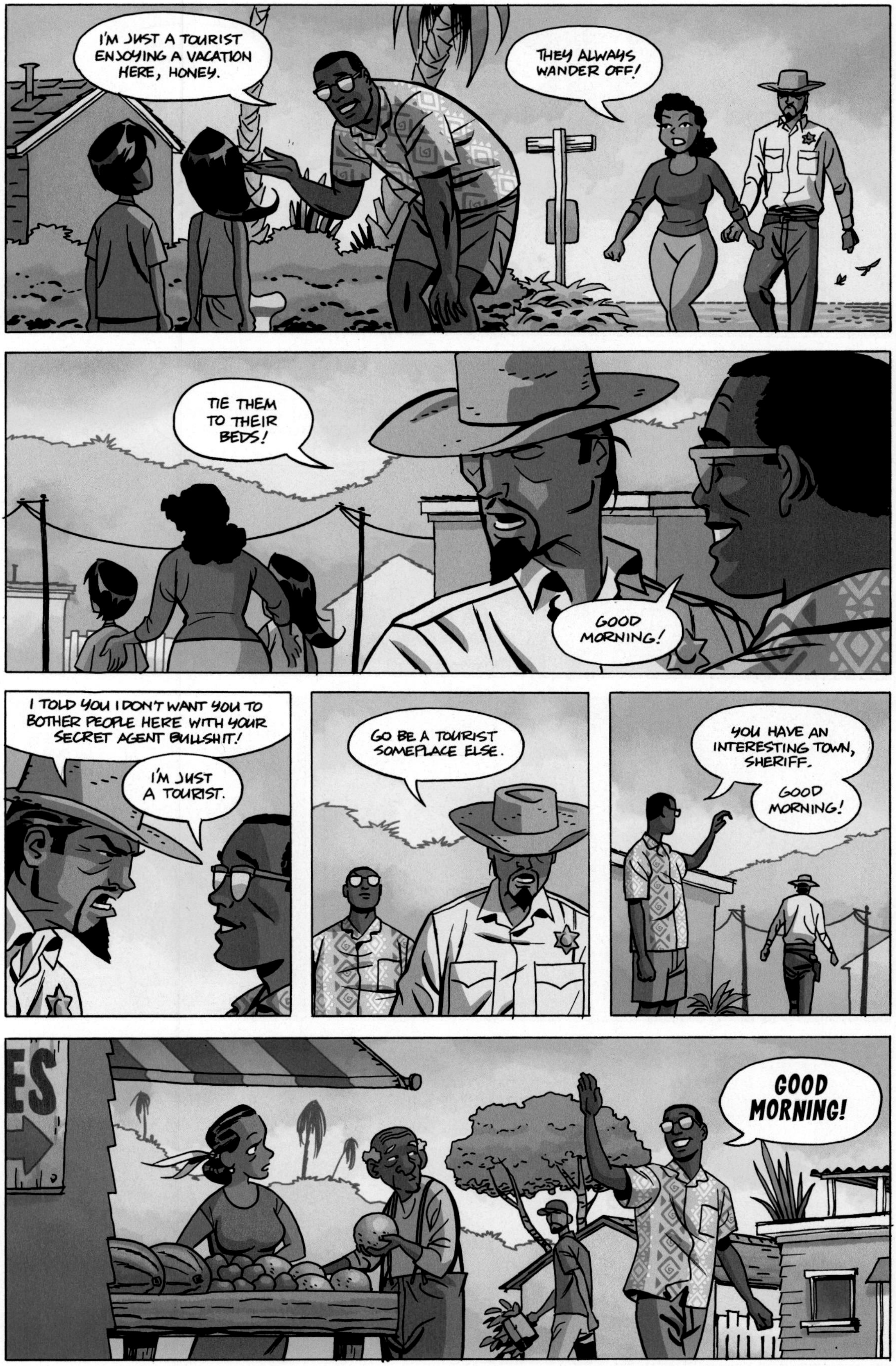
I'M JUST A TOURIST ENJOYING A VACATION HERE, HONEY.
THEY ALWAYS WANDER OFF!
TIE THEM TO THEIR BEDS!
GOOD MORNING!
I TOLD YOU I DON'T WANT YOU TO BOTHER PEOPLE HERE WITH YOUR SECRET AGENT BULLSHIT!
I'M JUST A TOURIST.
GO BE A TOURIST SOMEPLACE ELSE.
YOU HAVE AN INTERESTING TOWN, SHERIFF.
GOOD MORNING!
ES
GOOD MORNING!

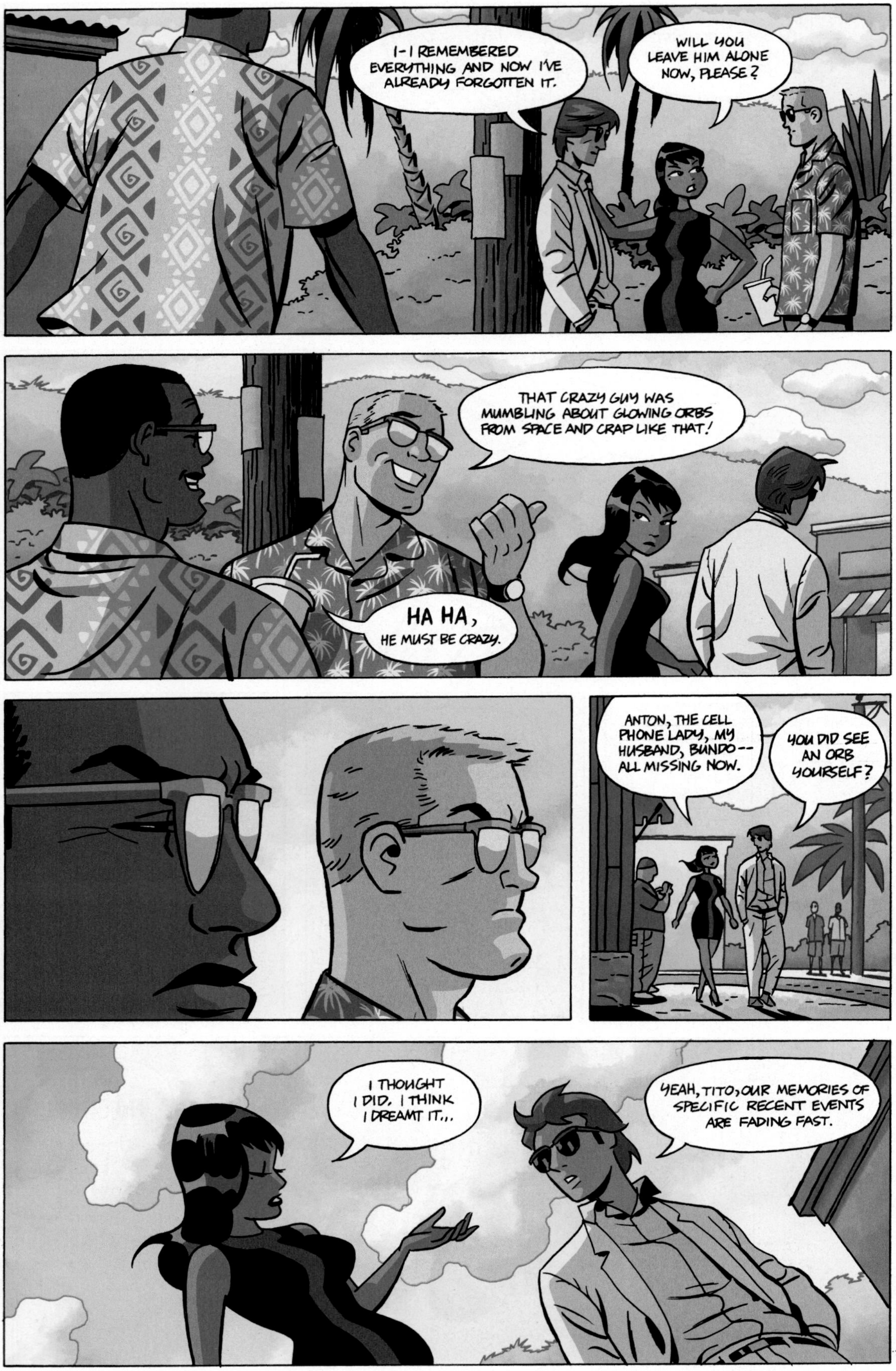
I-I REMEMBERED EVERYTHING AND NOW I'VE ALREADY FORGOTTEN IT.
WILL YOU LEAVE HIM ALONE NOW, PLEASE?
THAT CRAZY GUY WAS MUMBLING ABOUT GLOWING ORBS FROM SPACE AND CRAP LIKE THAT!
HA HA, HE MUST BE CRAZY.
ANTON, THE CELL PHONE LADY, MY HUSBAND, BUNDO-- ALL MISSING NOW.
YOU DID SEE AN ORB YOURSELF?
I THOUGHT I DID, I THINK I DREAMT IT...
YEAH, TITO, OUR MEMORIES OF SPECIFIC RECENT EVENTS ARE FADING FAST.

YOU GO AWAY! YOU'VE CAUSED ENOUGH TROUBLE!

WHO...WAS THAT?

I DON'T REMEM-- I DON'T KNOW.

BUT YOU SAID SHE CAUSED ENOUGH TROUBLE.

DID I?

SHE JUST LOOKS THE TYPE.

HA HA!

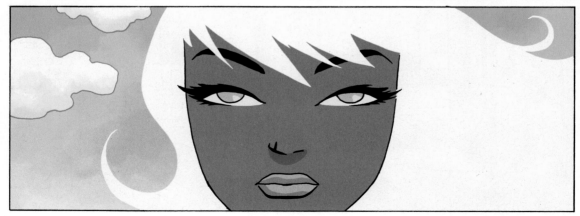

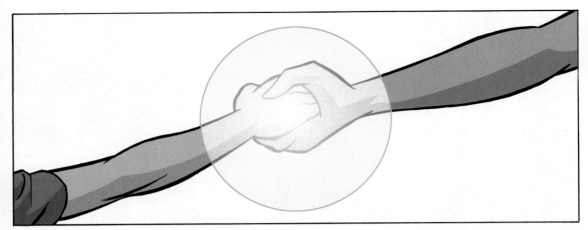

HEY, YOU!

OH, LET THEM HAVE FUN TOGETHER. HE SEEMS HAPPY WITH HER.

SHE DOES SEEM LIKE A CHILD, DOESN'T SHE?

IF YOU CAN CALL THAT A CHILD.

HARUMF.

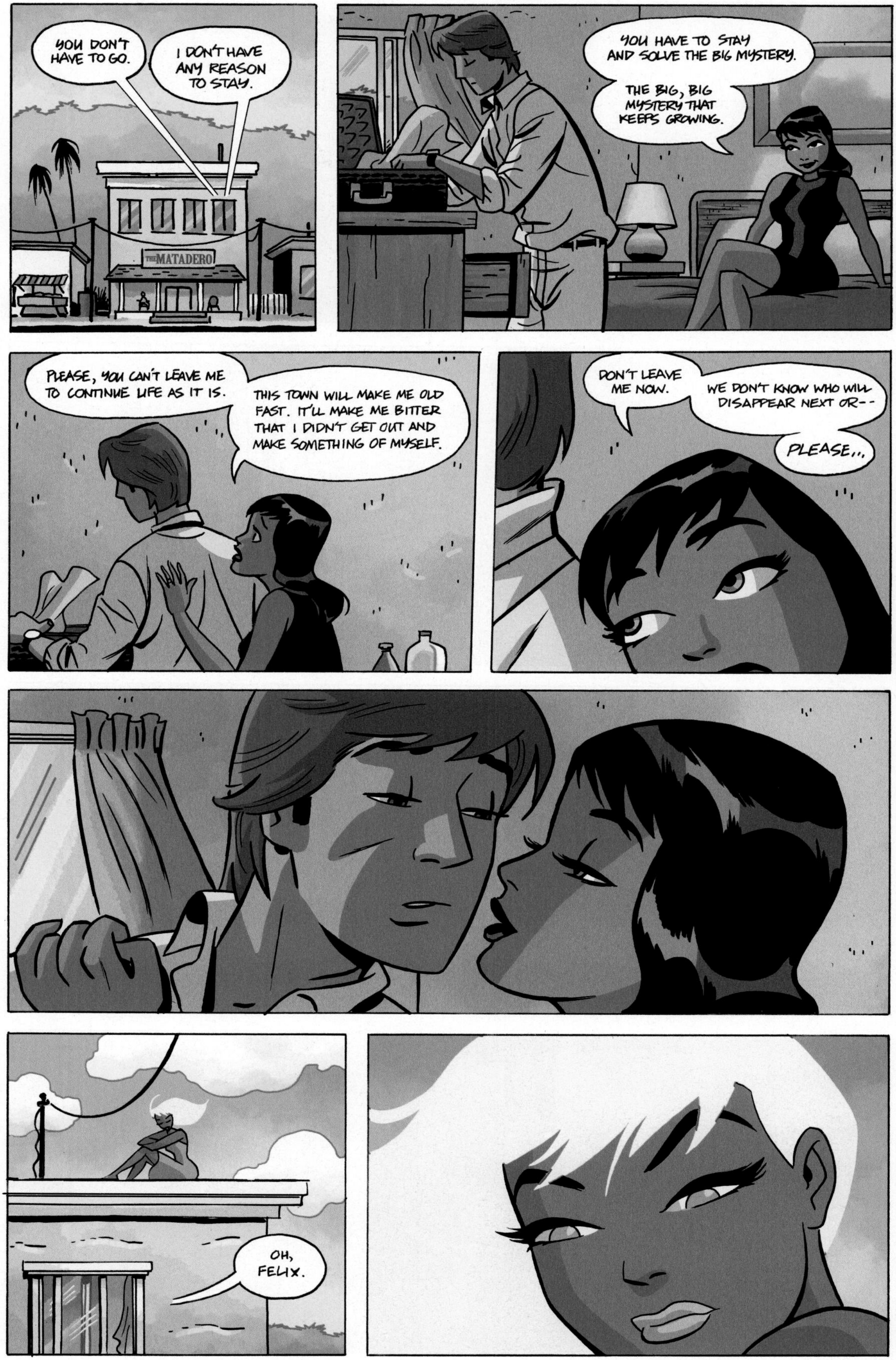
YOU DON'T HAVE TO GO.
I DON'T HAVE ANY REASON TO STAY.
THE MATADERO
YOU HAVE TO STAY AND SOLVE THE BIG MYSTERY.
THE BIG, BIG MYSTERY THAT KEEPS GROWING.
PLEASE, YOU CAN'T LEAVE ME TO CONTINUE LIFE AS IT IS.
THIS TOWN WILL MAKE ME OLD FAST. IT'LL MAKE ME BITTER THAT I DIDN'T GET OUT AND MAKE SOMETHING OF MYSELF.
DON'T LEAVE ME NOW.
WE DON'T KNOW WHO WILL DISAPPEAR NEXT OR--
PLEASE...
OH, FELIX.

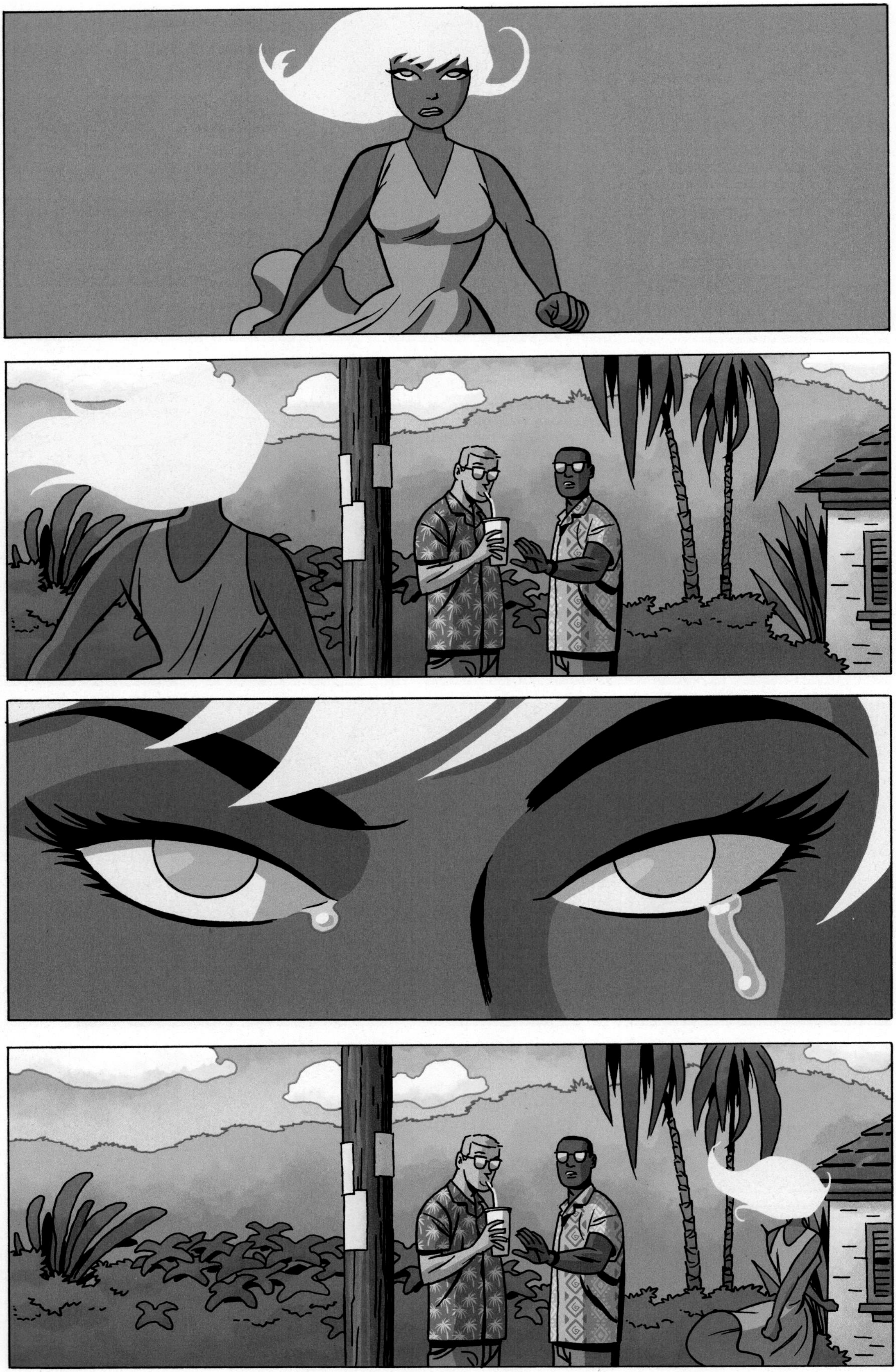

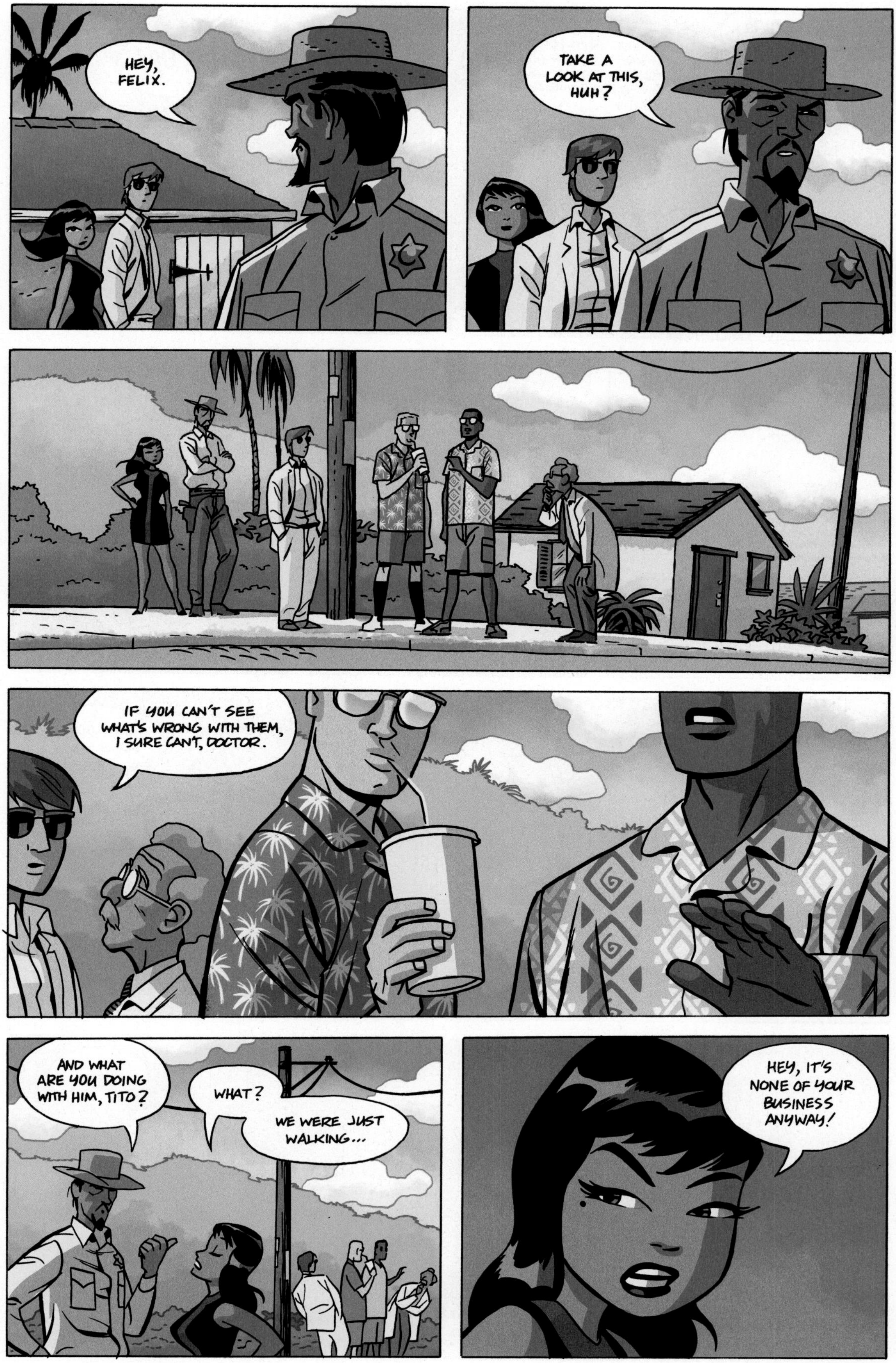
HEY, FELIX.
TAKE A LOOK AT THIS, HUH?
IF YOU CAN'T SEE WHAT'S WRONG WITH THEM, I SURE CAN'T, DOCTOR.
AND WHAT ARE YOU DOING WITH HIM, TITO?
WHAT?
WE WERE JUST WALKING...
HEY, IT'S NONE OF YOUR BUSINESS ANYWAY!

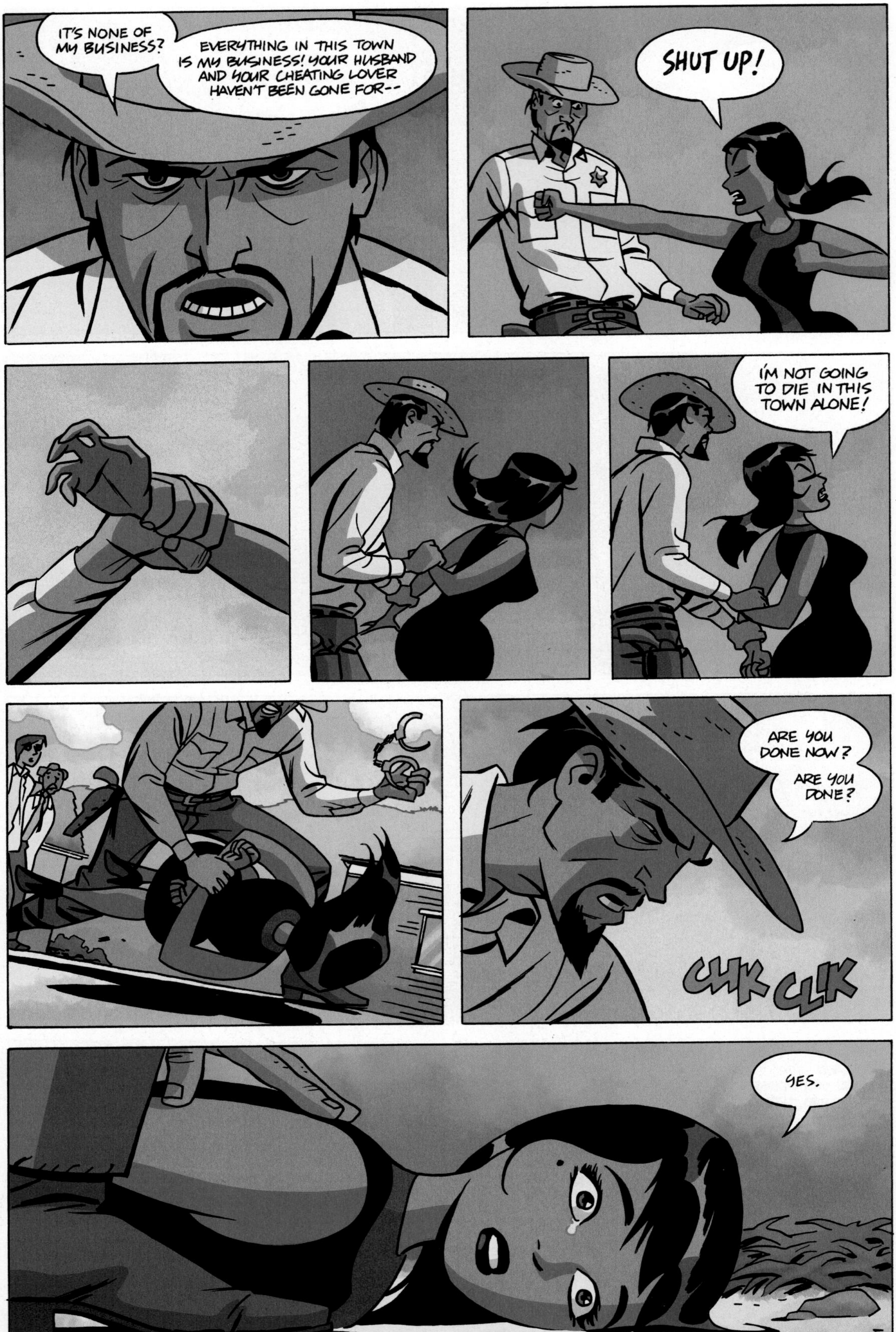
IT'S NONE OF MY BUSINESS?
EVERYTHING IN THIS TOWN IS MY BUSINESS! YOUR HUSBAND AND YOUR CHEATING LOVER HAVEN'T BEEN GONE FOR--
SHUT UP!
I'M NOT GOING TO DIE IN THIS TOWN ALONE!
ARE YOU DONE NOW?
ARE YOU DONE?
CLIK CLIK
YES.

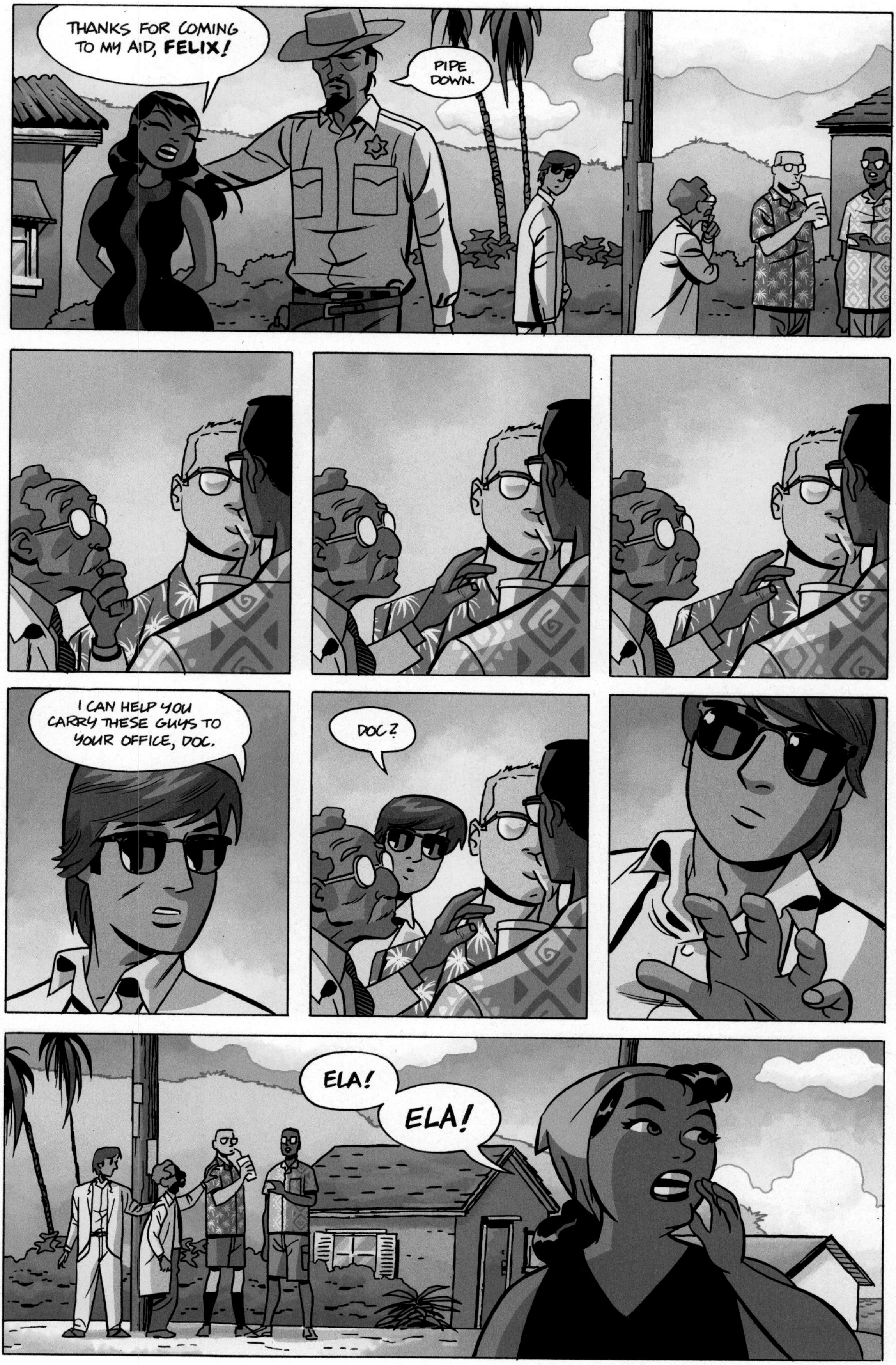
THANKS FOR COMING TO MY AID, FELIX!
PIPE DOWN.
I CAN HELP YOU CARRY THESE GUYS TO YOUR OFFICE, DOC.
DOC?
ELA!
ELA!

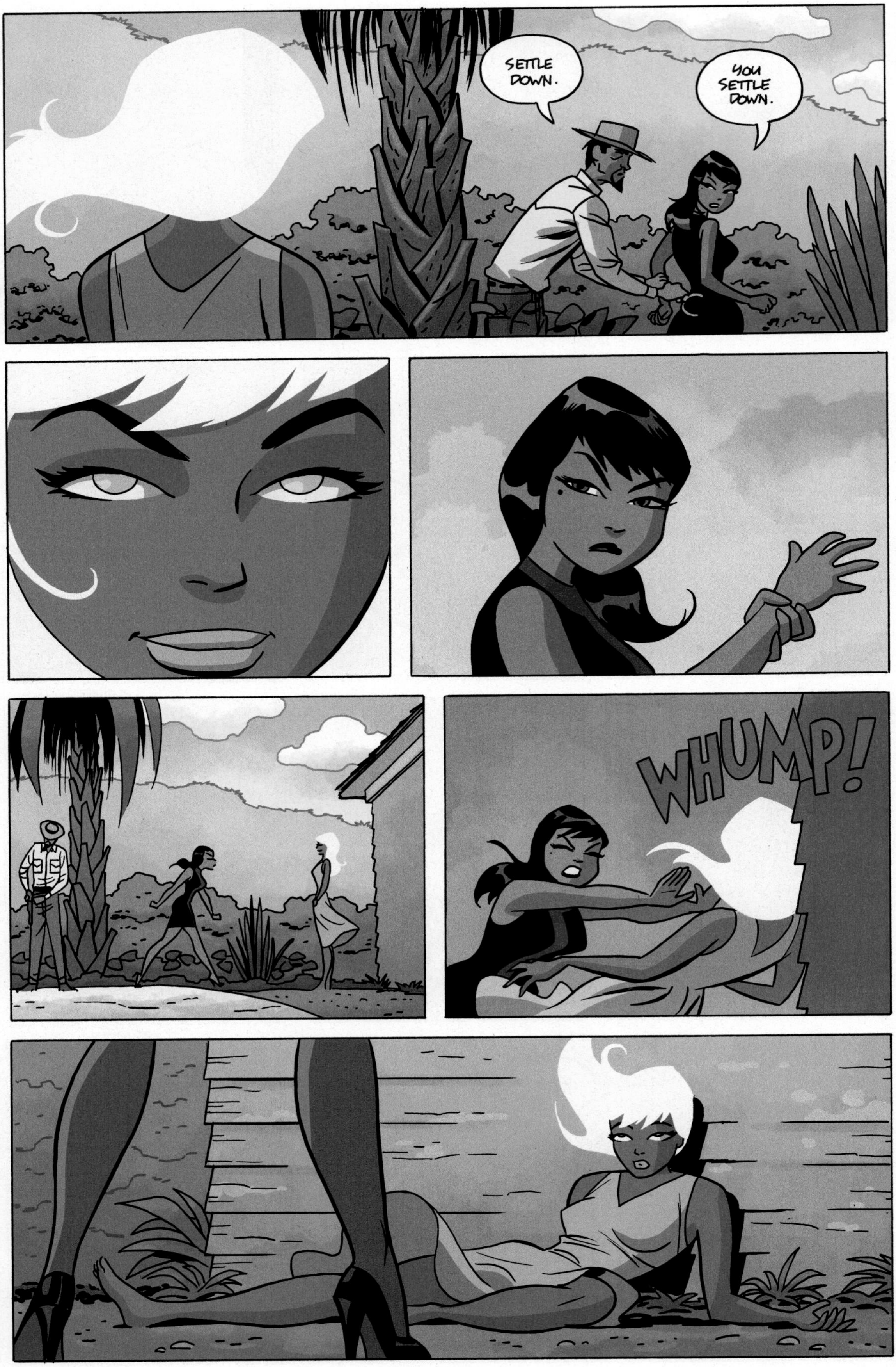
SETTLE DOWN.
YOU SETTLE DOWN.
WHUMP!

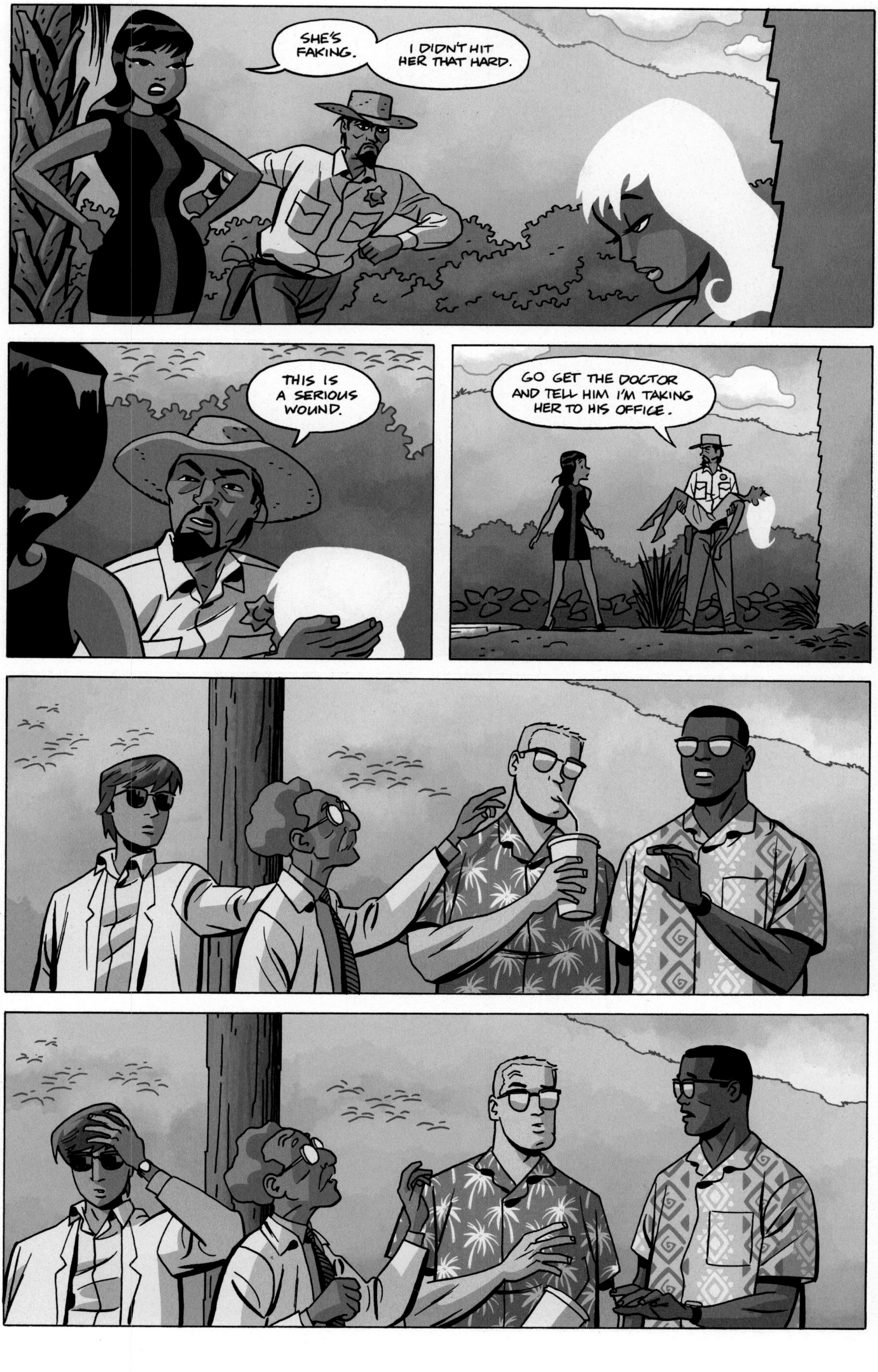
SHE'S FAKING.
I DIDN'T HIT HER THAT HARD.
THIS IS A SERIOUS WOUND.
GO GET THE DOCTOR AND TELL HIM I'M TAKING HER TO HIS OFFICE.

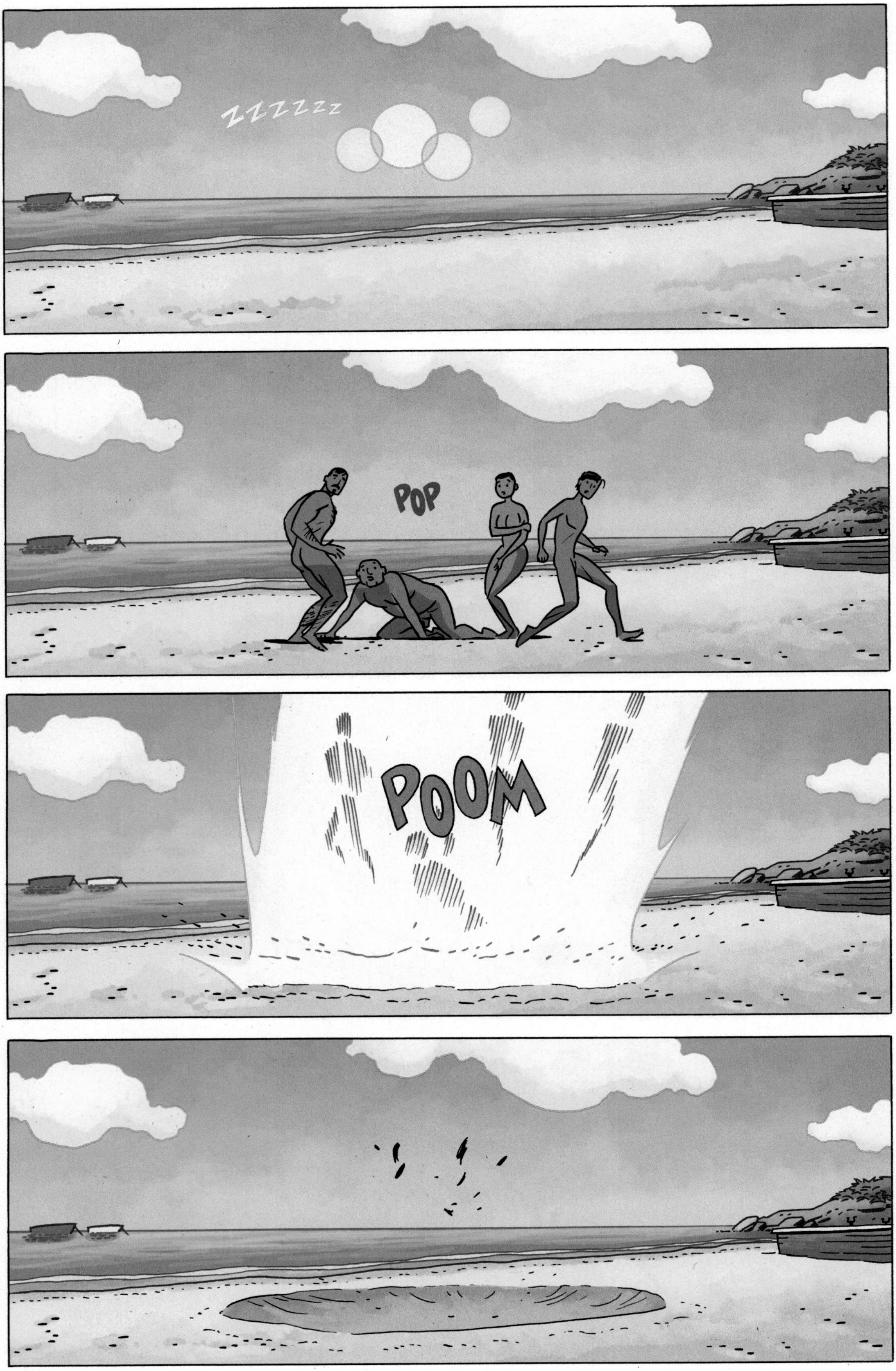
ZZZZZzz
POP
POOM

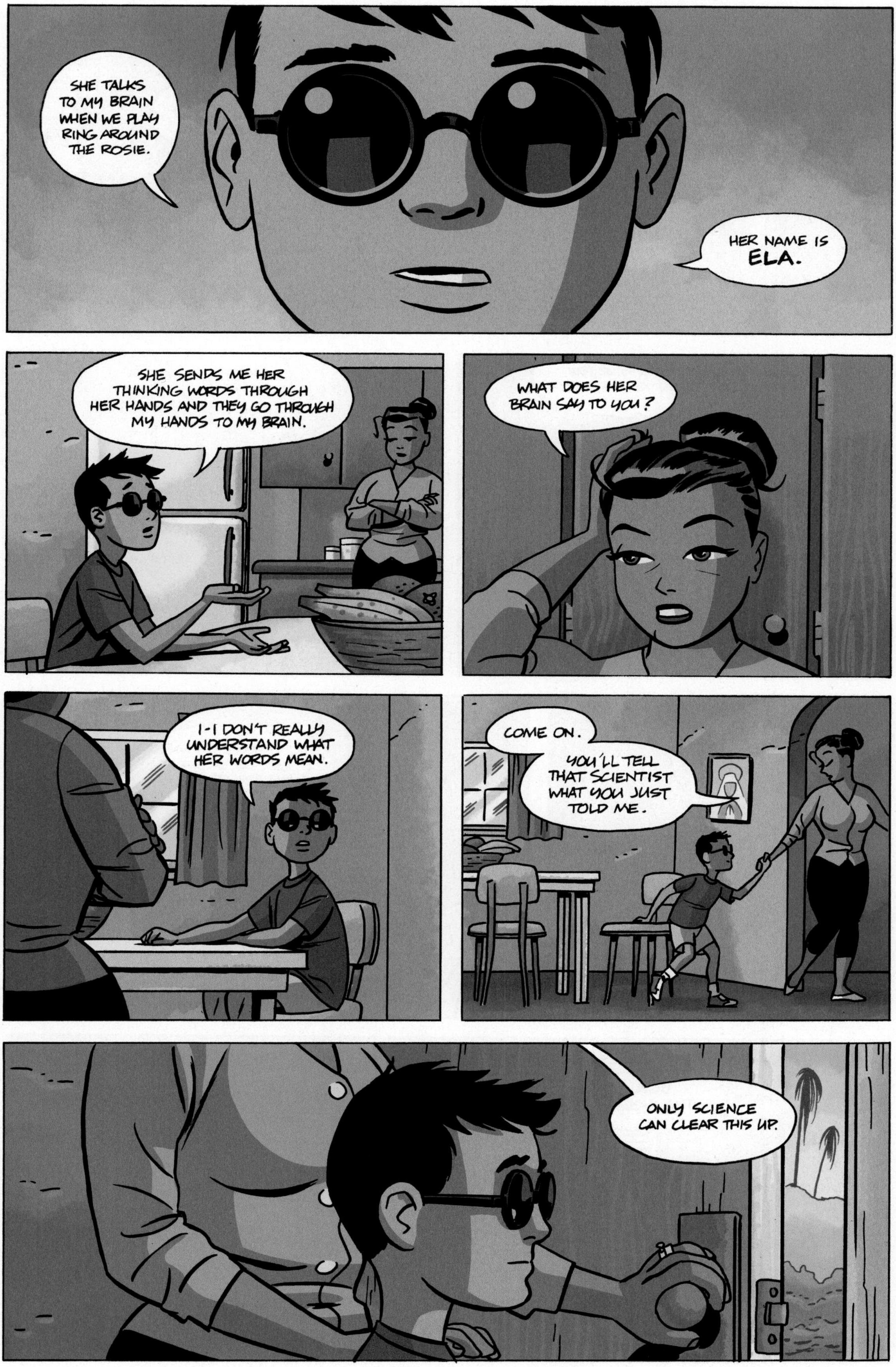
SHE TALKS TO MY BRAIN WHEN WE PLAY RING AROUND THE ROSIE.
HER NAME IS ELA.
SHE SENDS ME HER THINKING WORDS THROUGH HER HANDS AND THEY GO THROUGH MY HANDS TO MY BRAIN.
WHAT DOES HER BRAIN SAY TO YOU?
I-I DON'T REALLY UNDERSTAND WHAT HER WORDS MEAN.
COME ON.
YOU'LL TELL THAT SCIENTIST WHAT YOU JUST TOLD ME.
ONLY SCIENCE CAN CLEAR THIS UP.

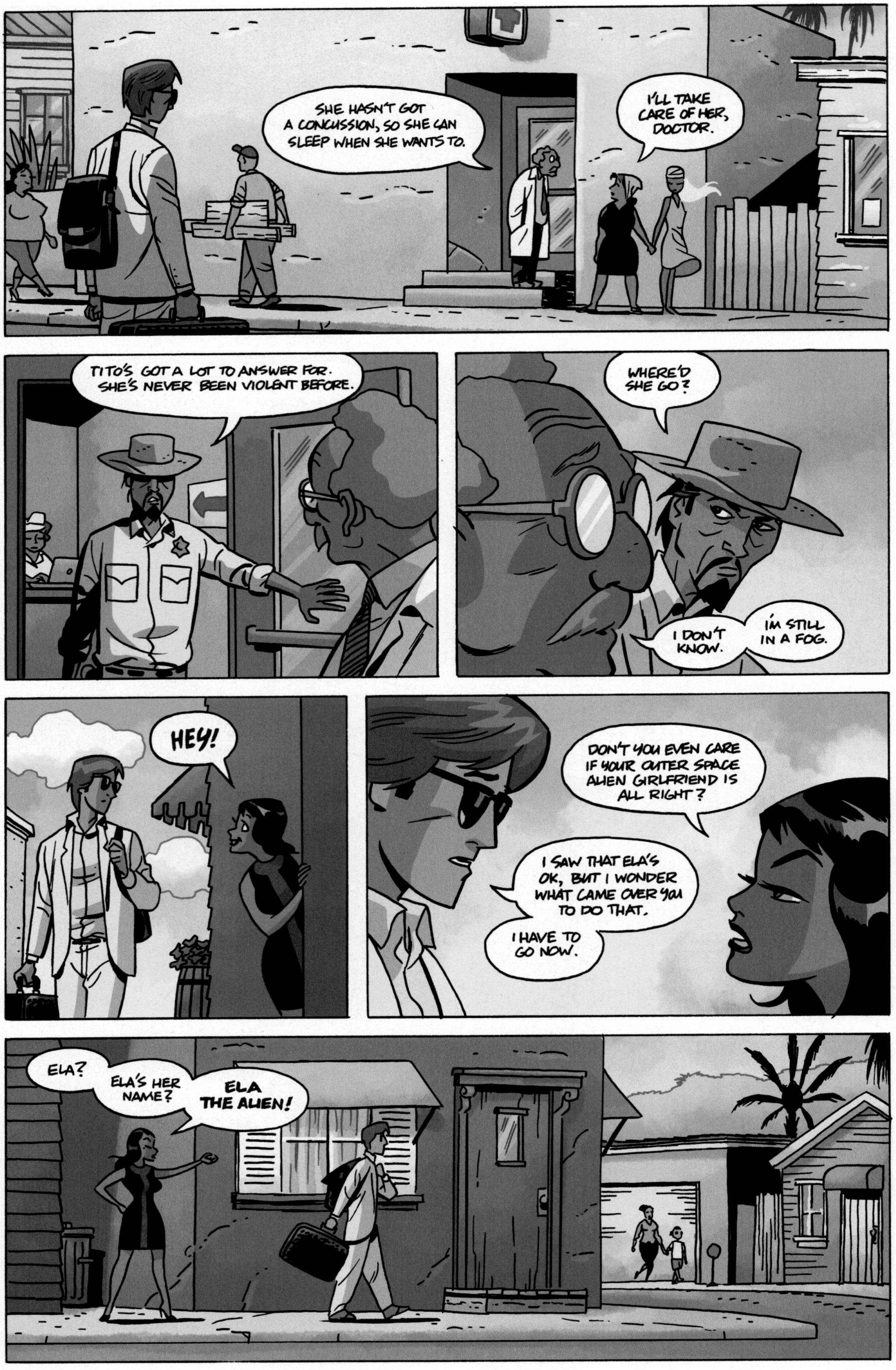
SHE HASN'T GOT A CONCUSSION, SO SHE CAN SLEEP WHEN SHE WANTS TO.
I'LL TAKE CARE OF HER, DOCTOR.
TITO'S GOT A LOT TO ANSWER FOR. SHE'S NEVER BEEN VIOLENT BEFORE.
WHERE'D SHE GO?
I DON'T KNOW.
I'M STILL IN A FOG.
HEY!
DON'T YOU EVEN CARE IF YOUR OUTER SPACE ALIEN GIRLFRIEND IS ALL RIGHT?
I SAW THAT ELA'S OK, BUT I WONDER WHAT CAME OVER YOU TO DO THAT.
I HAVE TO GO NOW.
ELA?
ELA'S HER NAME?
ELA THE ALIEN!

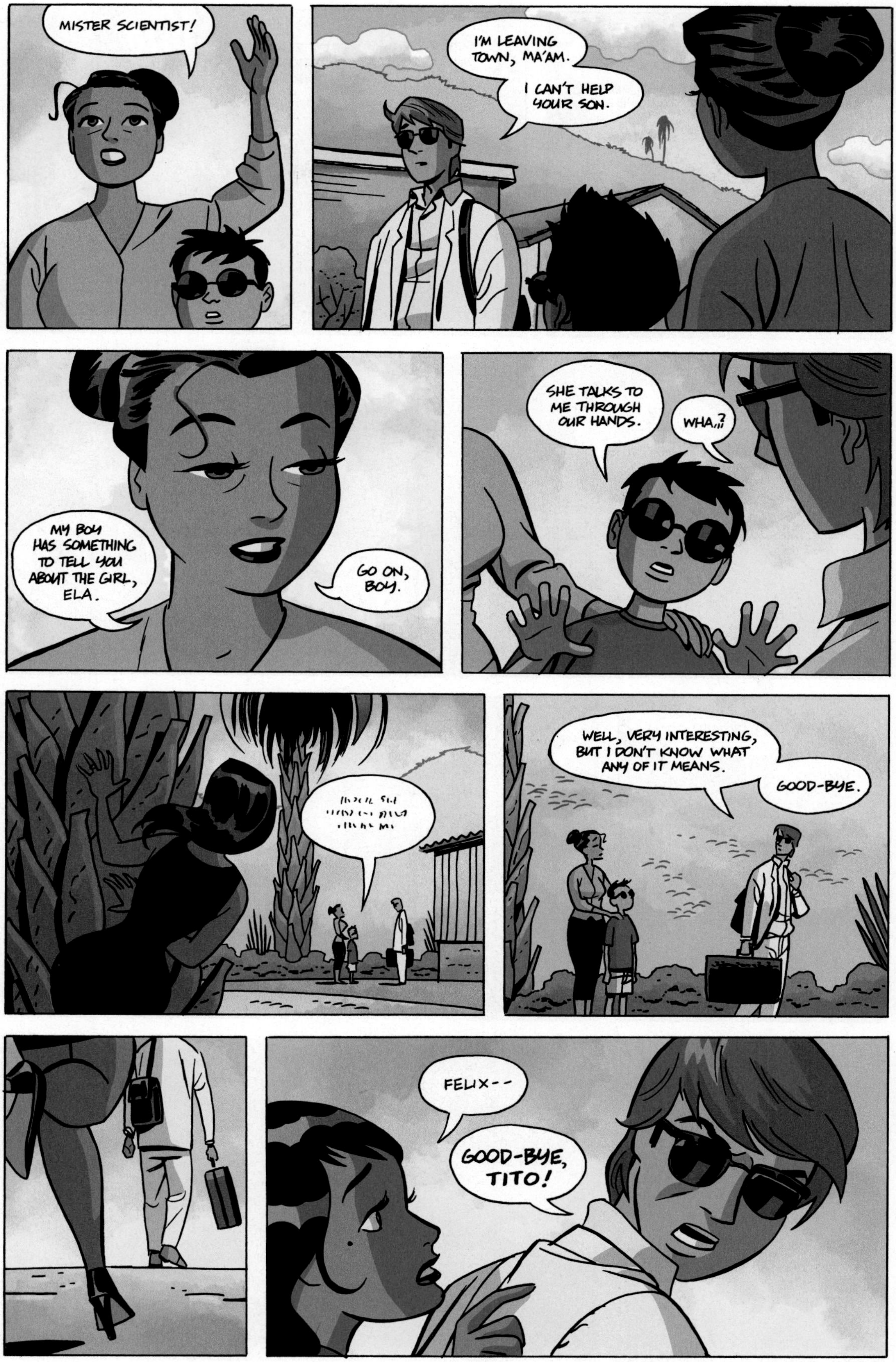
MISTER SCIENTIST!
I'M LEAVING TOWN, MA'AM.
I CAN'T HELP YOUR SON.
MY BOY HAS SOMETHING TO TELL YOU ABOUT THE GIRL, ELA.
GO ON, BOY.
SHE TALKS TO ME THROUGH OUR HANDS.
WHA..?
WELL, VERY INTERESTING, BUT I DON'T KNOW WHAT ANY OF IT MEANS.
GOOD-BYE.
FELIX--
GOOD-BYE, TITO!

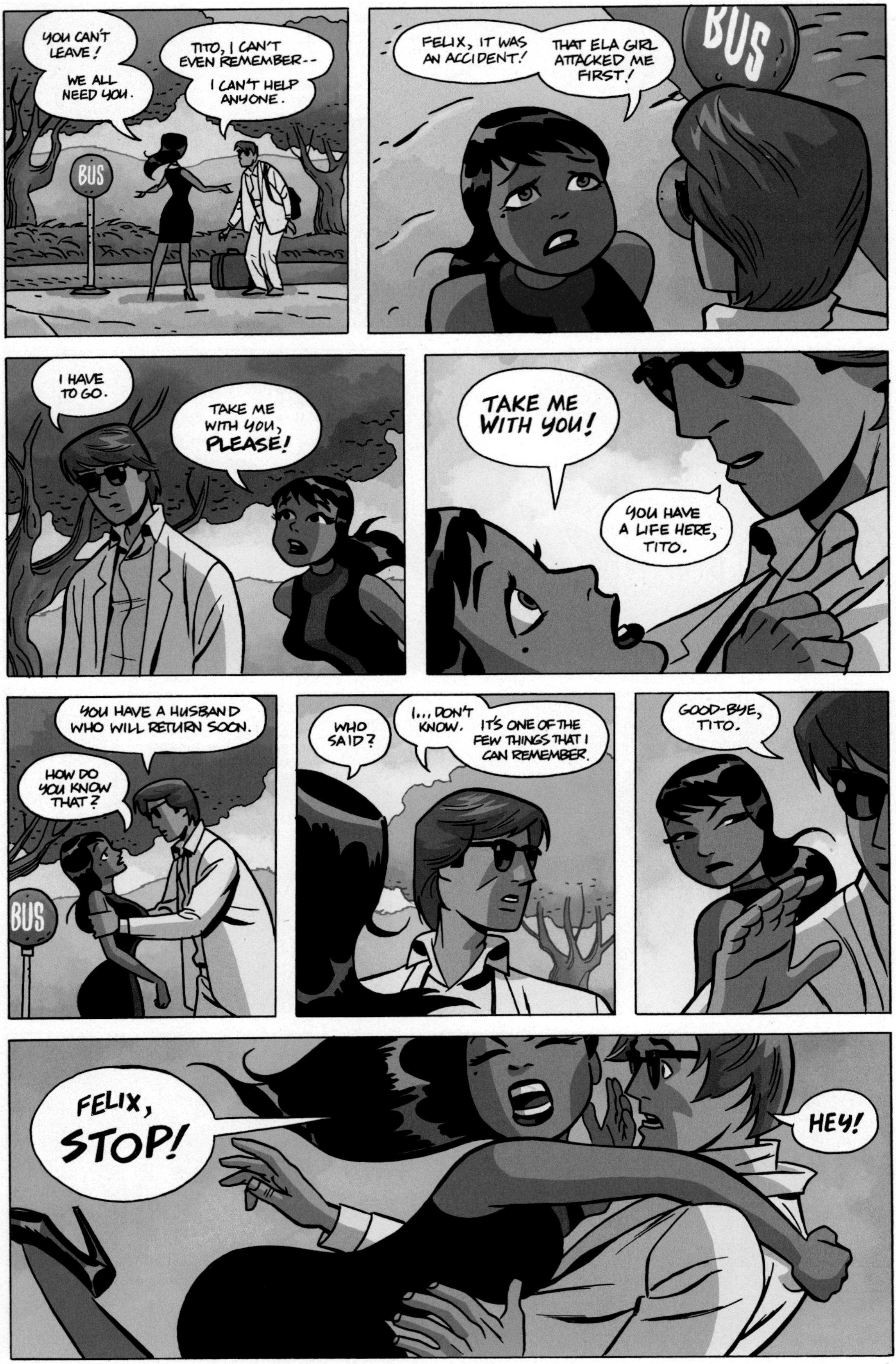
YOU CAN'T LEAVE!
WE ALL NEED YOU.
TITO, I CAN'T EVEN REMEMBER--
I CAN'T HELP ANYONE.
BUS
FELIX, IT WAS AN ACCIDENT!
THAT ELA GIRL ATTACKED ME FIRST!
BUS
I HAVE TO GO.
TAKE ME WITH YOU, PLEASE!
TAKE ME WITH YOU!
YOU HAVE A LIFE HERE, TITO.
YOU HAVE A HUSBAND WHO WILL RETURN SOON.
HOW DO YOU KNOW THAT?
BUS
WHO SAID?
I... DON'T KNOW.
IT'S ONE OF THE FEW THINGS THAT I CAN REMEMBER.
GOOD-BYE, TITO.
FELIX, STOP!
HEY!

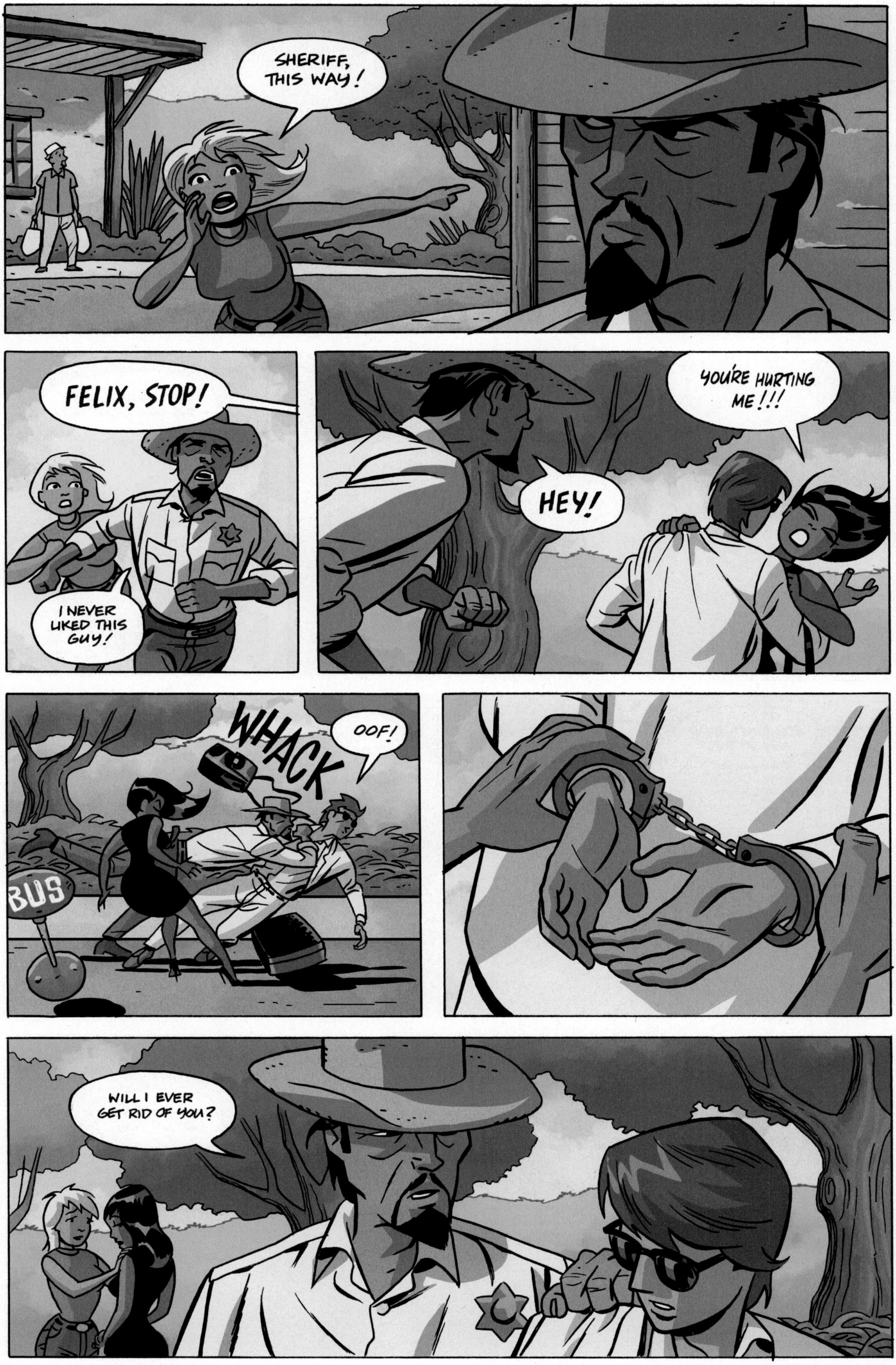
SHERIFF, THIS WAY!
FELIX, STOP!
I NEVER LIKED THIS GUY!
YOU'RE HURTING ME!!!
HEY!
WHACK
OOF!
BUS
WILL I EVER GET RID OF YOU?

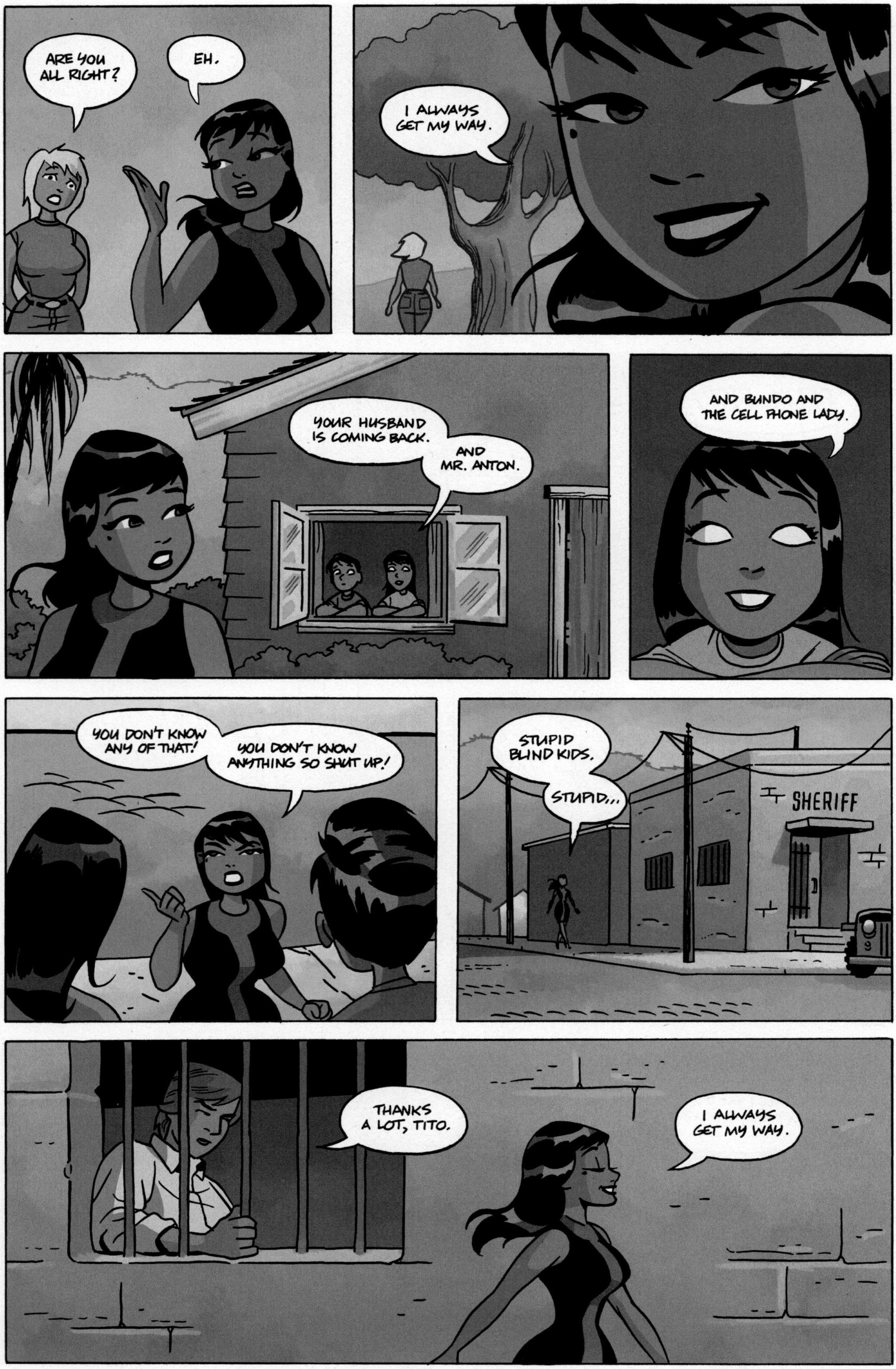
ARE YOU ALL RIGHT?
EH.
I ALWAYS GET MY WAY.
YOUR HUSBAND IS COMING BACK.
AND MR. ANTON.
AND BUNDO AND THE CELL PHONE LADY.
YOU DON'T KNOW ANY OF THAT!
YOU DON'T KNOW ANYTHING SO SHUT UP!
STUPID BLIND KIDS.
STUPID...
SHERIFF
THANKS A LOT, TITO.
I ALWAYS GET MY WAY.

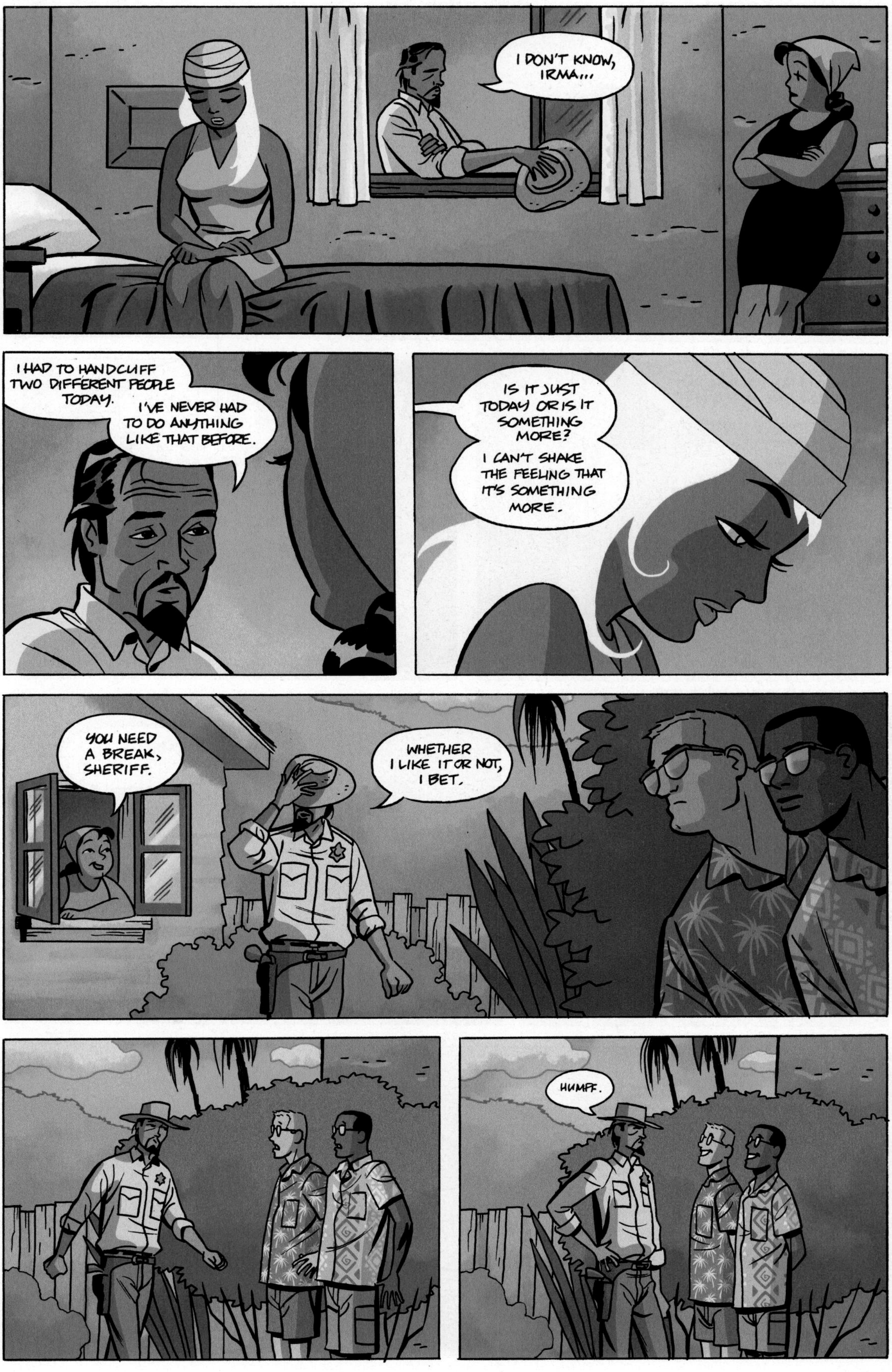
I DON'T KNOW, IRMA...
I HAD TO HANDCUFF TWO DIFFERENT PEOPLE TODAY.
I'VE NEVER HAD TO DO ANYTHING LIKE THAT BEFORE.
IS IT JUST TODAY OR IS IT SOMETHING MORE?
I CAN'T SHAKE THE FEELING THAT IT'S SOMETHING MORE.
YOU NEED A BREAK, SHERIFF.
WHETHER I LIKE IT OR NOT, I BET.
HUMFF.

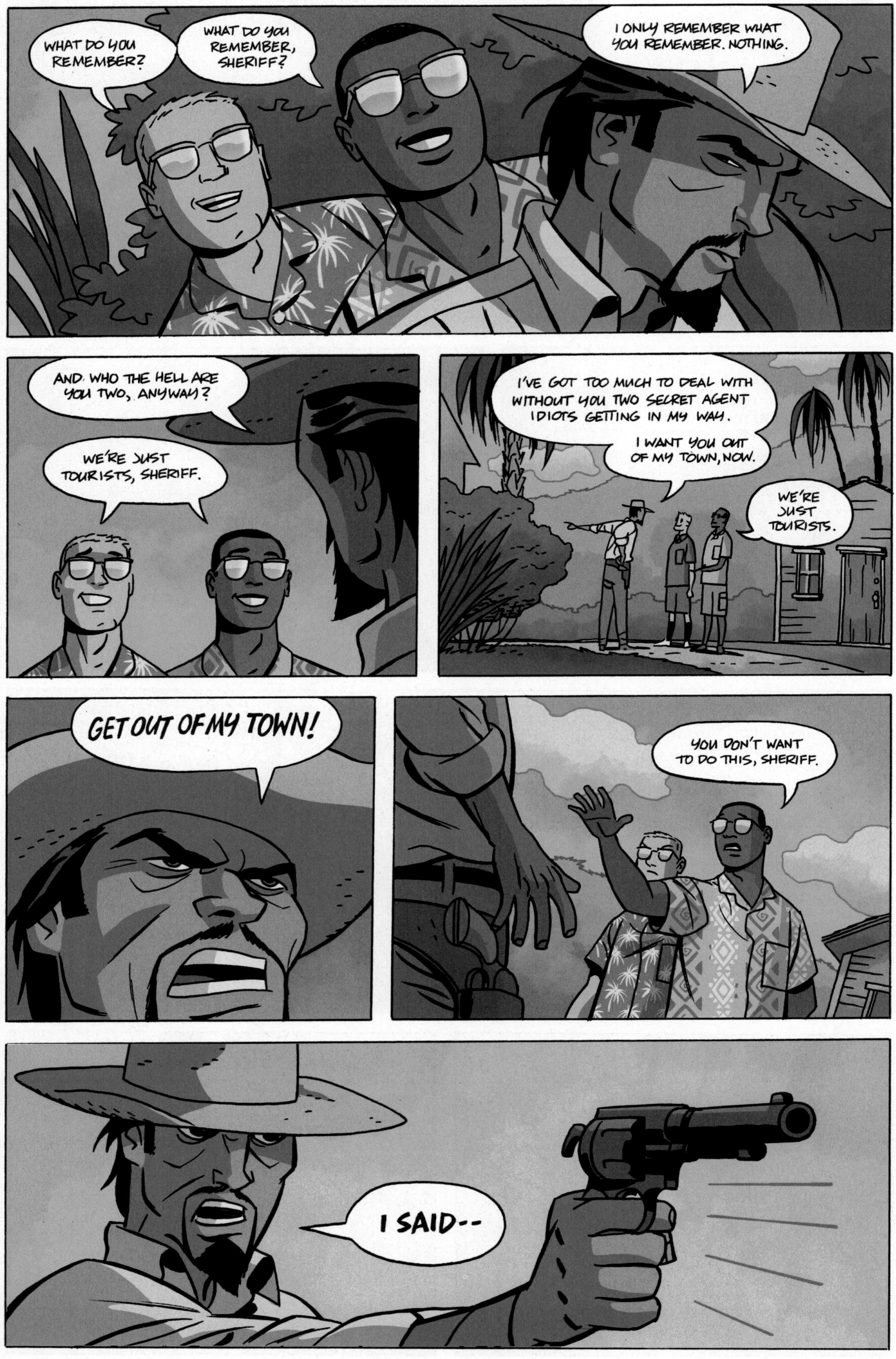
WHAT DO YOU REMEMBER?
WHAT DO YOU REMEMBER, SHERIFF?
I ONLY REMEMBER WHAT YOU REMEMBER. NOTHING.
AND WHO THE HELL ARE YOU TWO, ANYWAY?
WE'RE JUST TOURISTS, SHERIFF.
I'VE GOT TOO MUCH TO DEAL WITH WITHOUT YOU TWO SECRET AGENT IDIOTS GETTING IN MY WAY.
I WANT YOU OUT OF MY TOWN, NOW.
WE'RE JUST TOURISTS.
GET OUT OF MY TOWN!
YOU DON'T WANT TO DO THIS, SHERIFF.
I SAID--

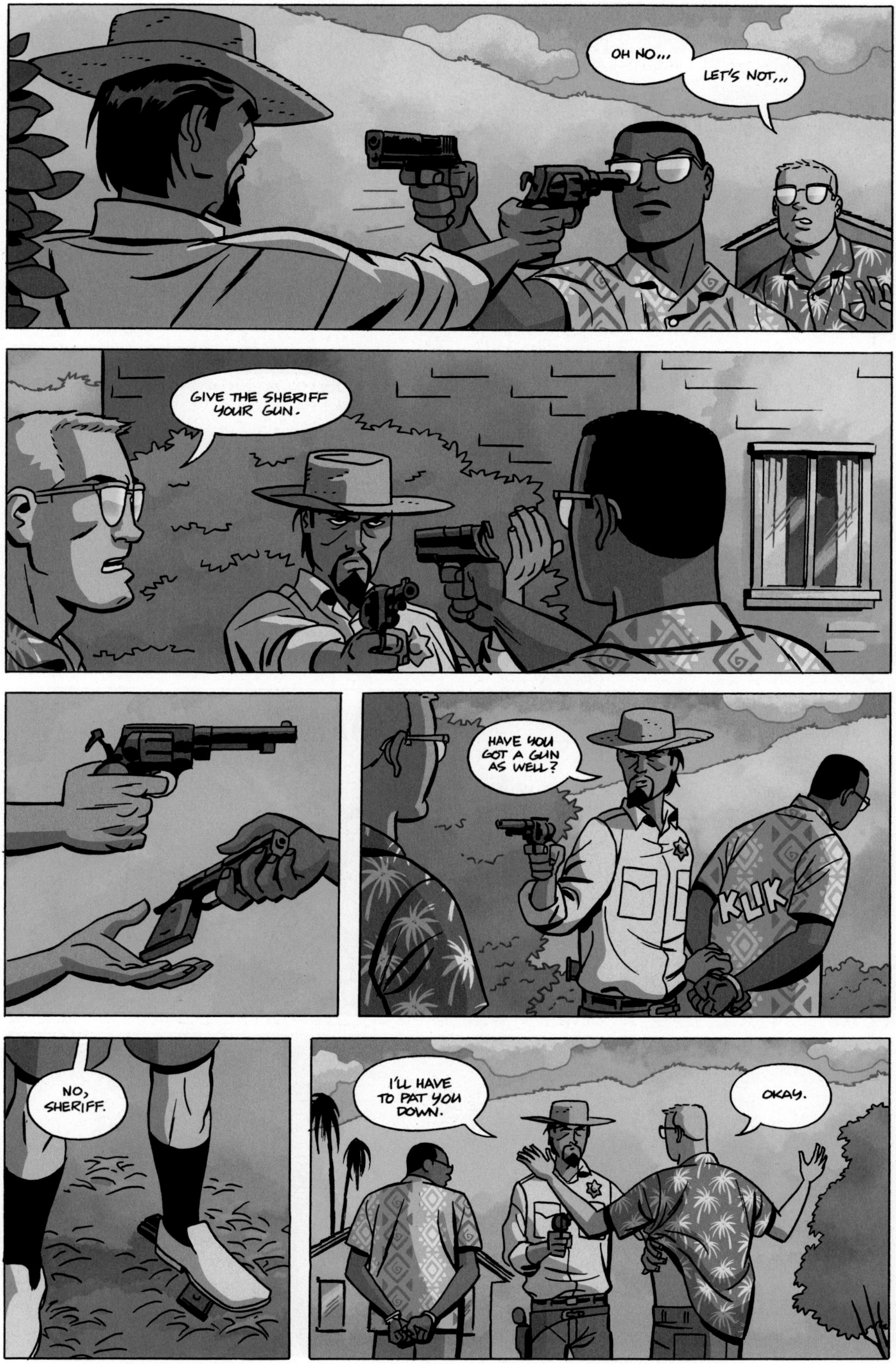

OH NO...
LET'S NOT...
GIVE THE SHERIFF YOUR GUN.
HAVE YOU GOT A GUN AS WELL?
KLIK
NO, SHERIFF.
I'LL HAVE TO PAT YOU DOWN.
OKAY.

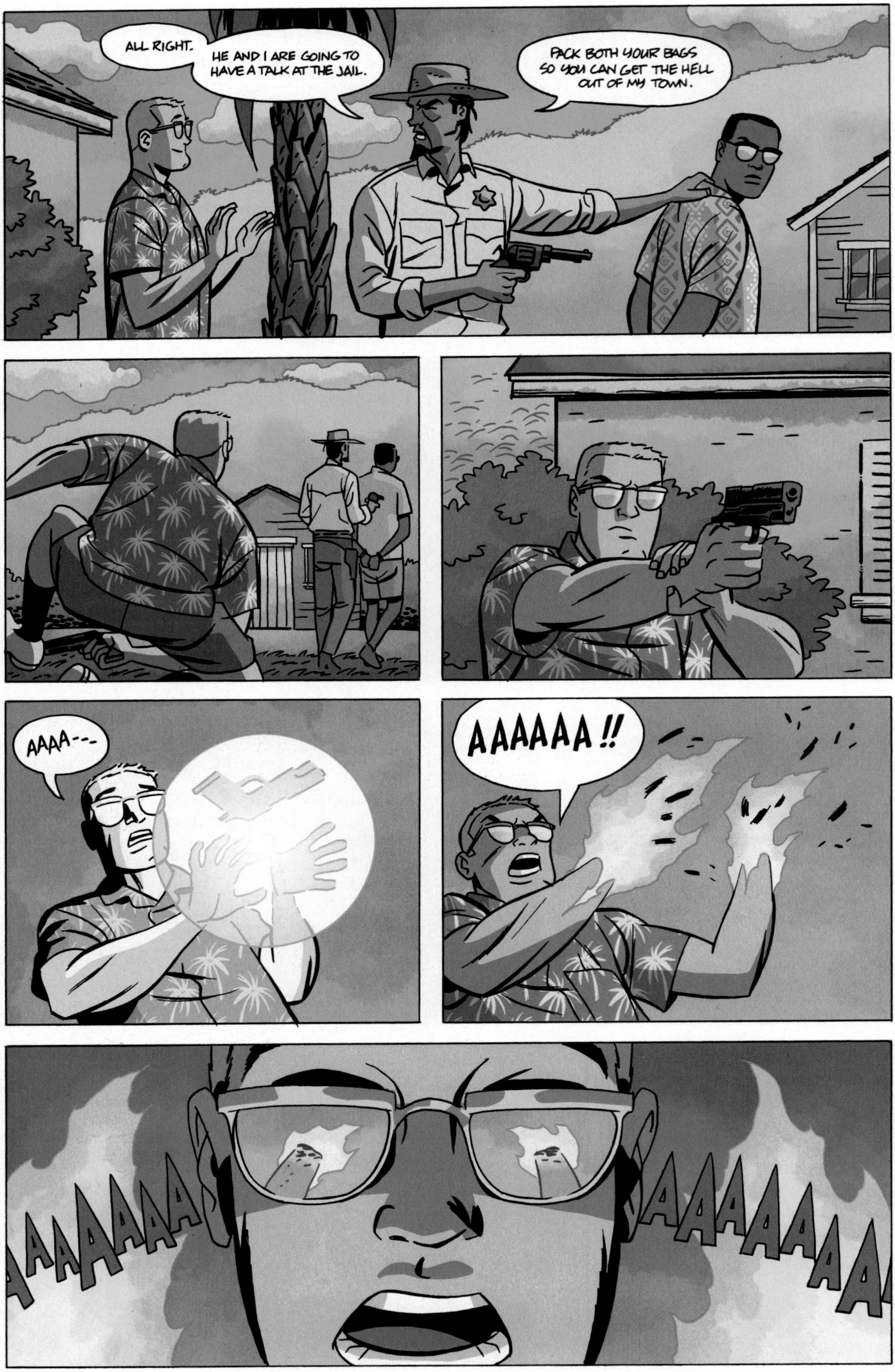
ALL RIGHT.
HE AND I ARE GOING TO HAVE A TALK AT THE JAIL.
PACK BOTH YOUR BAGS SO YOU CAN GET THE HELL OUT OF MY TOWN.
AAAA---
AAAAAA!!
AAAAAAAA
AAAAAAAAAAAA

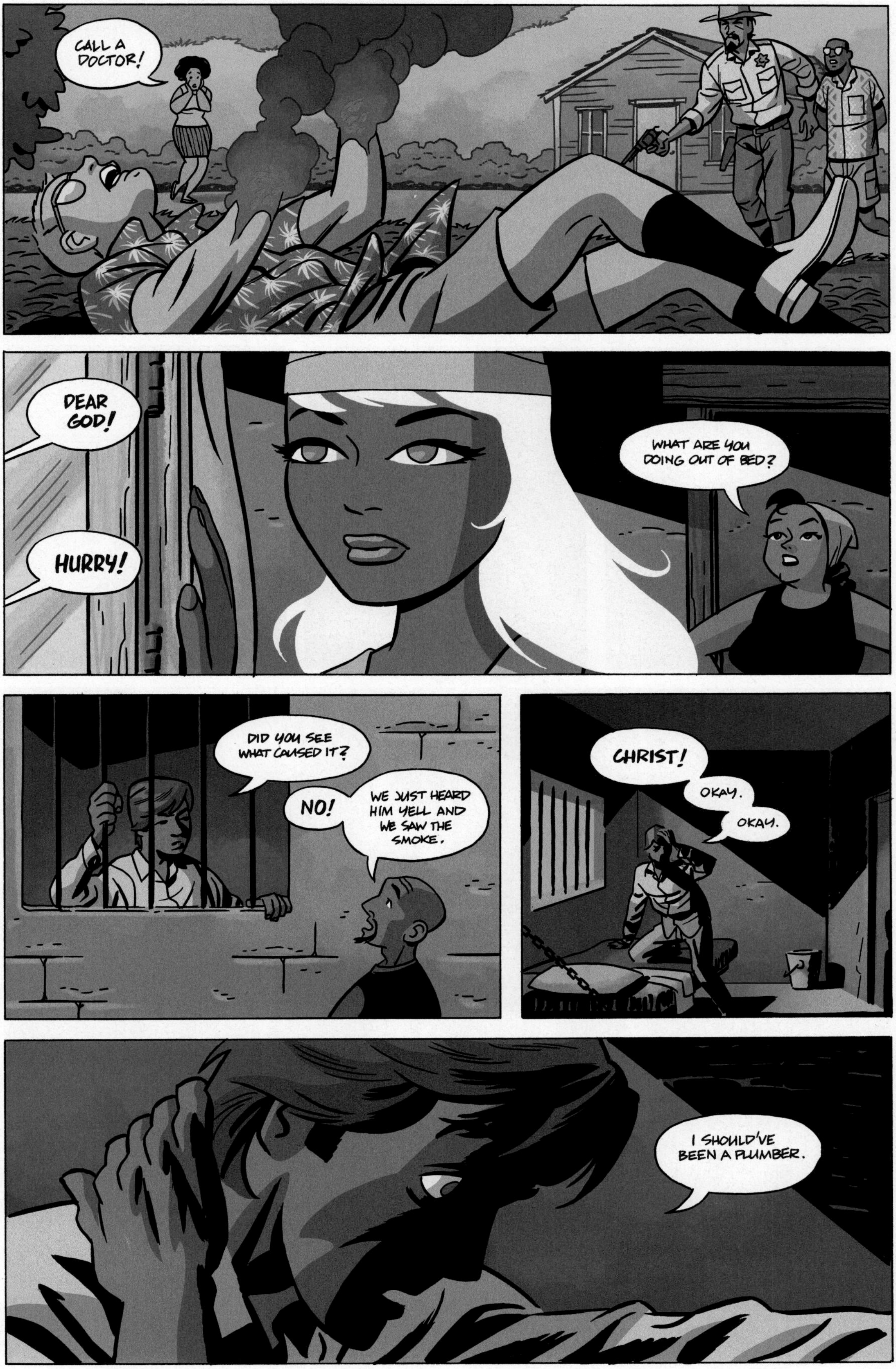
CALL A DOCTOR!
DEAR GOD!
HURRY!
WHAT ARE YOU DOING OUT OF BED?
DID YOU SEE WHAT CAUSED IT?
NO!
WE JUST HEARD HIM YELL AND WE SAW THE SMOKE.
CHRIST!
OKAY.
OKAY.
I SHOULD'VE BEEN A PLUMBER.

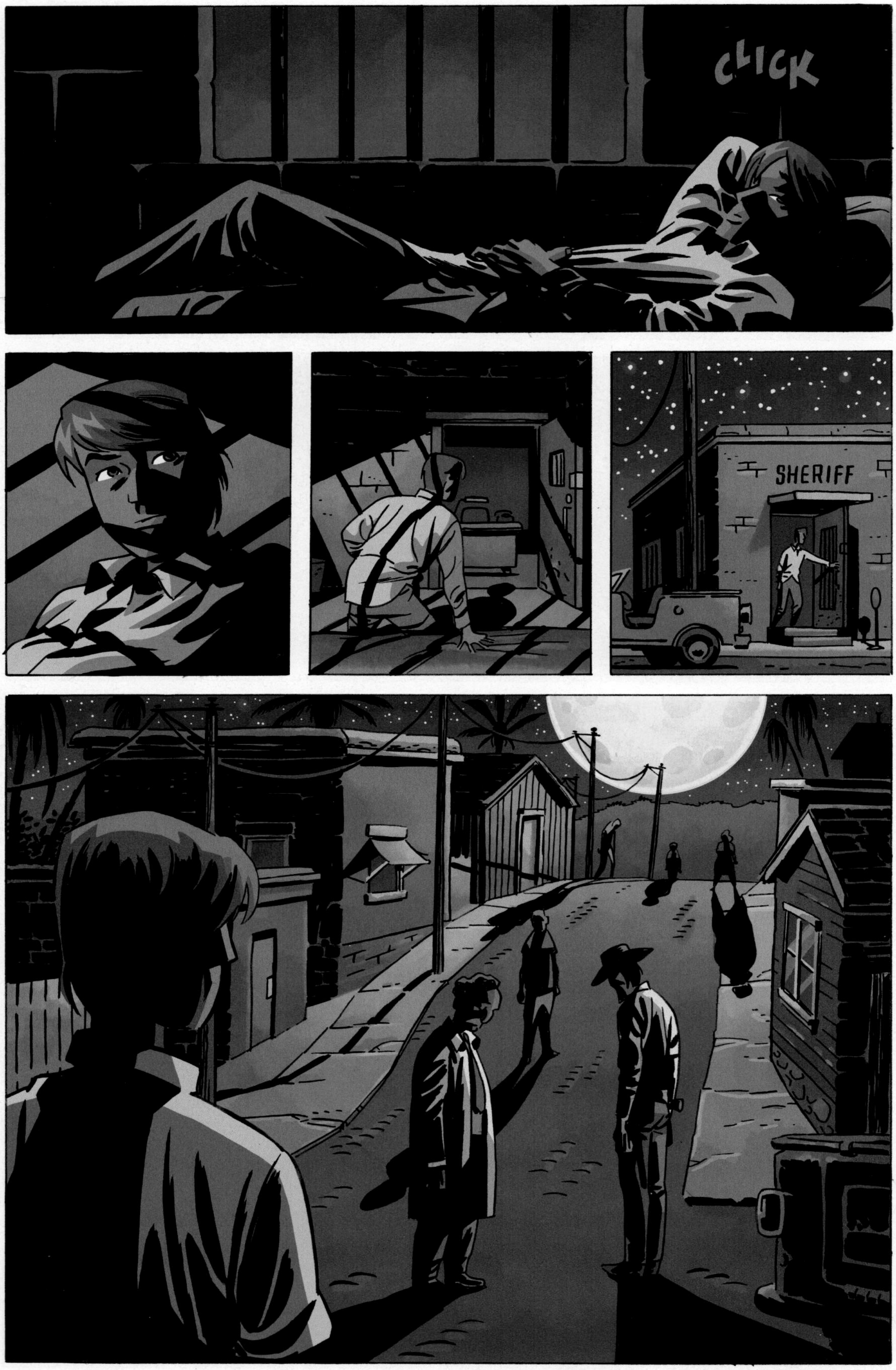
CLICK
SHERIFF

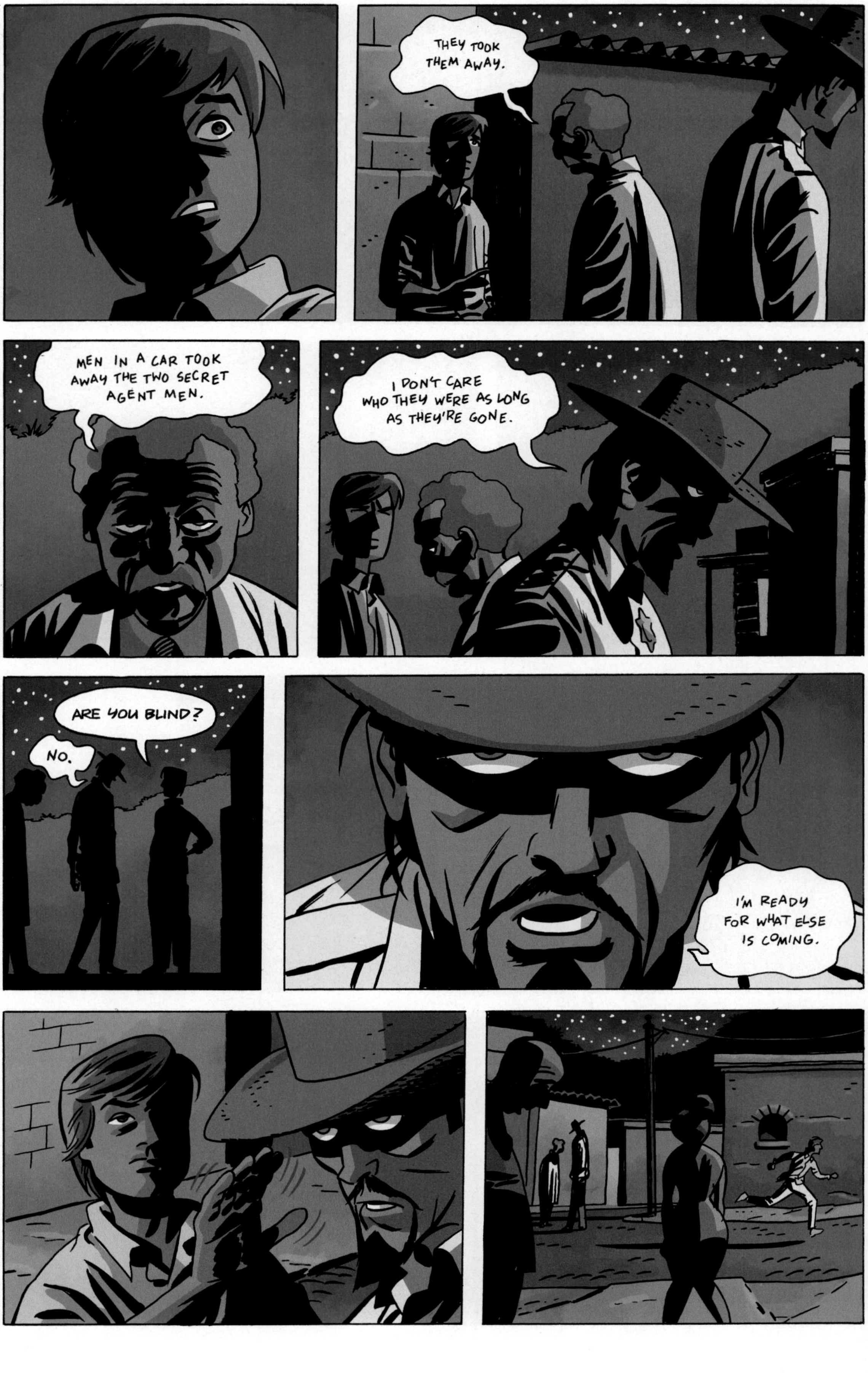
THEY TOOK THEM AWAY.
MEN IN A CAR TOOK AWAY THE TWO SECRET AGENT MEN.
I DON'T CARE WHO THEY WERE AS LONG AS THEY'RE GONE.
ARE YOU BLIND?
NO.
I'M READY FOR WHAT ELSE IS COMING.

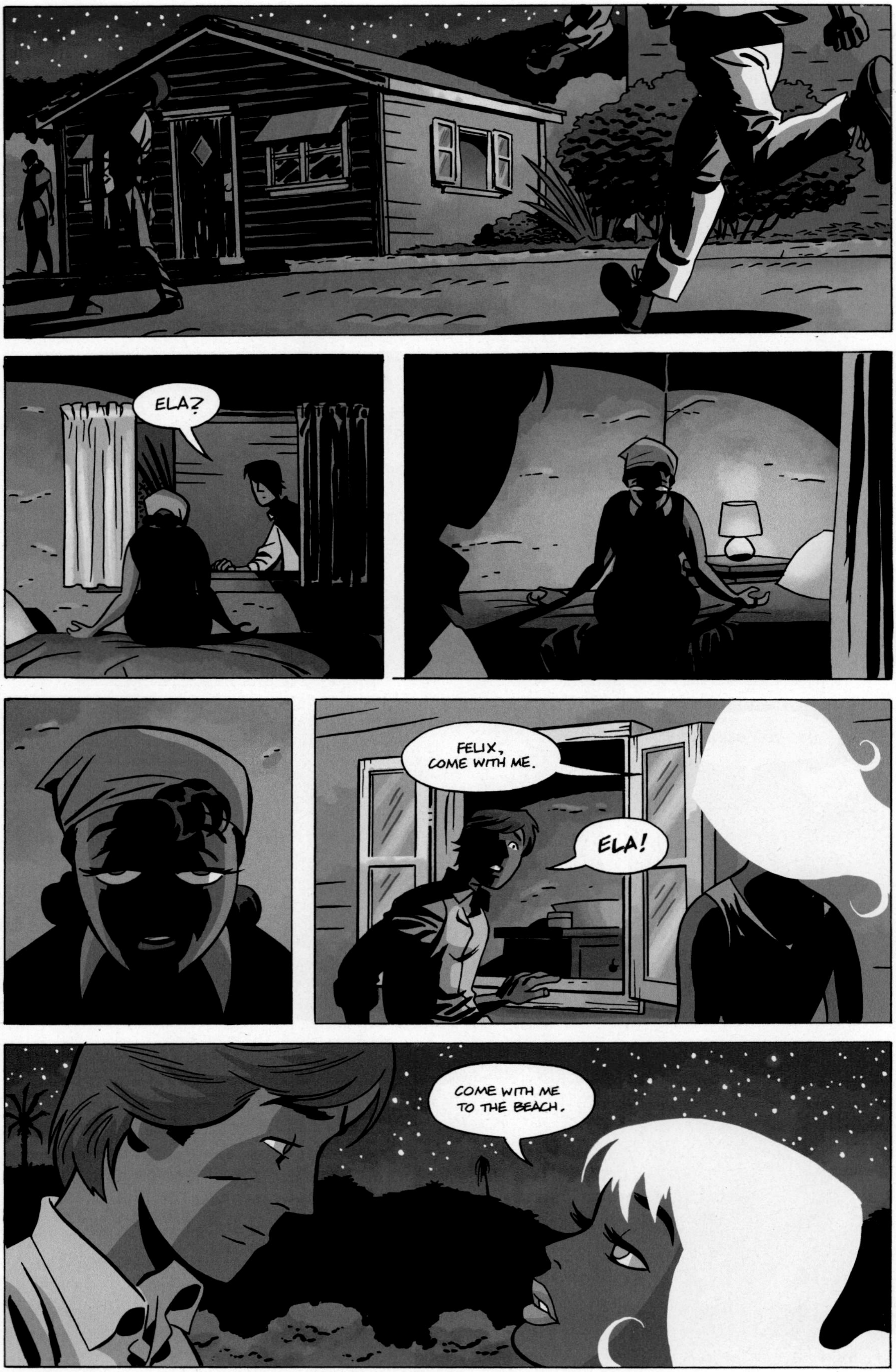
ELA?
FELIX, COME WITH ME.
ELA!
COME WITH ME TO THE BEACH.

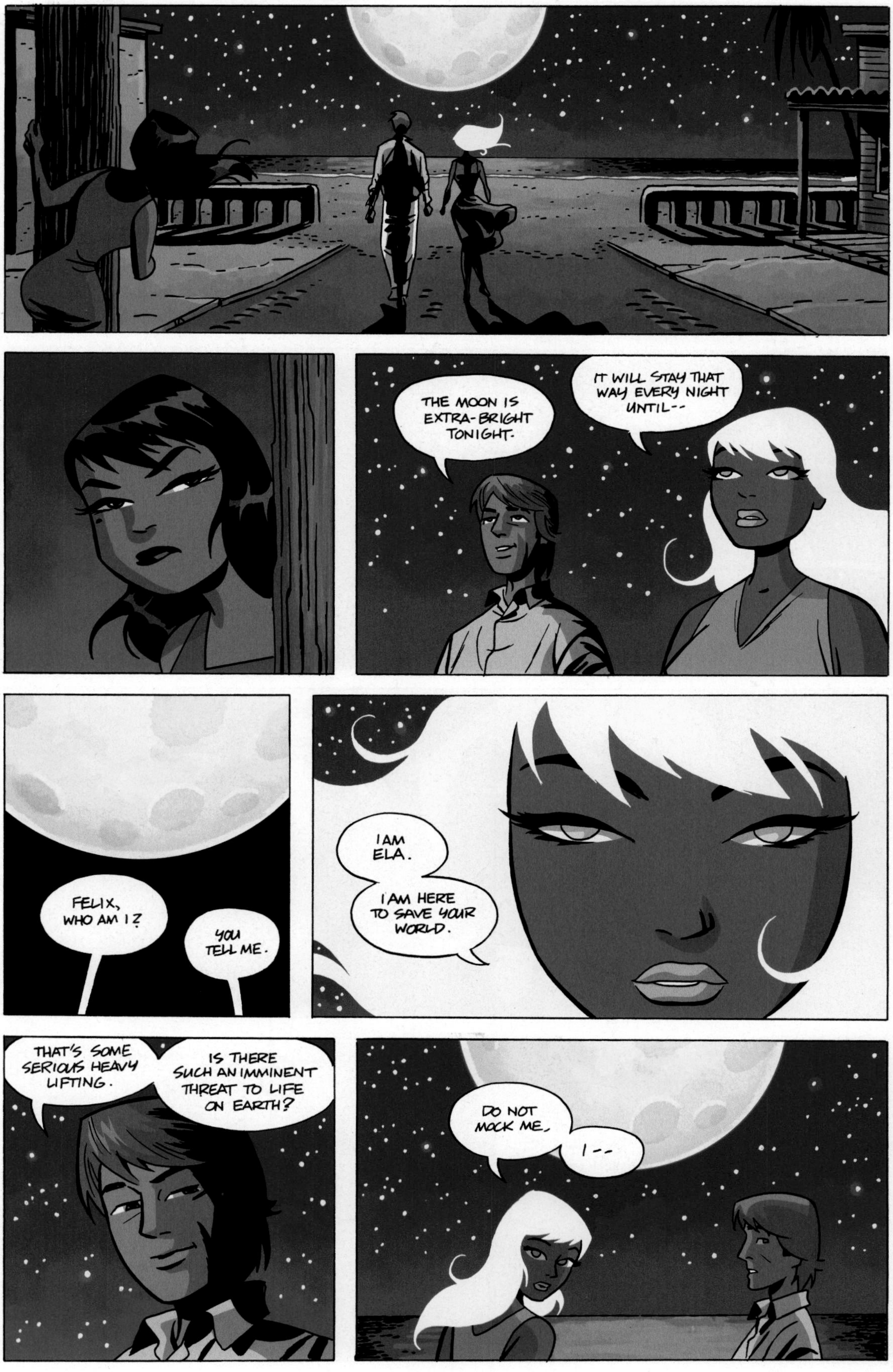
THE MOON IS EXTRA-BRIGHT TONIGHT.
IT WILL STAY THAT WAY EVERY NIGHT UNTIL--
FELIX, WHO AM I?
YOU TELL ME.
I AM ELA.
I AM HERE TO SAVE YOUR WORLD.
THAT'S SOME SERIOUS HEAVY LIFTING.
IS THERE SUCH AN IMMINENT THREAT TO LIFE ON EARTH?
DO NOT MOCK ME.
I--

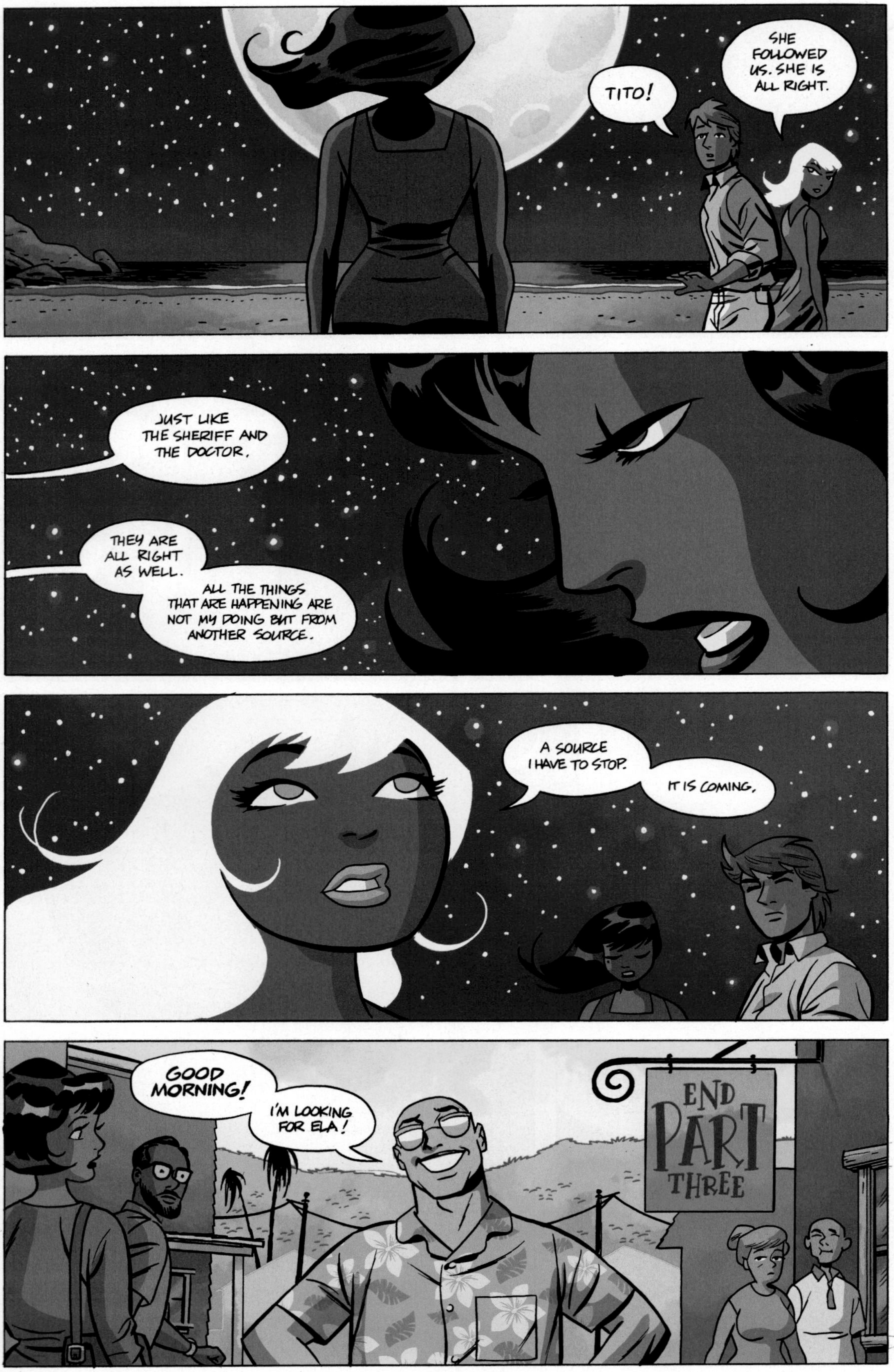

TITO!
SHE FOLLOWED US. SHE IS ALL RIGHT.
JUST LIKE THE SHERIFF AND THE DOCTOR.
THEY ARE ALL RIGHT AS WELL.
ALL THE THINGS THAT ARE HAPPENING ARE NOT MY DOING BUT FROM ANOTHER SOURCE.
A SOURCE I HAVE TO STOP.
IT IS COMING.
GOOD MORNING!
I'M LOOKING FOR ELA!
END PART THREE

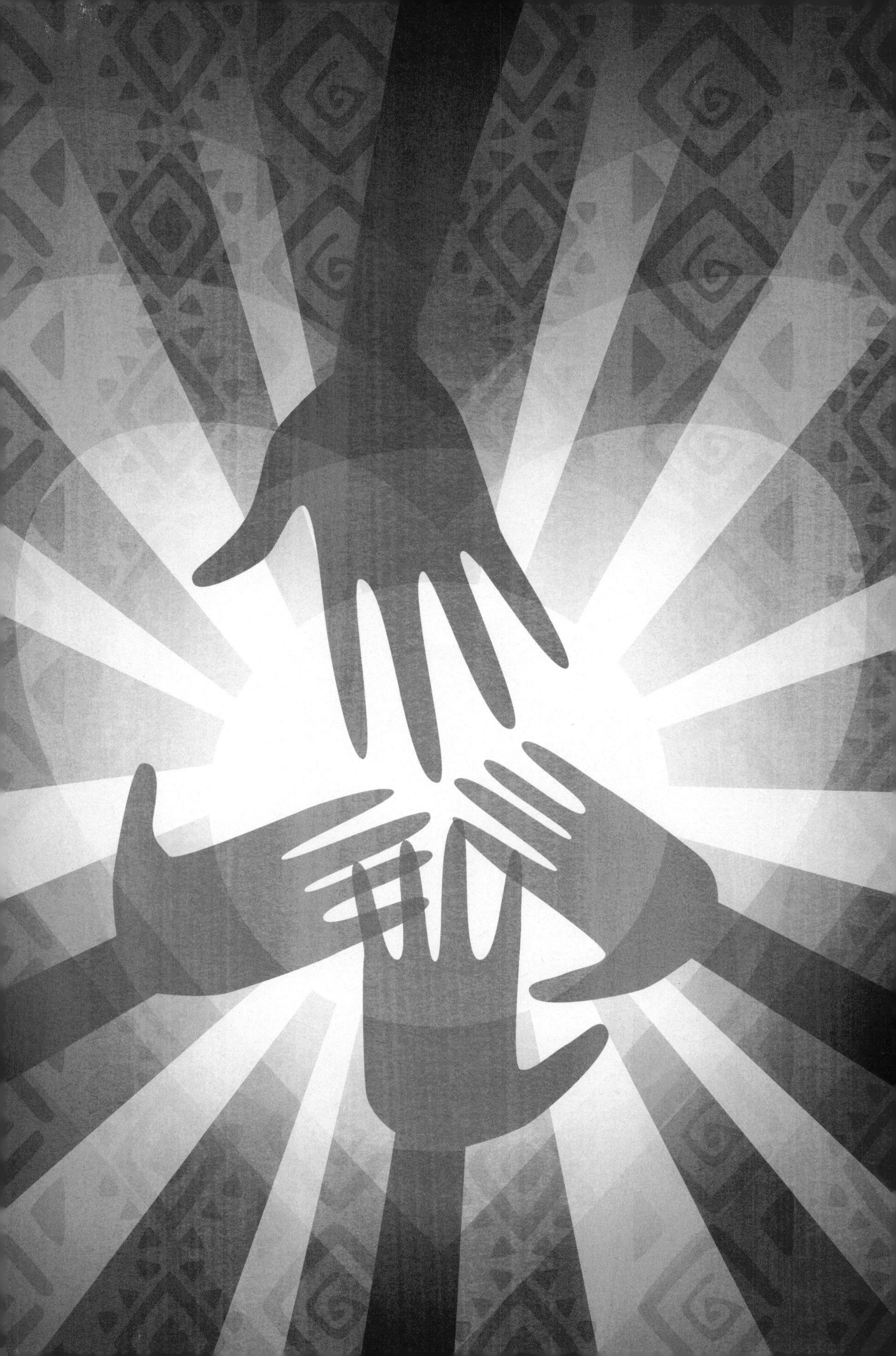

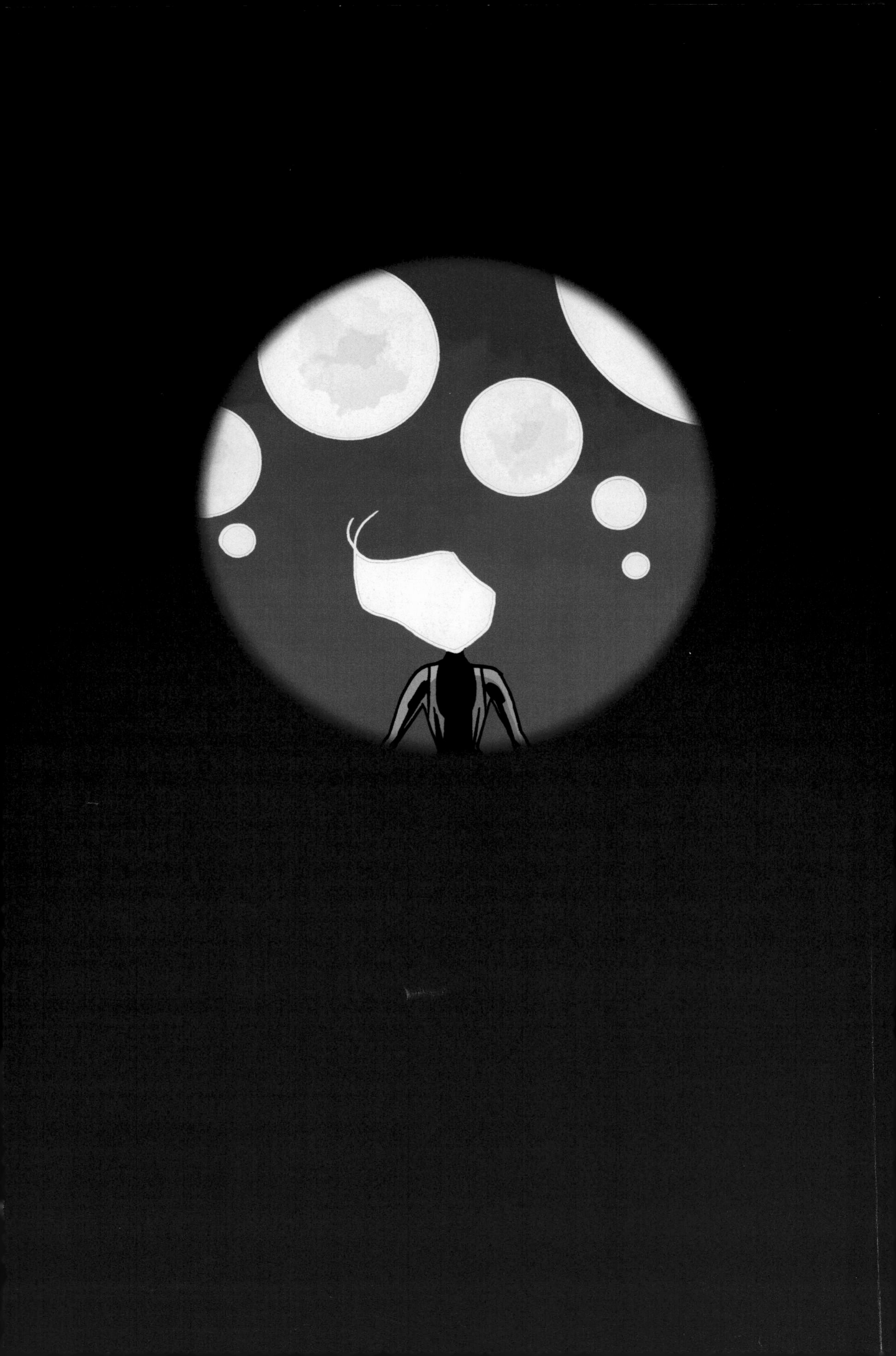

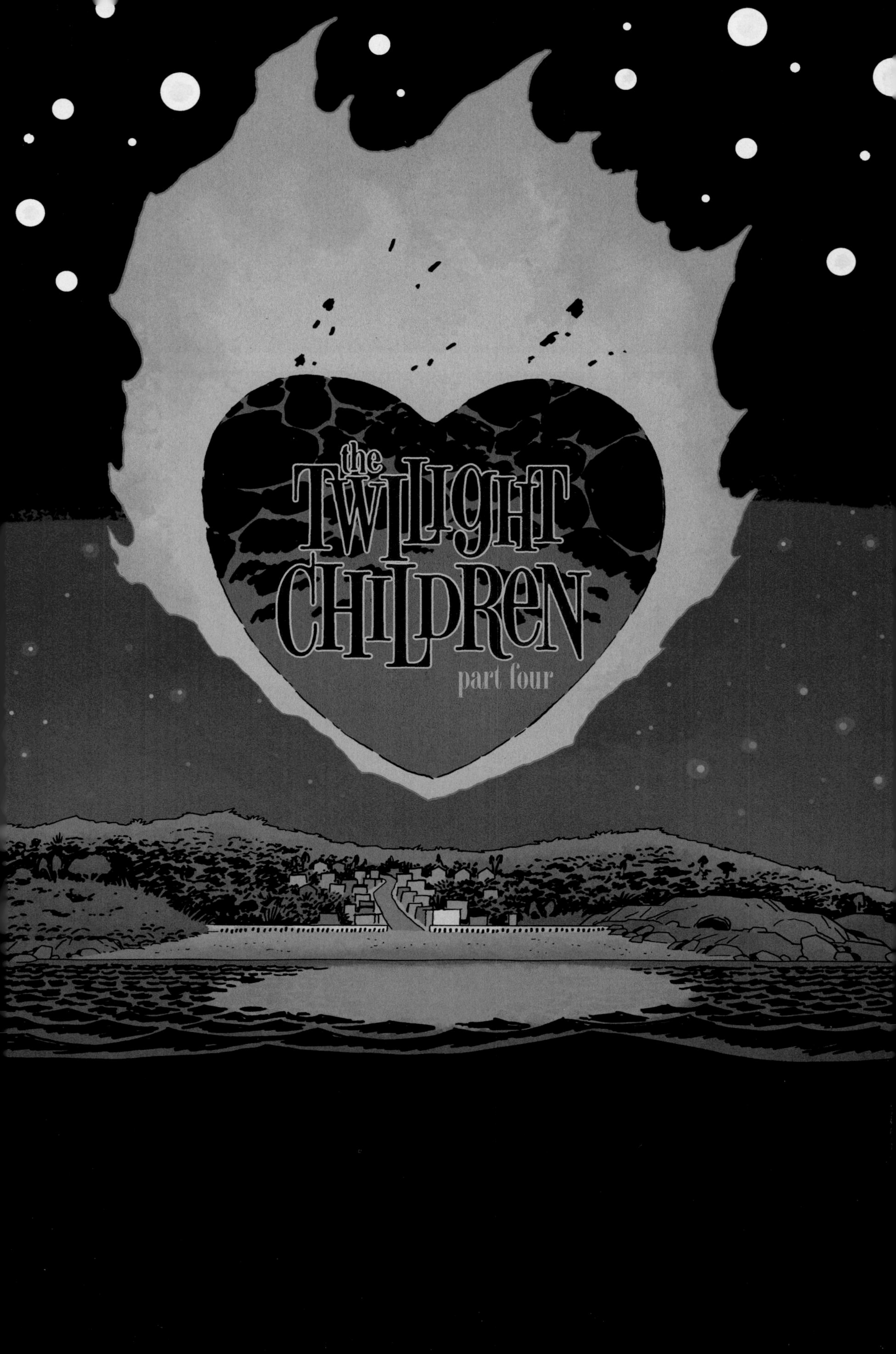
the TWILIGHT CHILDREN
part four

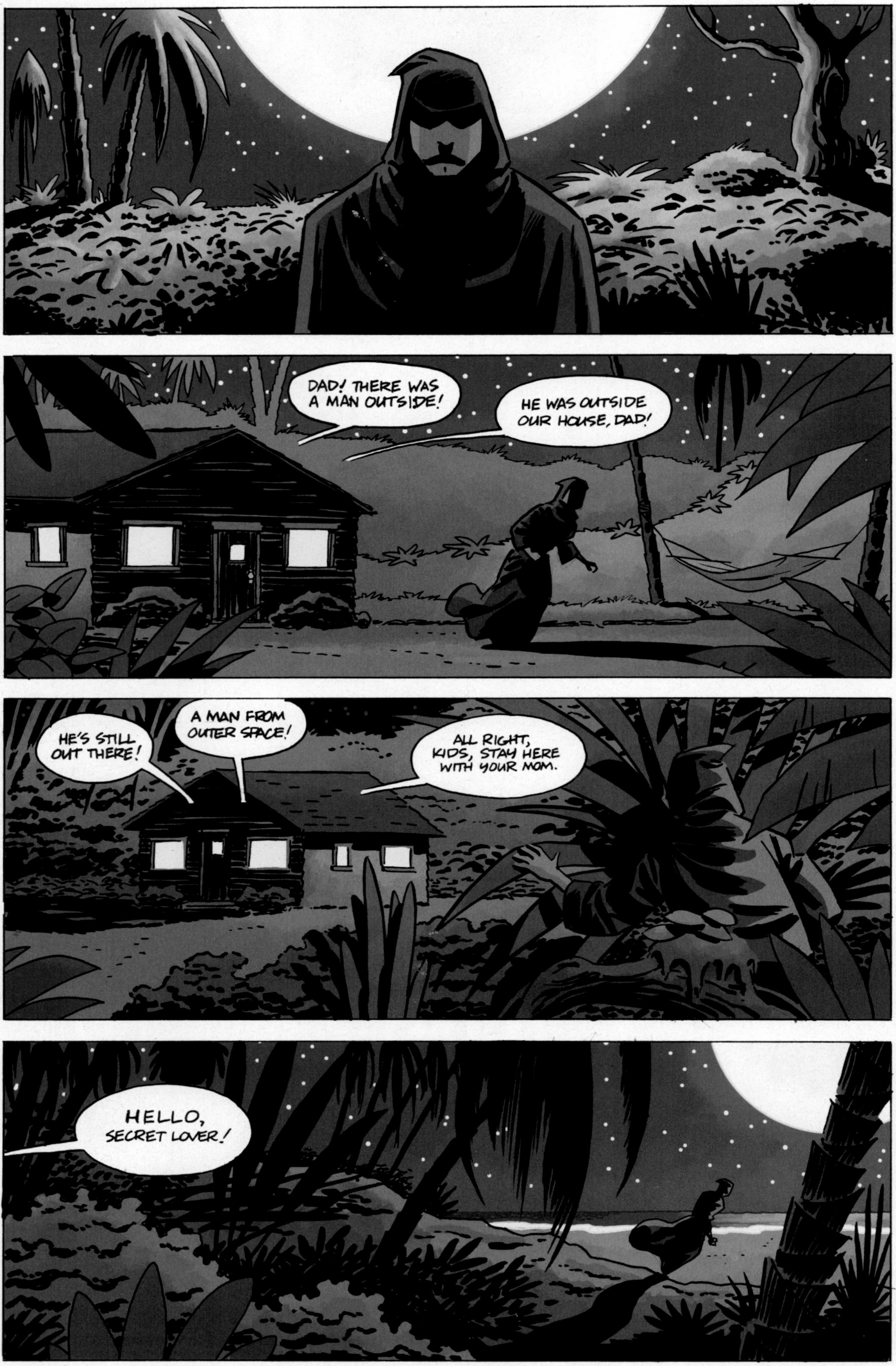
DAD! THERE WAS A MAN OUTSIDE!
HE WAS OUTSIDE OUR HOUSE, DAD!
HE'S STILL OUT THERE!
A MAN FROM OUTER SPACE!
ALL RIGHT, KIDS, STAY HERE WITH YOUR MOM.
HELLO, SECRET LOVER!

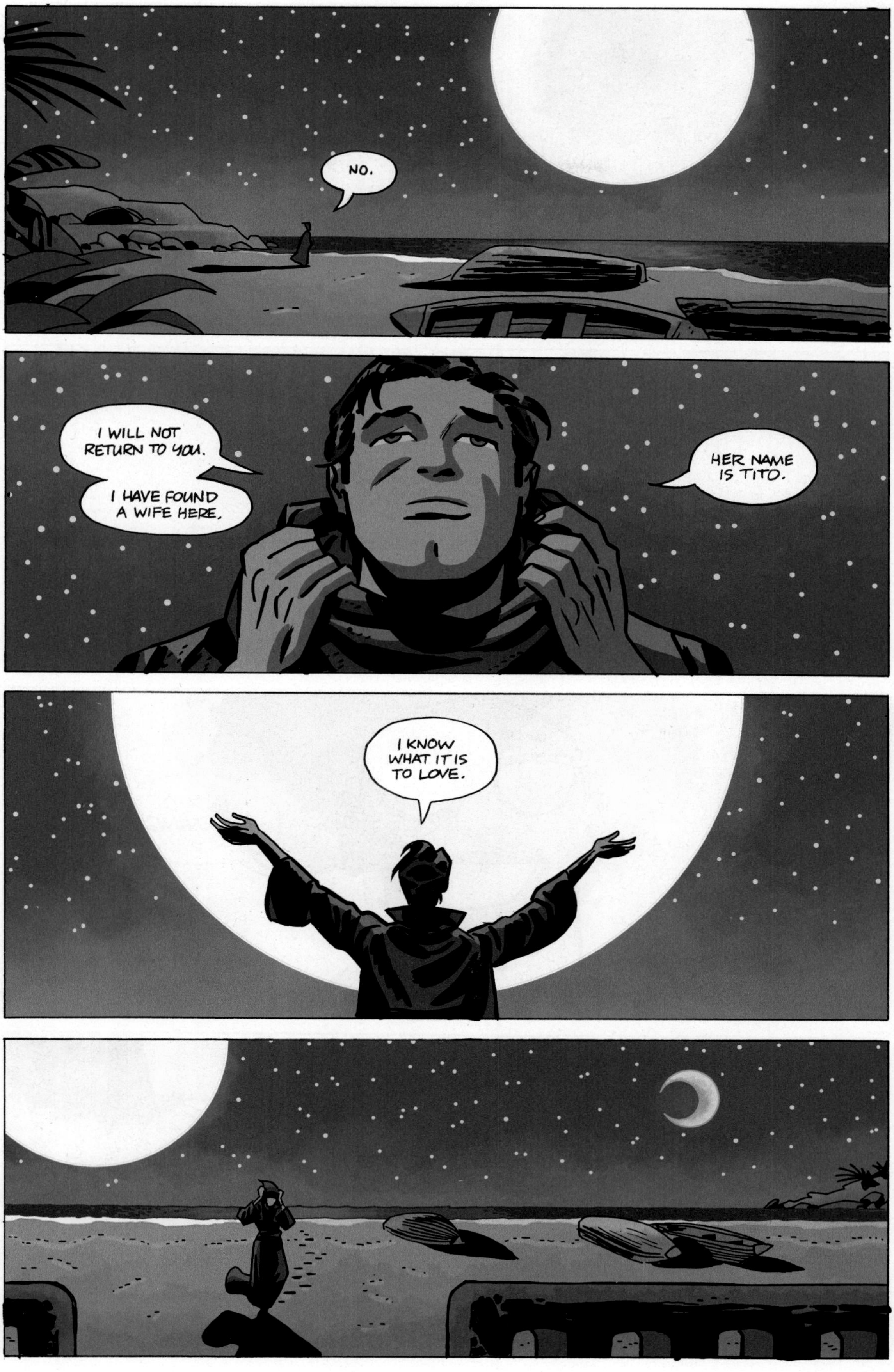
NO.
I WILL NOT RETURN TO YOU.
I HAVE FOUND A WIFE HERE.
HER NAME IS TITO.
I KNOW WHAT IT IS TO LOVE.

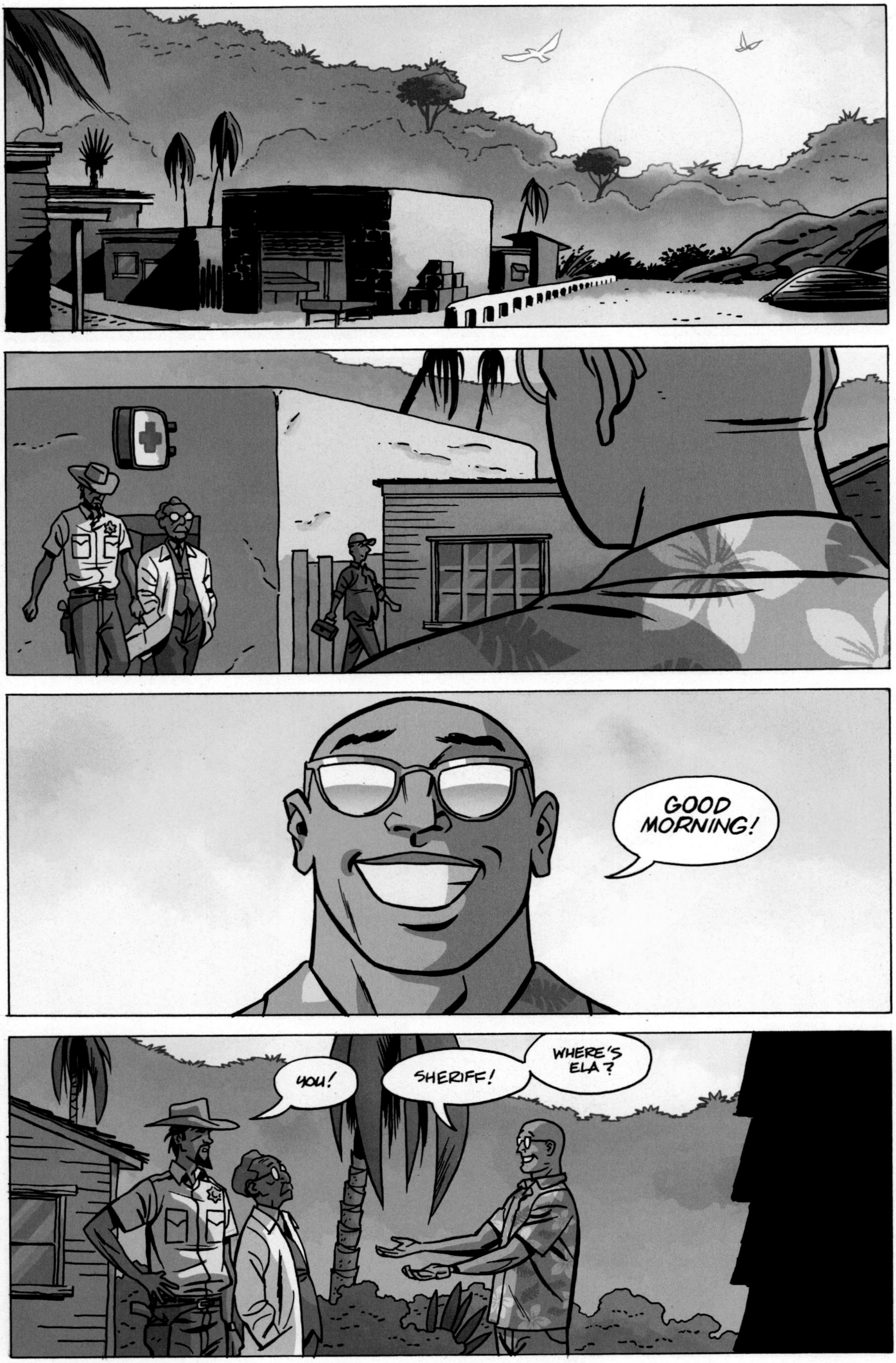
GOOD MORNING!
YOU!
SHERIFF!
WHERE'S ELA?

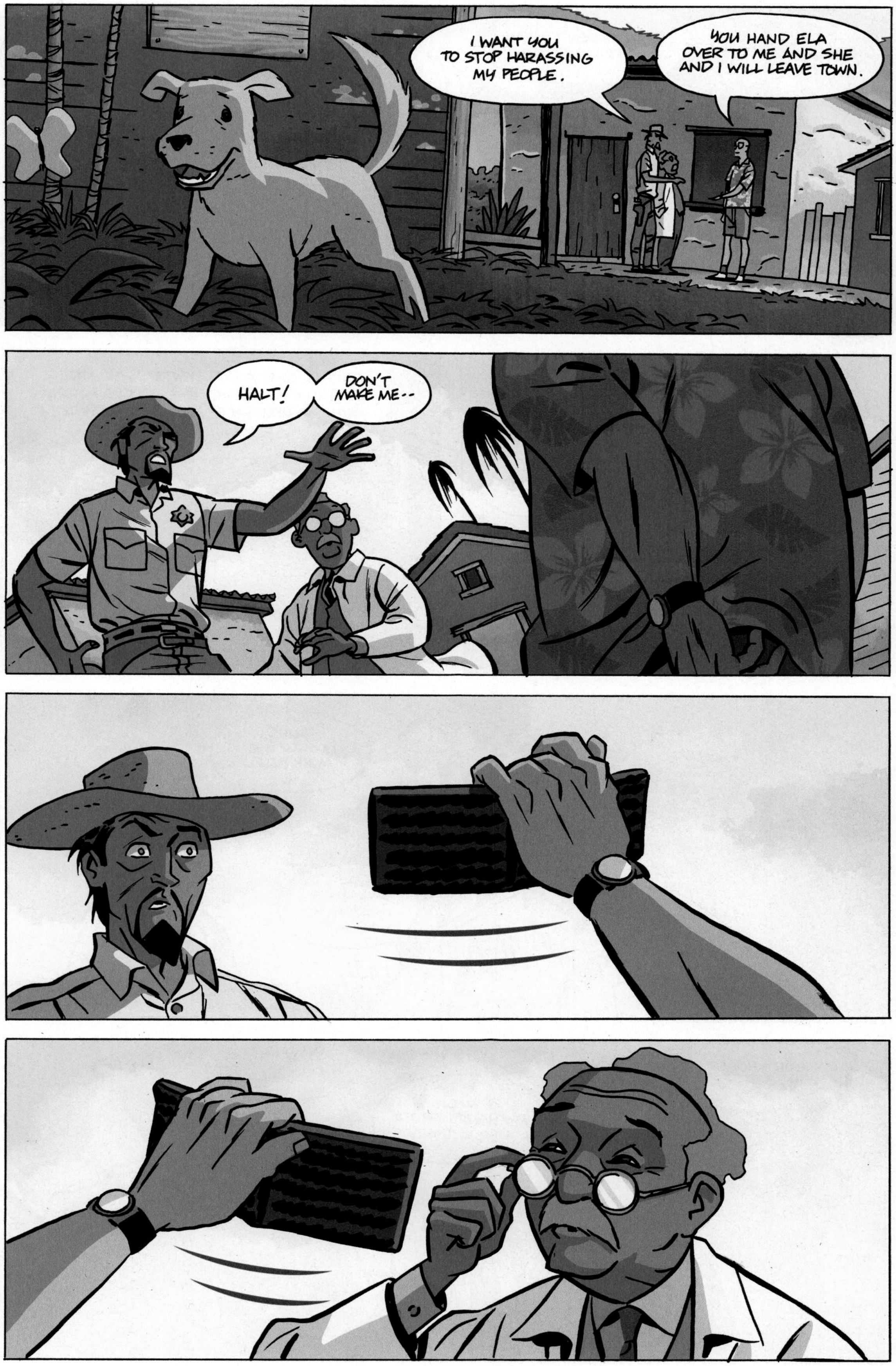
I WANT YOU TO STOP HARASSING MY PEOPLE.
YOU HAND ELA OVER TO ME AND SHE AND I WILL LEAVE TOWN.
HALT!
DON'T MAKE ME--

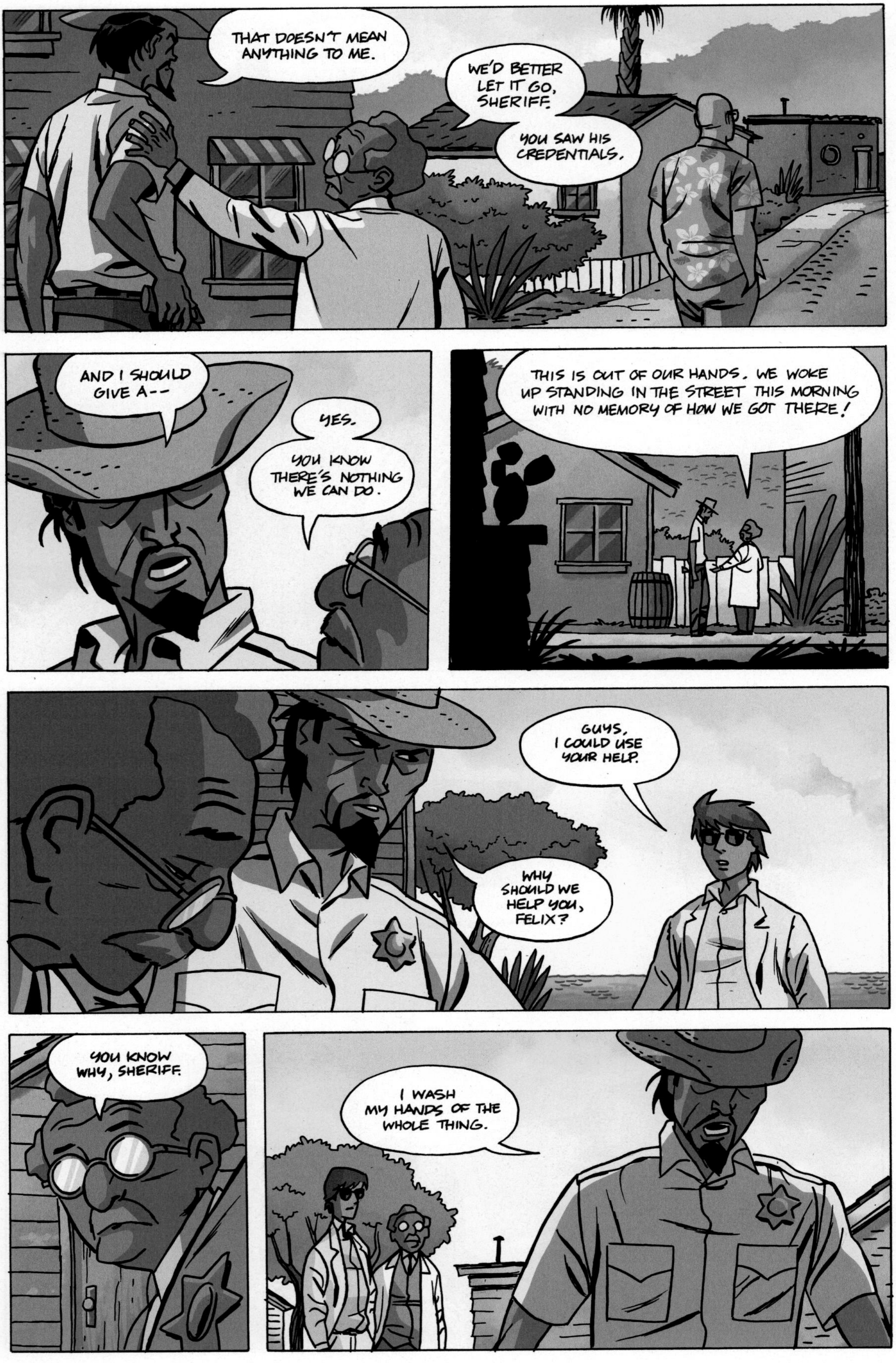
THAT DOESN'T MEAN ANYTHING TO ME.
WE'D BETTER LET IT GO, SHERIFF.
YOU SAW HIS CREDENTIALS.
AND I SHOULD GIVE A--
YES.
YOU KNOW THERE'S NOTHING WE CAN DO.
THIS IS OUT OF OUR HANDS. WE WOKE UP STANDING IN THE STREET THIS MORNING WITH NO MEMORY OF HOW WE GOT THERE!
GUYS, I COULD USE YOUR HELP.
WHY SHOULD WE HELP YOU, FELIX?
YOU KNOW WHY, SHERIFF.
I WASH MY HANDS OF THE WHOLE THING.

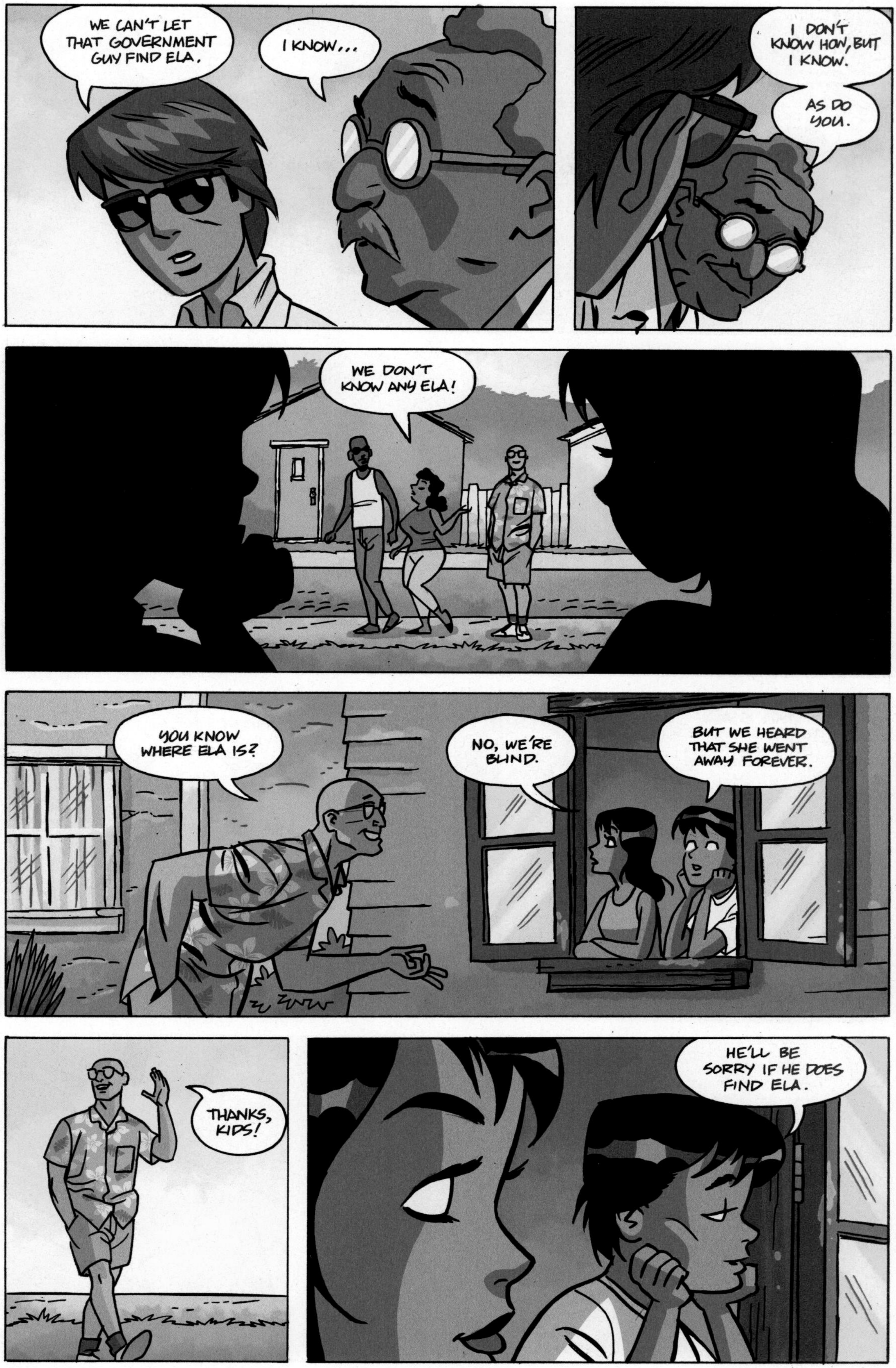
WE CAN'T LET THAT GOVERNMENT GUY FIND ELA.
I KNOW...
I DON'T KNOW HOW, BUT I KNOW.
AS DO YOU.
WE DON'T KNOW ANY ELA!
YOU KNOW WHERE ELA IS?
NO, WE'RE BLIND.
BUT WE HEARD THAT SHE WENT AWAY FOREVER.
THANKS, KIDS!
HE'LL BE SORRY IF HE DOES FIND ELA.

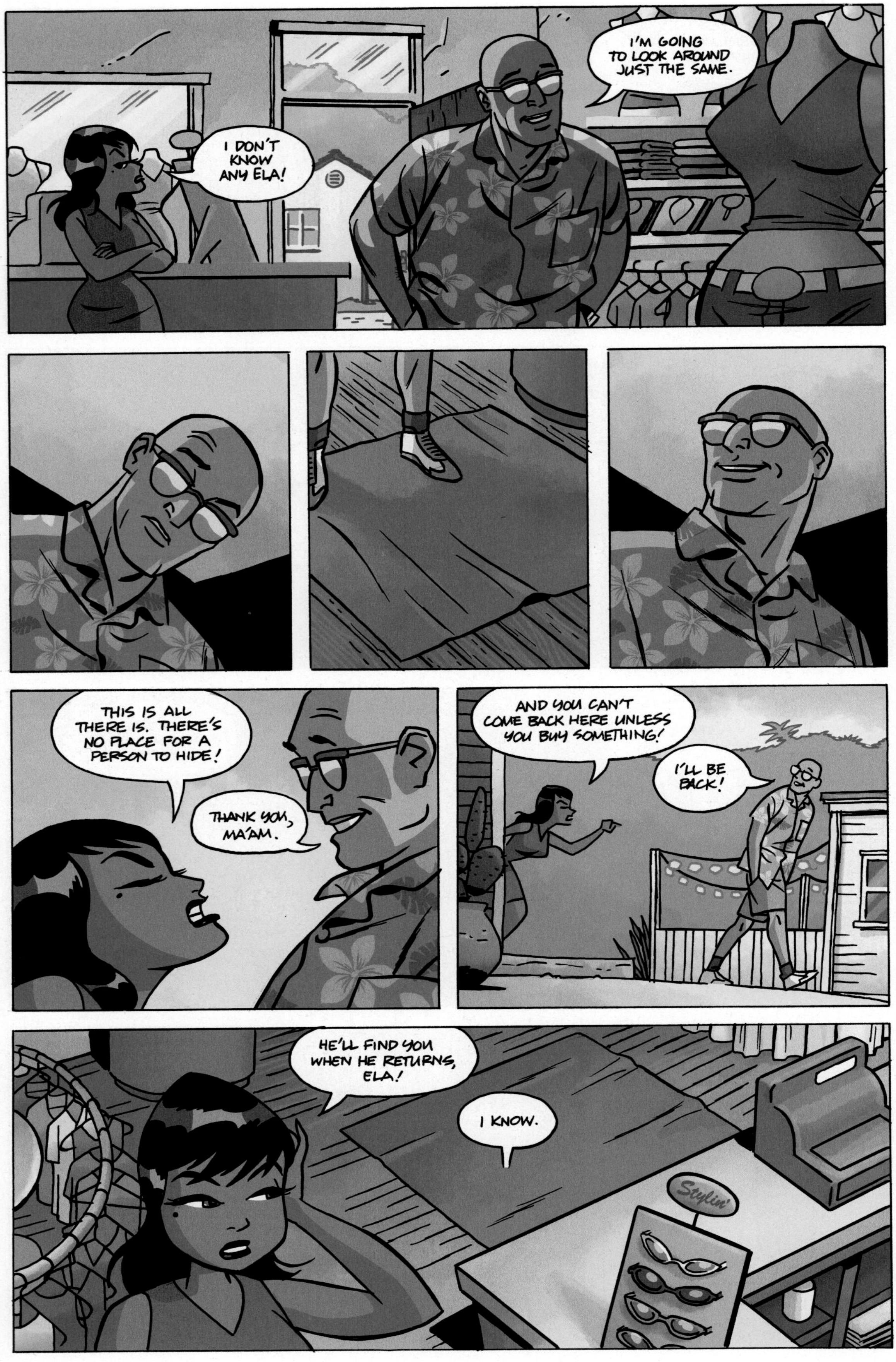
I DON'T KNOW ANY ELA!
I'M GOING TO LOOK AROUND JUST THE SAME.
THIS IS ALL THERE IS. THERE'S NO PLACE FOR A PERSON TO HIDE!
THANK YOU, MA'AM.
AND YOU CAN'T COME BACK HERE UNLESS YOU BUY SOMETHING!
I'LL BE BACK!
HE'LL FIND YOU WHEN HE RETURNS, ELA!
I KNOW.
Stylin'

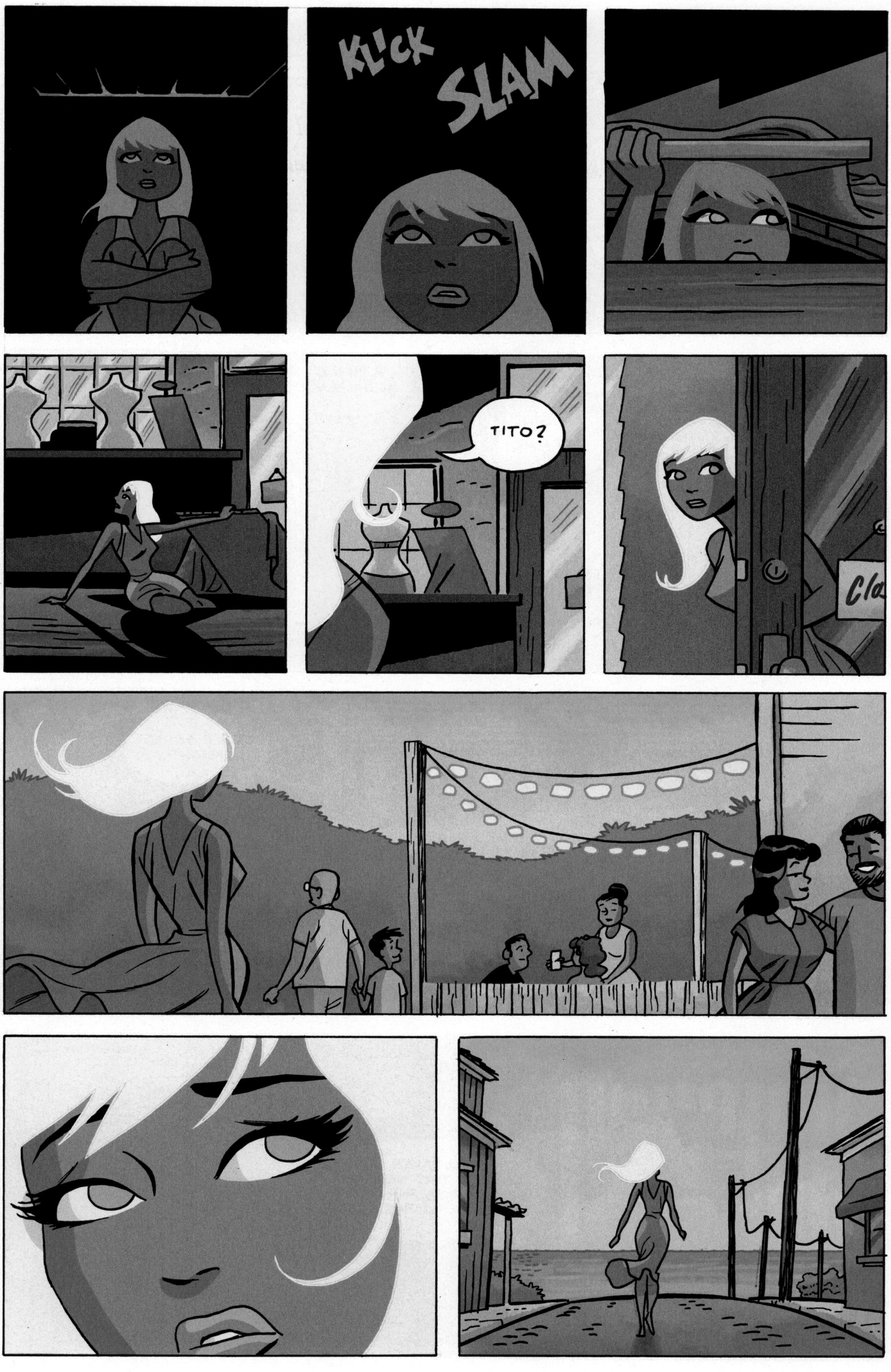
KLICK
SLAM
TITO?
Clo

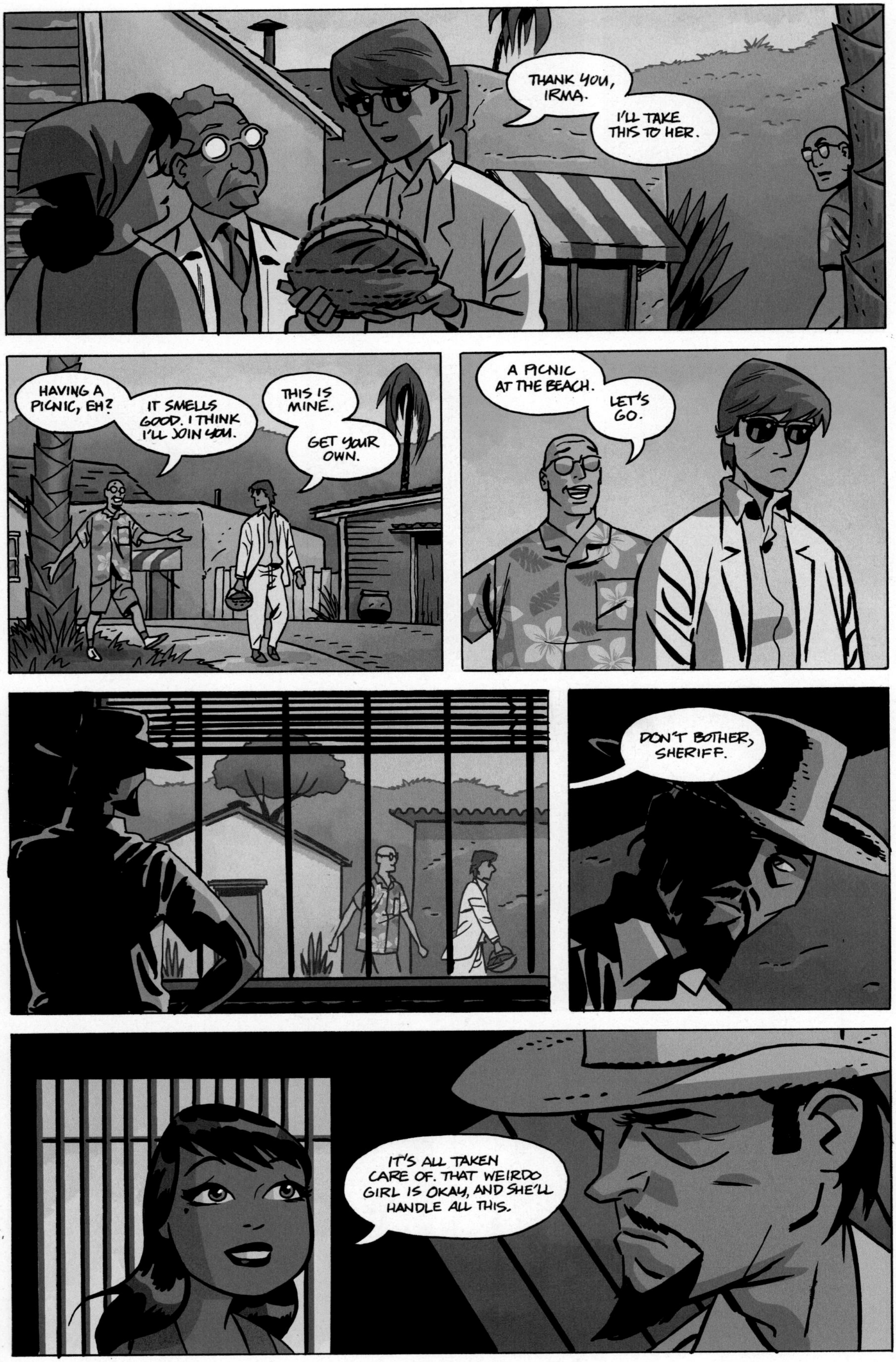
THANK YOU, IRMA.
I'LL TAKE THIS TO HER.
HAVING A PICNIC, EH?
IT SMELLS GOOD. I THINK I'LL JOIN YOU.
THIS IS MINE.
GET YOUR OWN.
A PICNIC AT THE BEACH.
LET'S GO.
DON'T BOTHER, SHERIFF.
IT'S ALL TAKEN CARE OF. THAT WEIRDO GIRL IS OKAY, AND SHE'LL HANDLE ALL THIS.

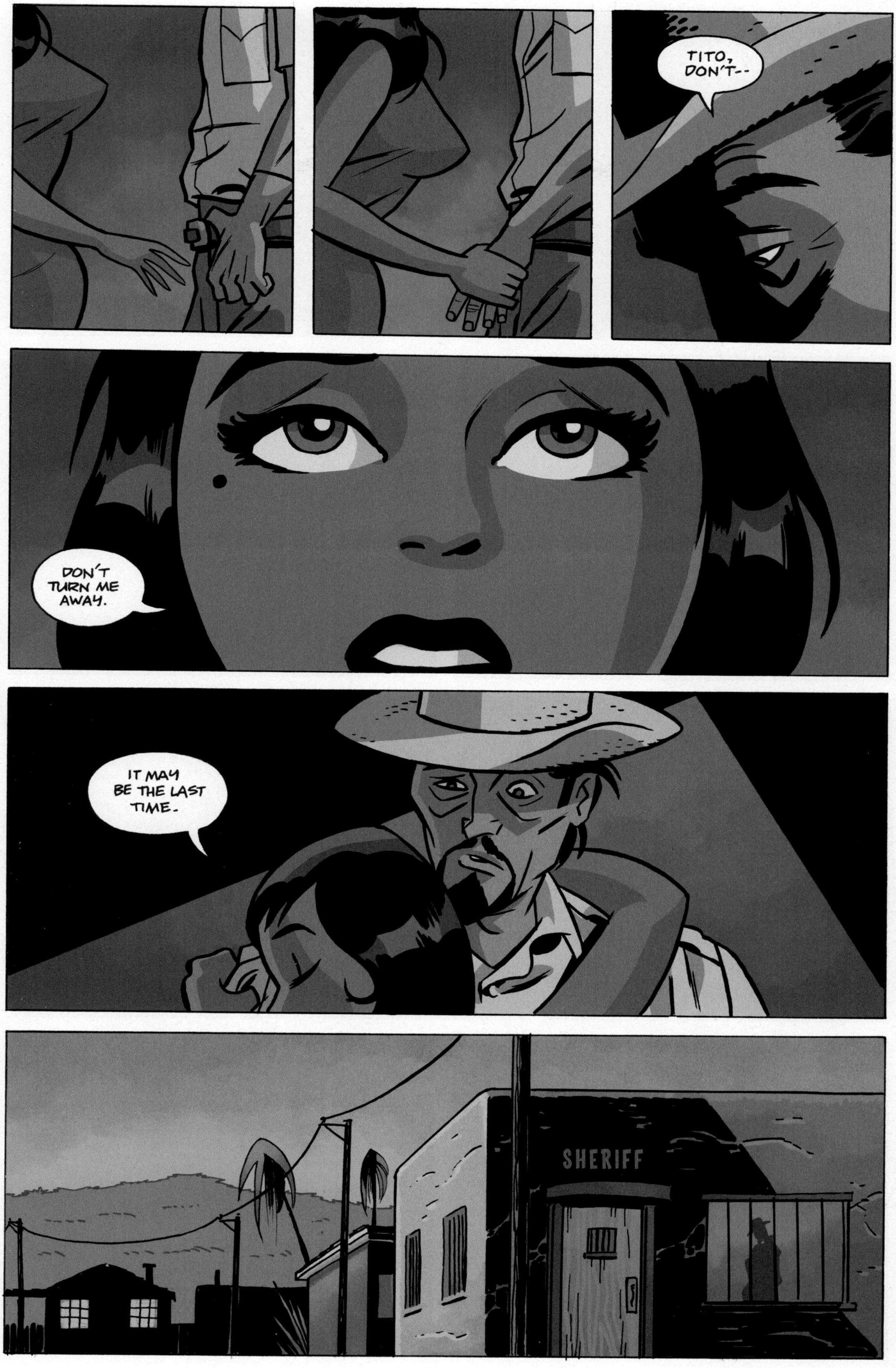
TITO, DON'T--
DON'T TURN ME AWAY.
IT MAY BE THE LAST TIME.
SHERIFF

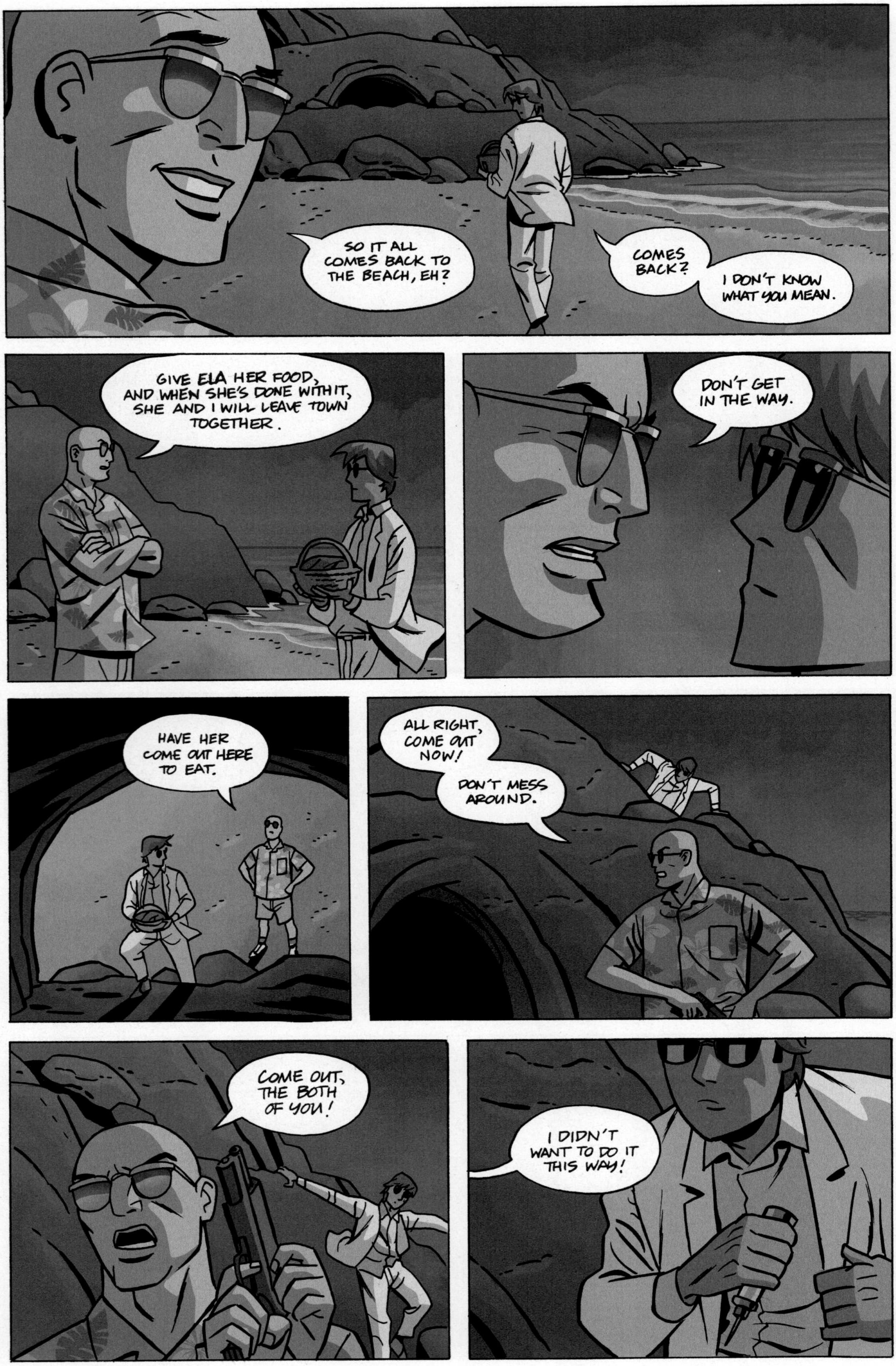
SO IT ALL COMES BACK TO THE BEACH, EH?
COMES BACK?
I DON'T KNOW WHAT YOU MEAN.
GIVE ELA HER FOOD, AND WHEN SHE'S DONE WITH IT, SHE AND I WILL LEAVE TOWN TOGETHER.
DON'T GET IN THE WAY.
HAVE HER COME OUT HERE TO EAT.
ALL RIGHT, COME OUT NOW!
DON'T MESS AROUND.
COME OUT, THE BOTH OF YOU!
I DIDN'T WANT TO DO IT THIS WAY!

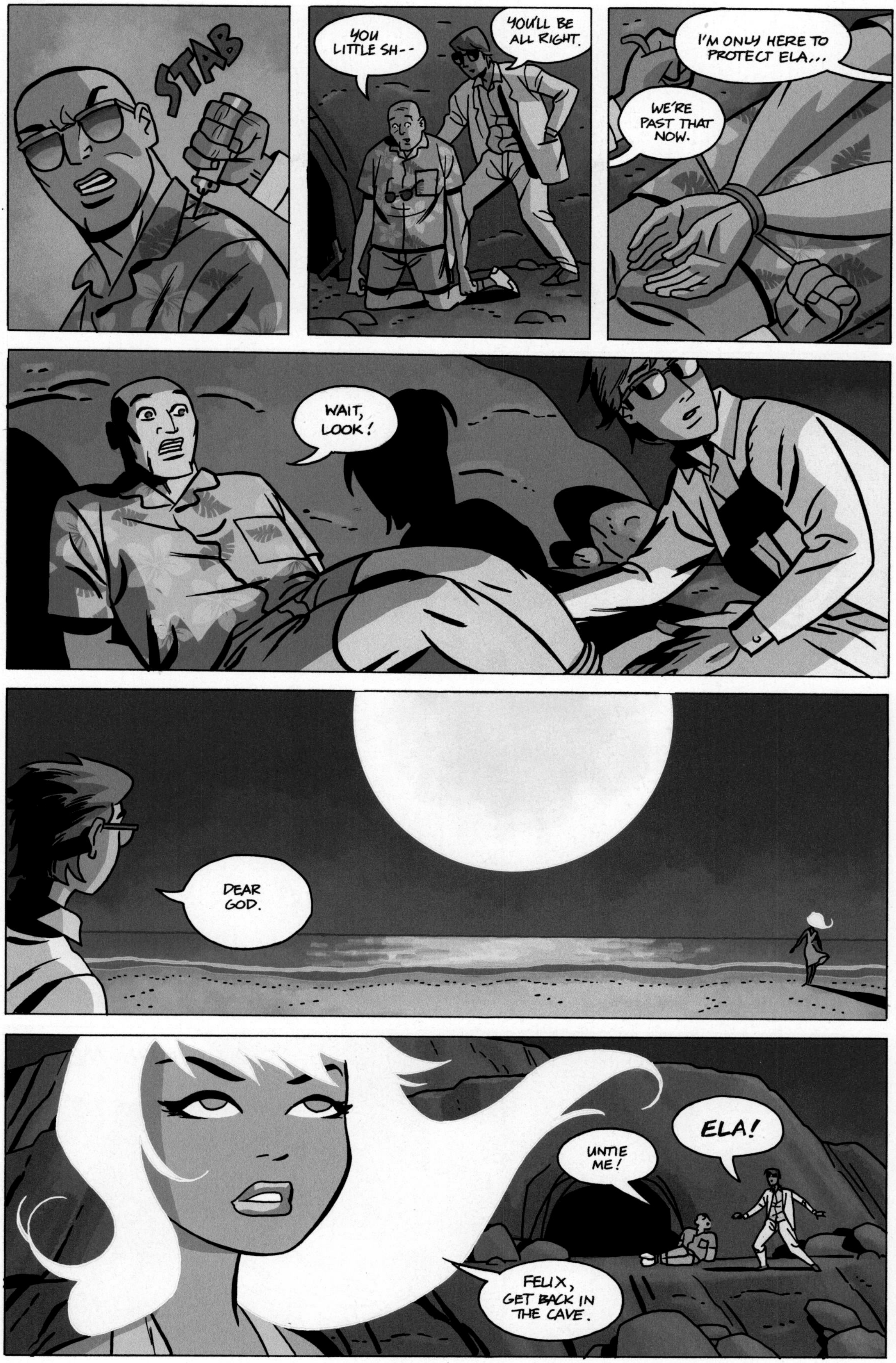
STAB
YOU LITTLE SH--
YOU'LL BE ALL RIGHT.
I'M ONLY HERE TO PROTECT ELA...
WE'RE PAST THAT NOW.
WAIT, LOOK!
DEAR GOD.
ELA!
UNTIE ME!
FELIX, GET BACK IN THE CAVE.

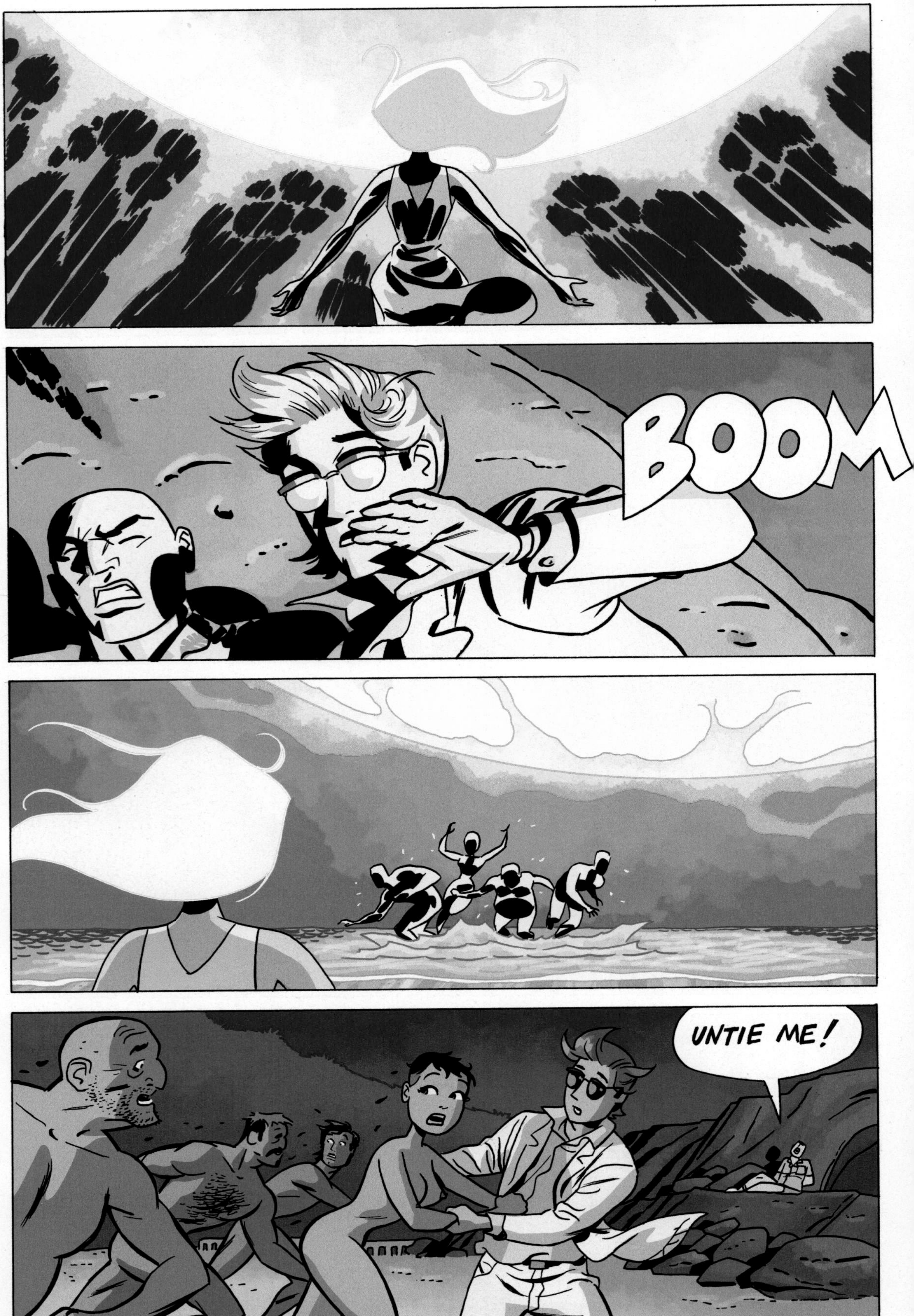
BOOM
UNTIE ME!

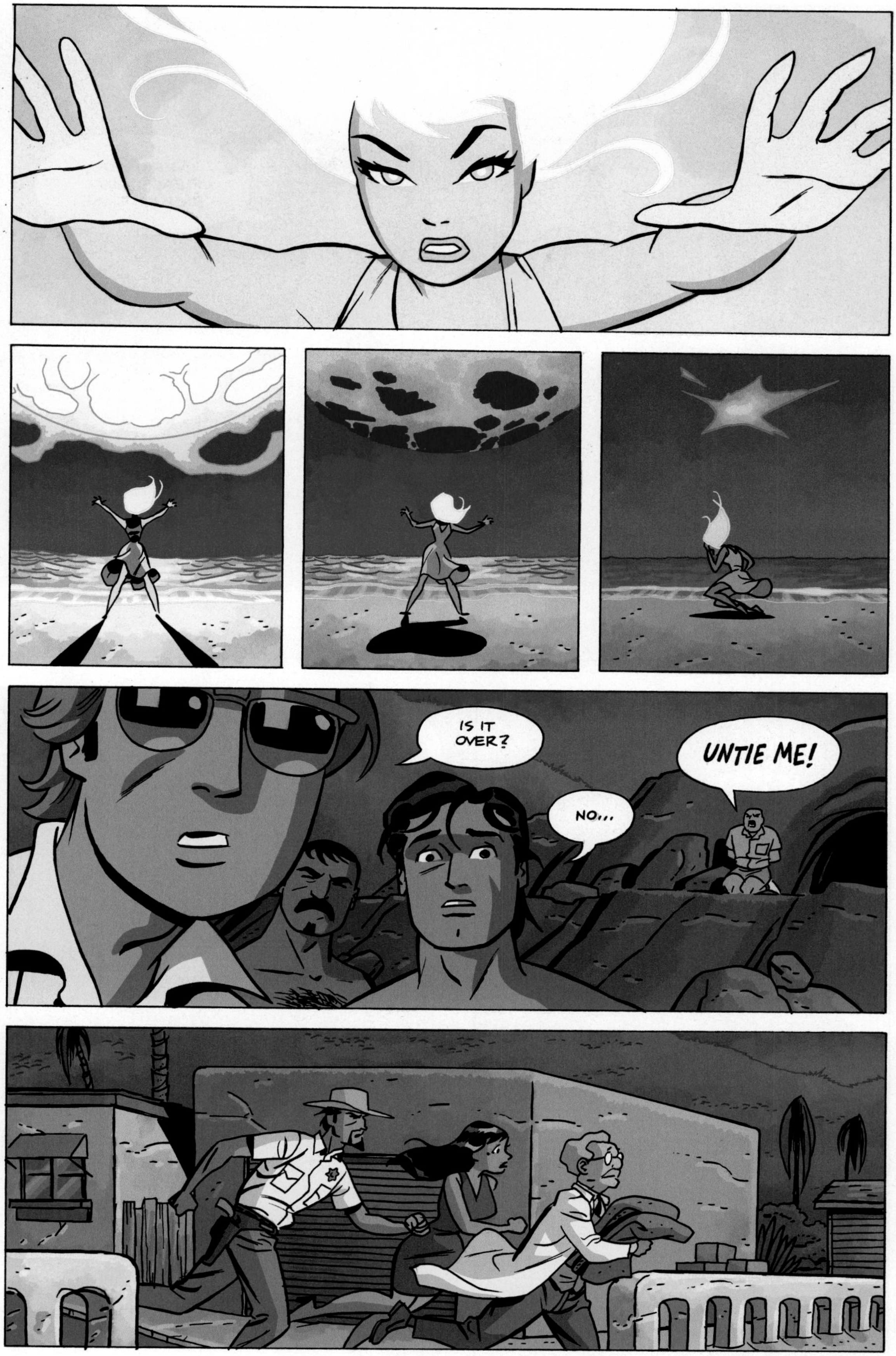
IS IT OVER?
NO...
UNTIE ME!

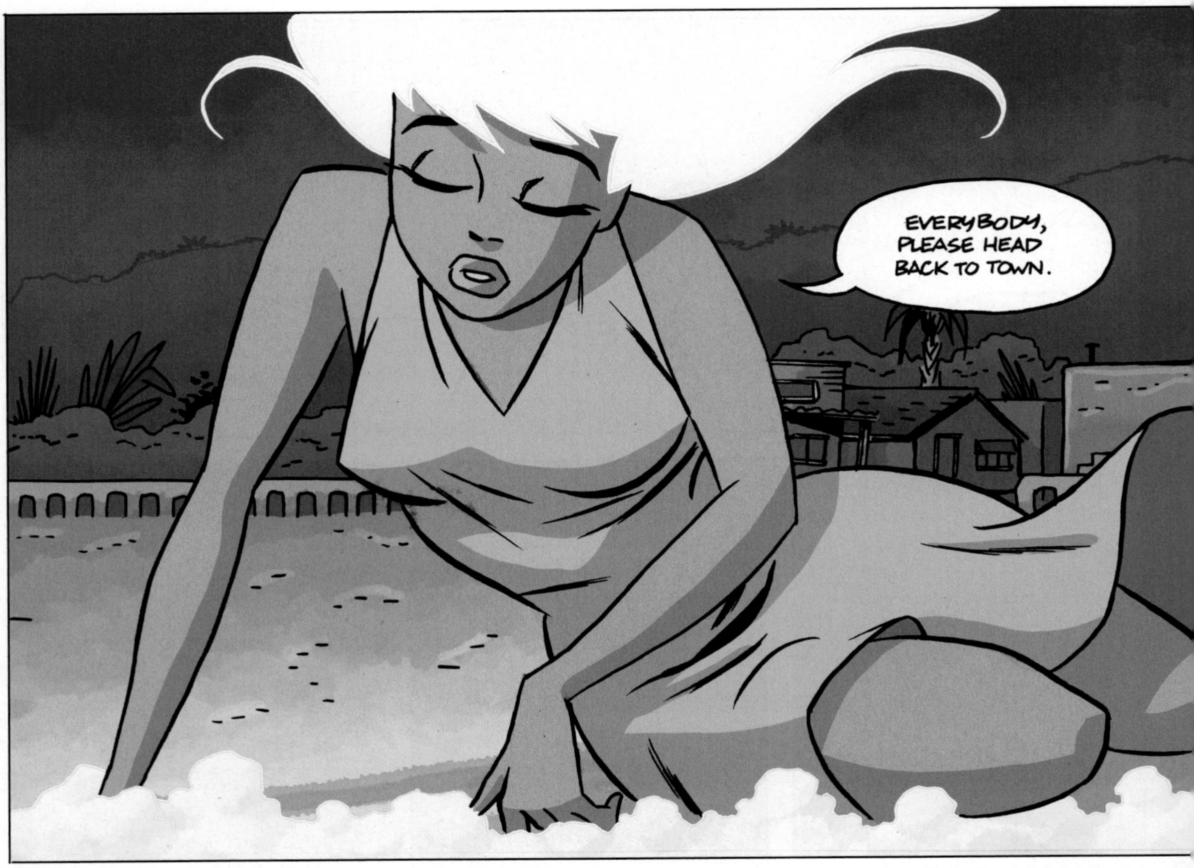
EVERYBODY, PLEASE HEAD BACK TO TOWN.

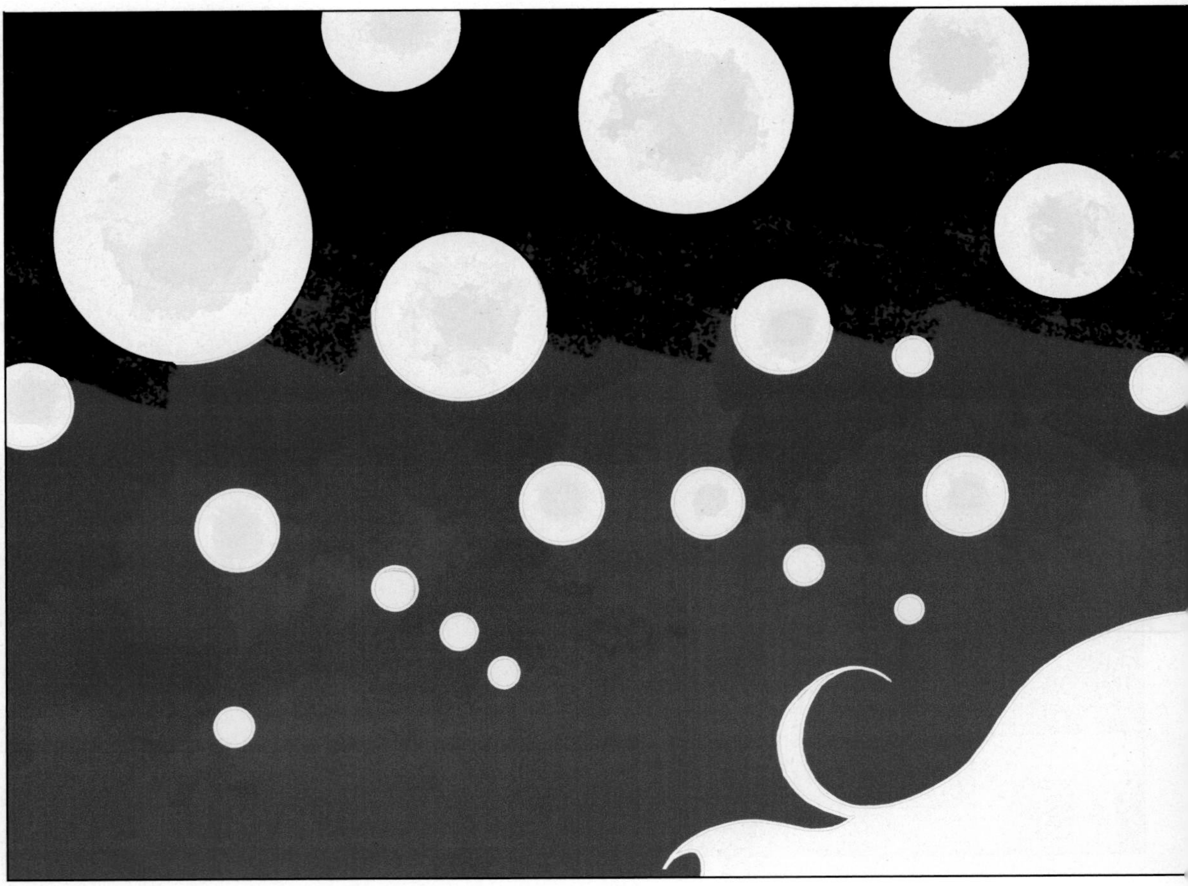

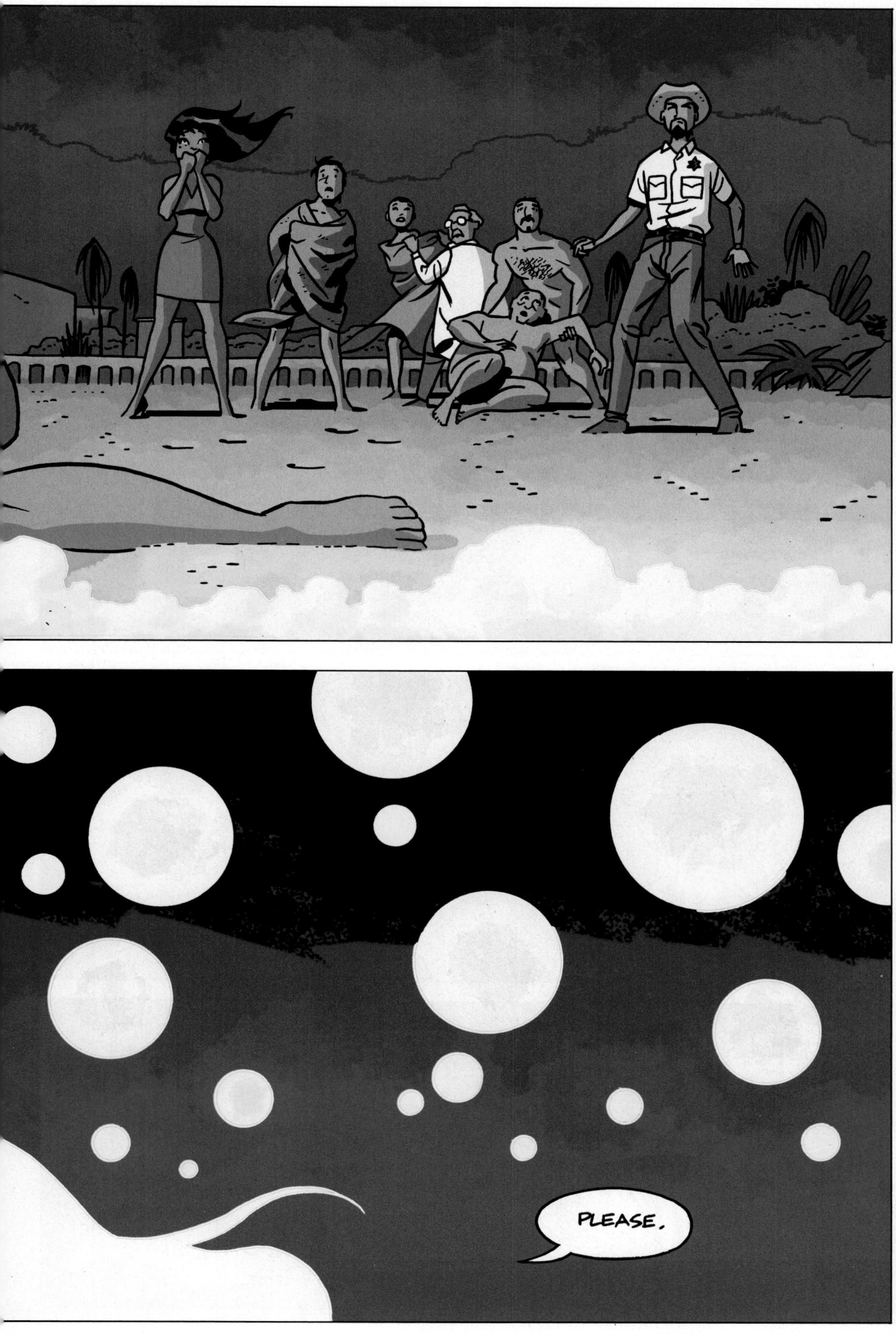
PLEASE.

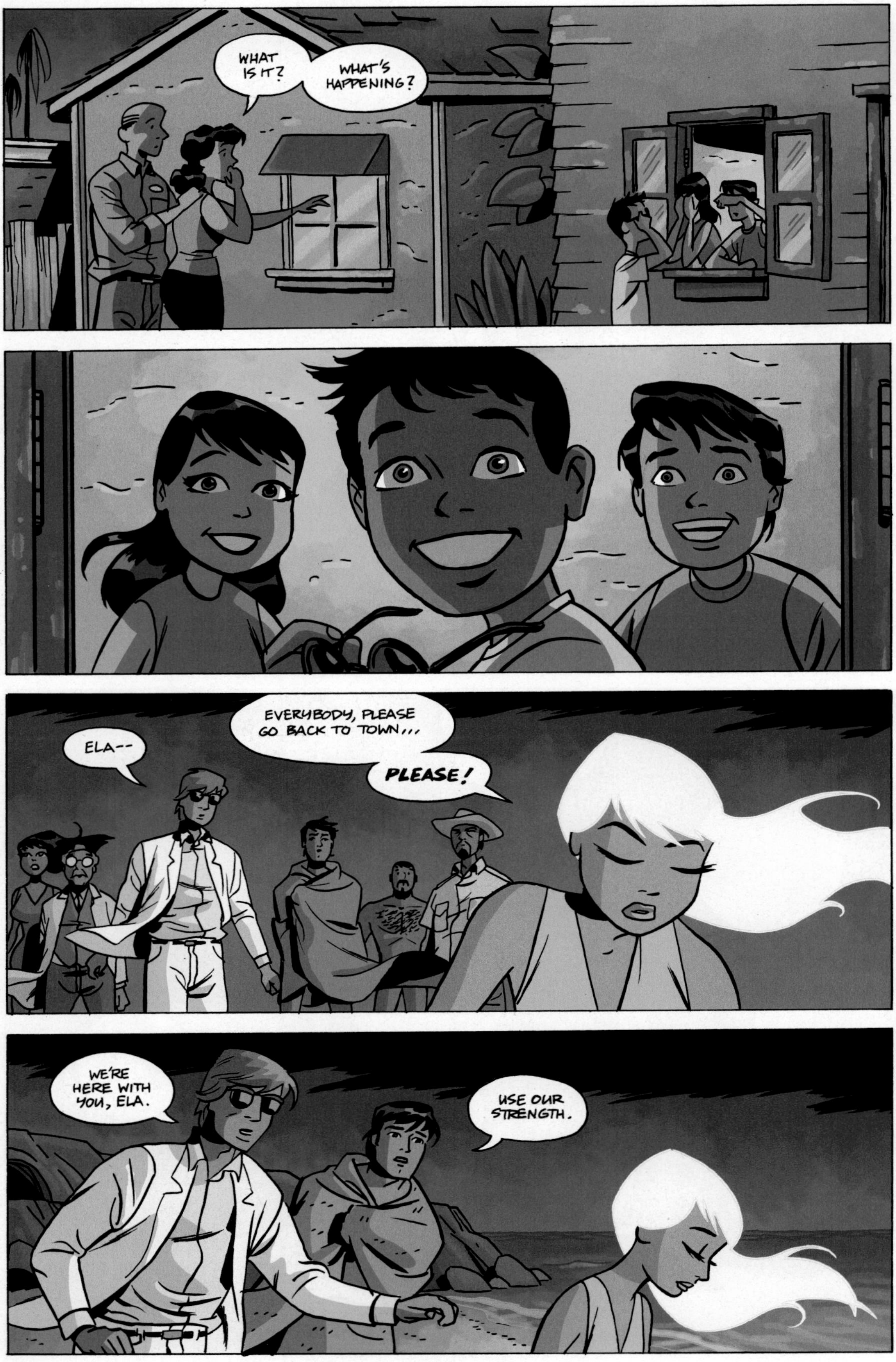
WHAT IS IT?
WHAT'S HAPPENING?
ELA--
EVERYBODY, PLEASE GO BACK TO TOWN...
PLEASE!
WE'RE HERE WITH YOU, ELA.
USE OUR STRENGTH.

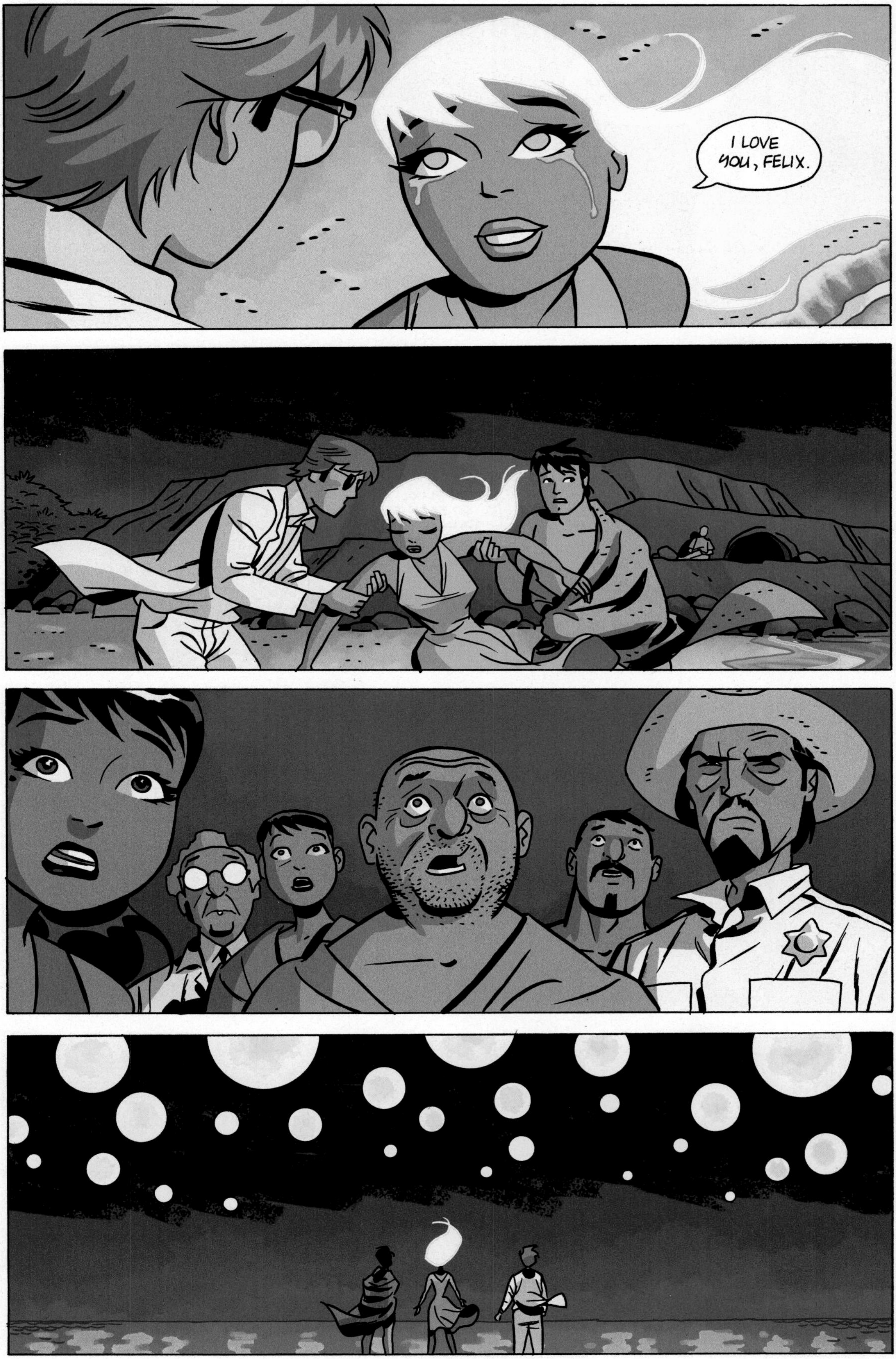
I LOVE YOU, FELIX.

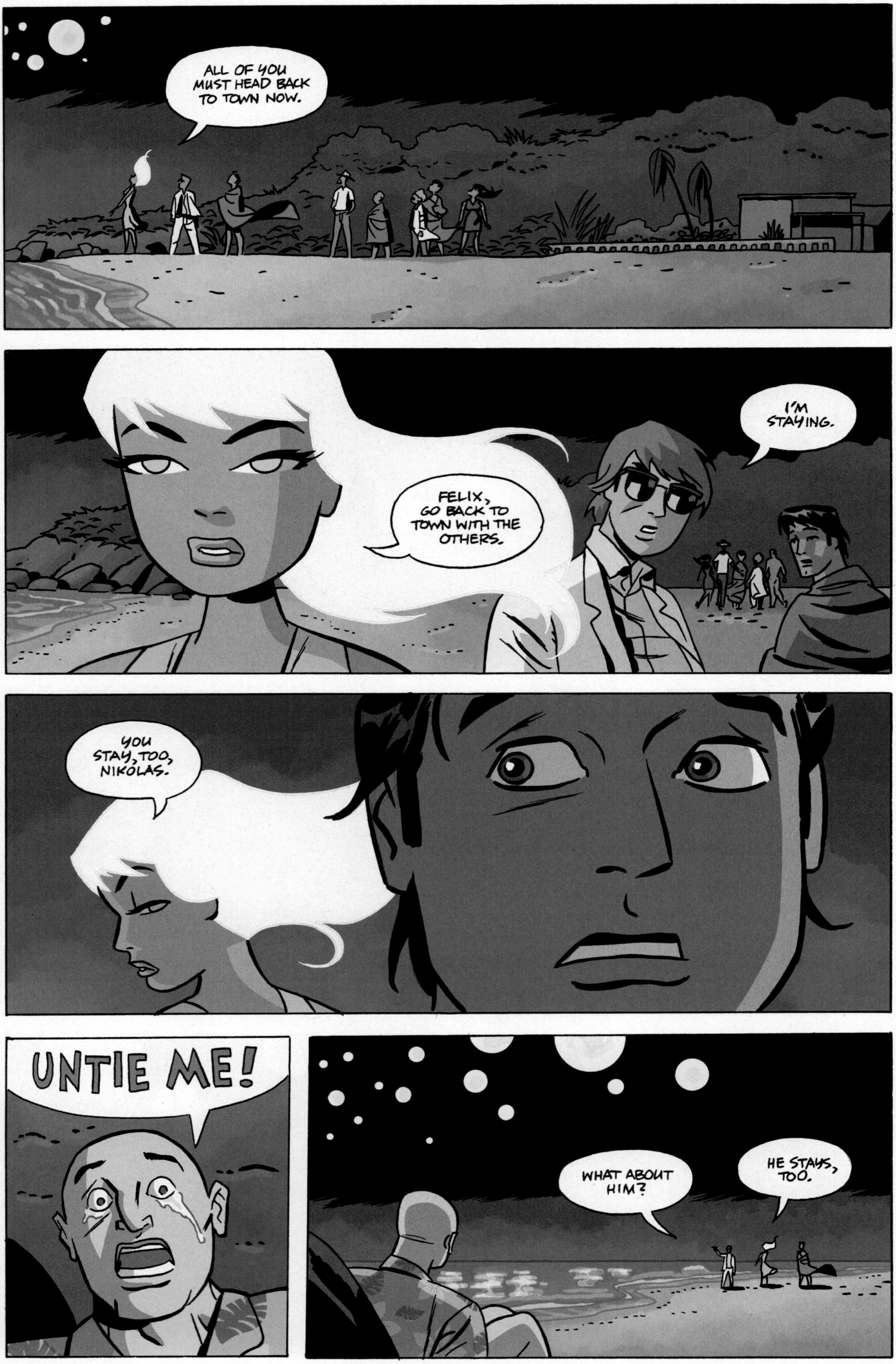
ALL OF YOU MUST HEAD BACK TO TOWN NOW.
FELIX, GO BACK TO TOWN WITH THE OTHERS.
I'M STAYING.
YOU STAY, TOO, NIKOLAS.
UNTIE ME!
WHAT ABOUT HIM?
HE STAYS, TOO.

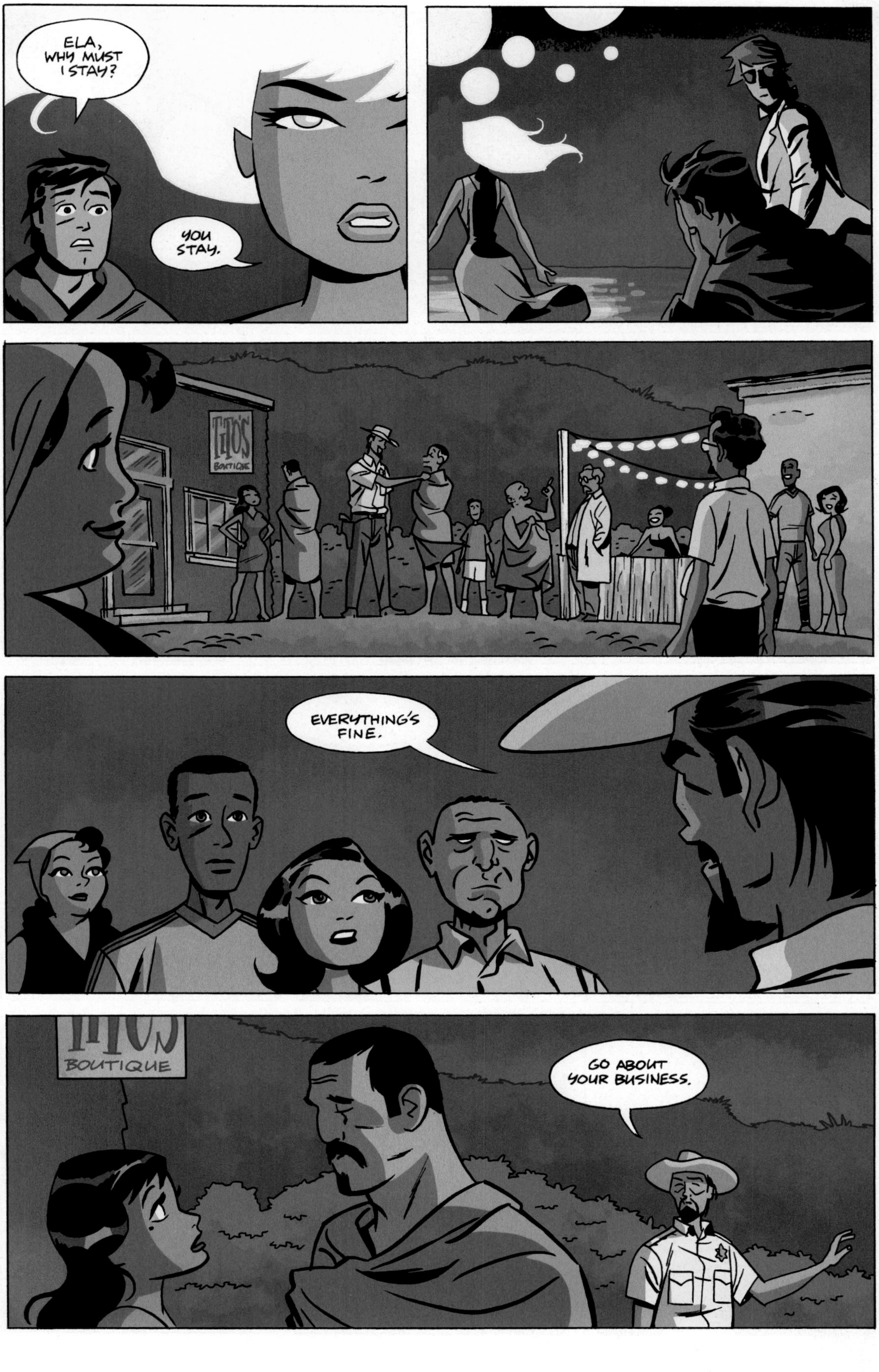
ELA, WHY MUST I STAY?
YOU STAY.
TITO'S BOUTIQUE
EVERYTHING'S FINE.
BOUTIQUE
GO ABOUT YOUR BUSINESS.

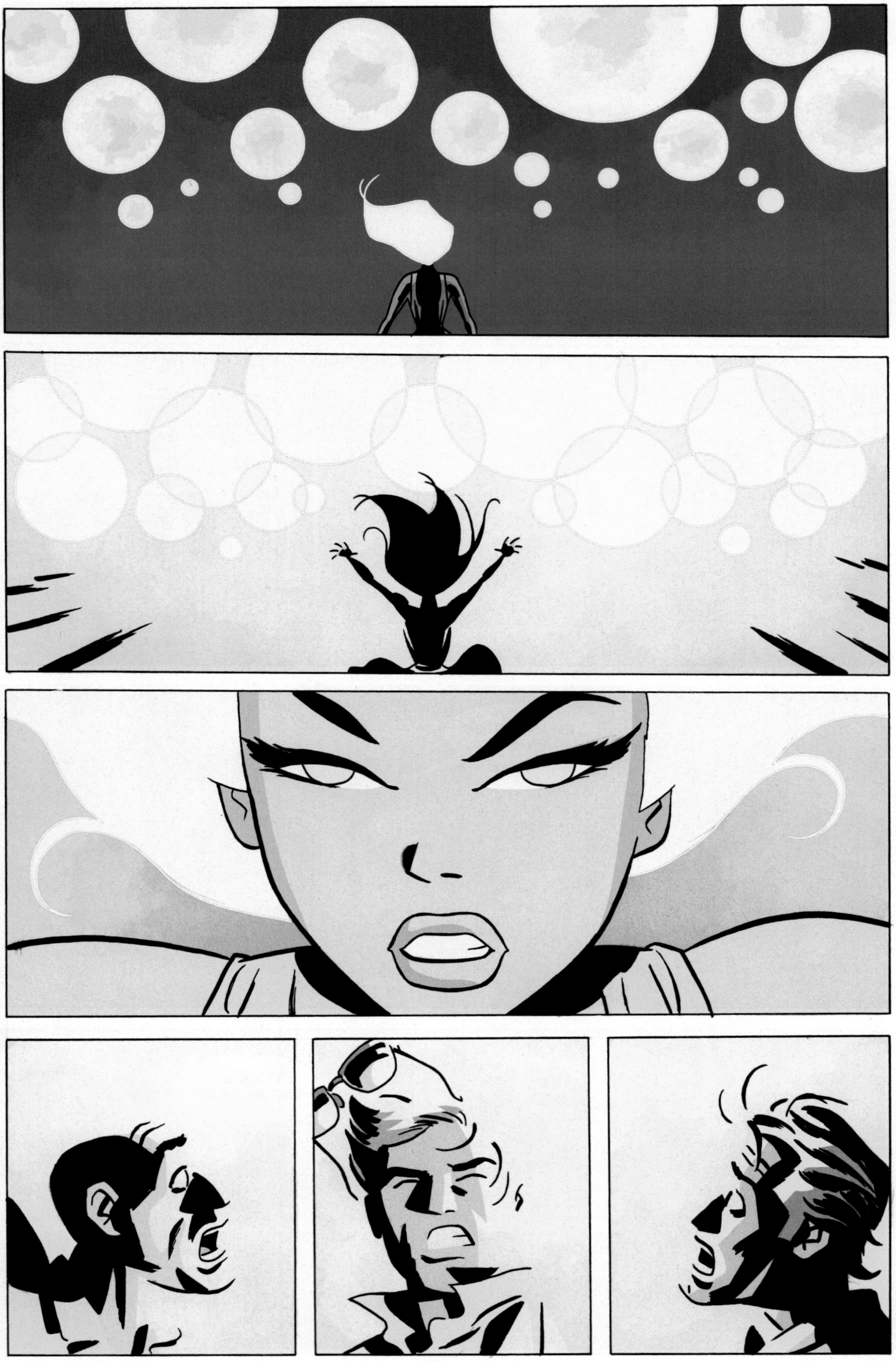

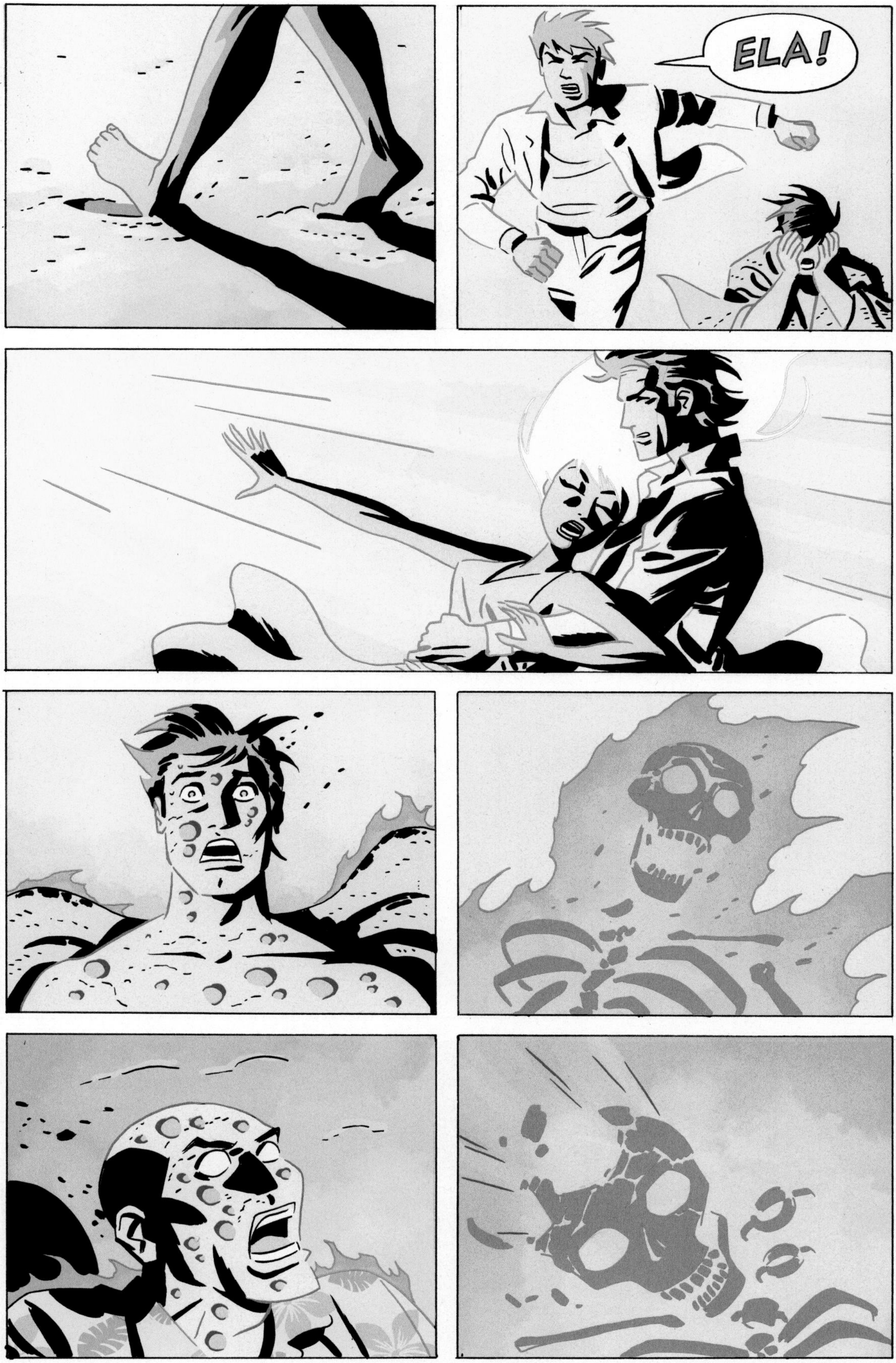
ELA!

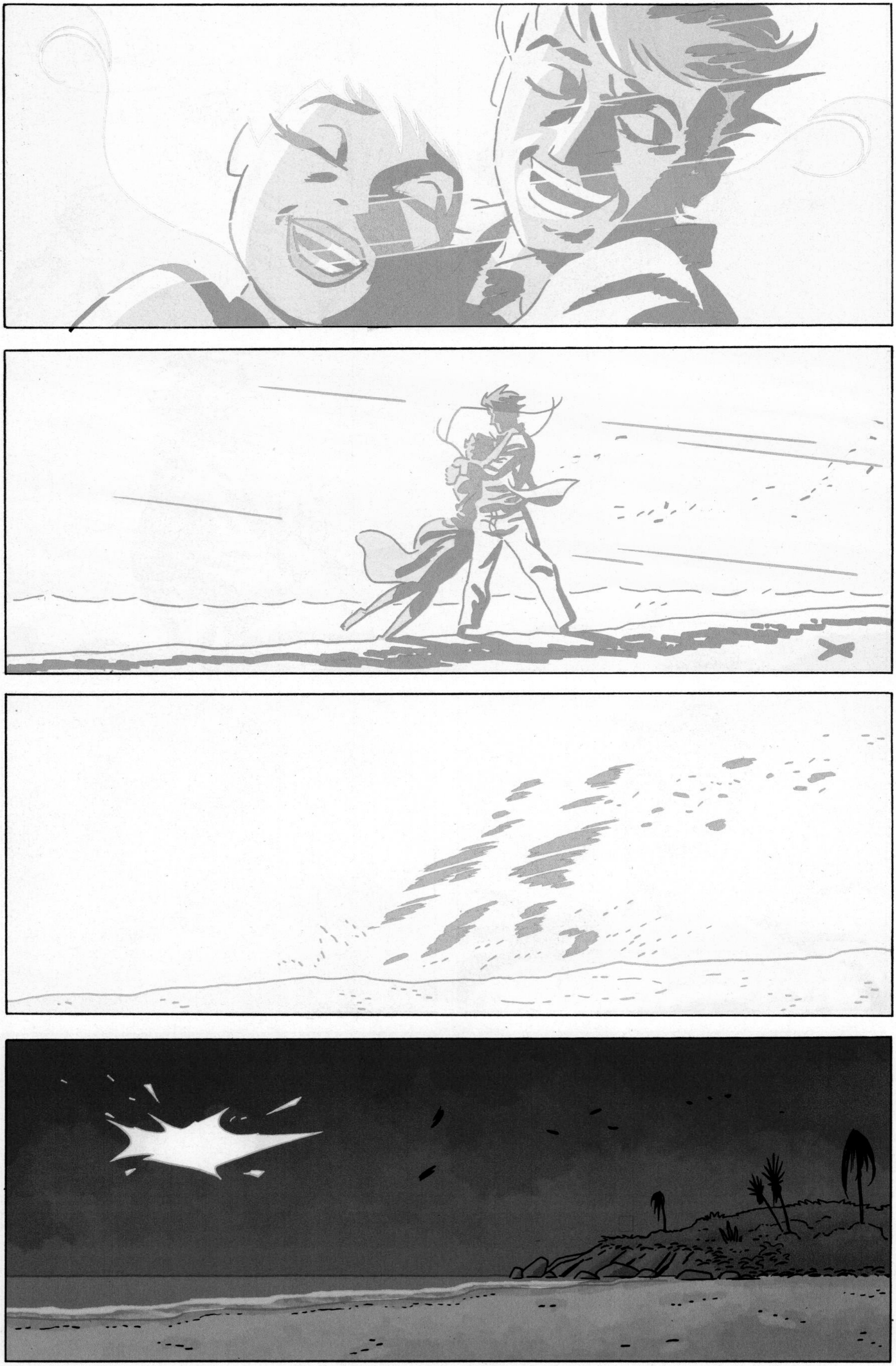

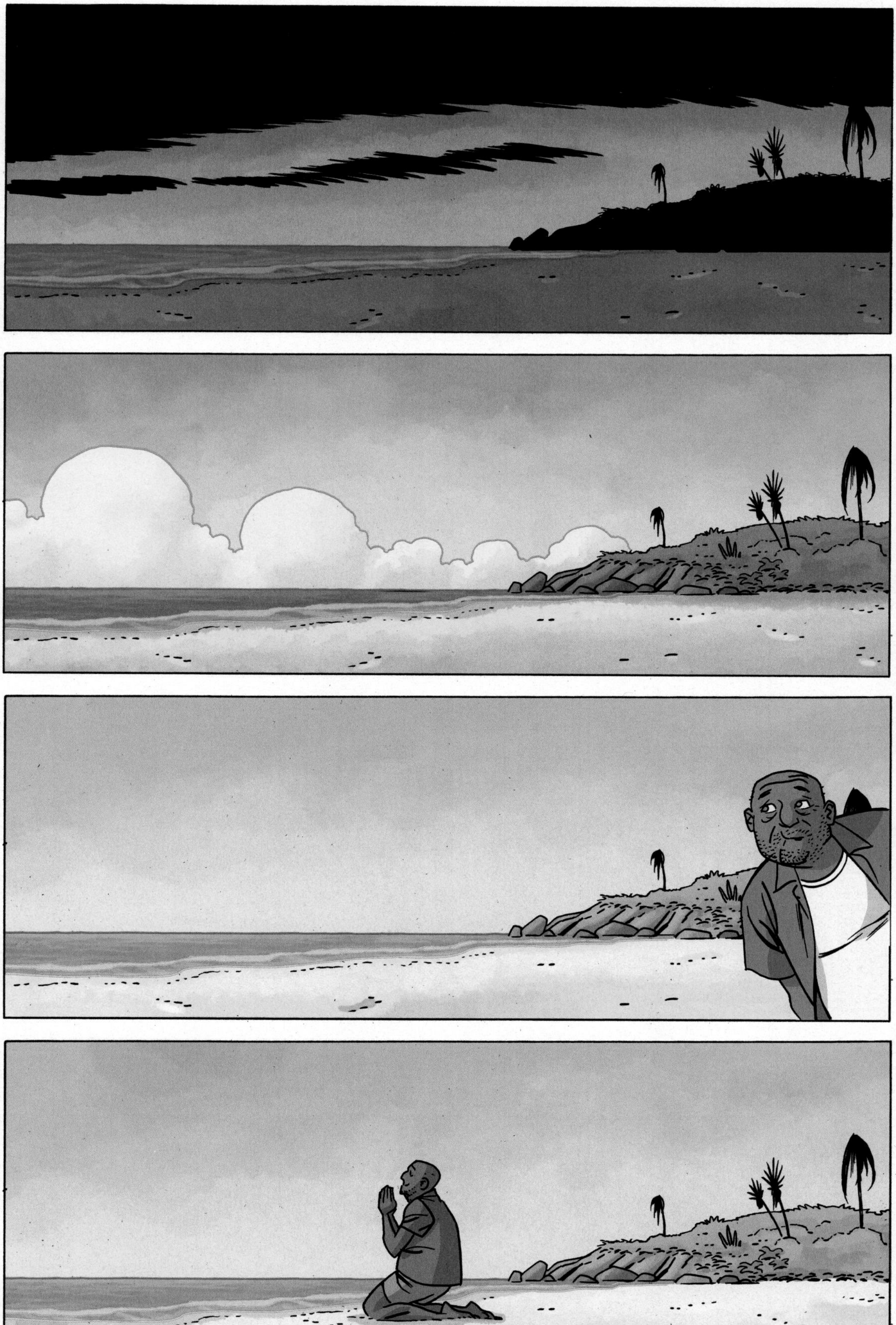

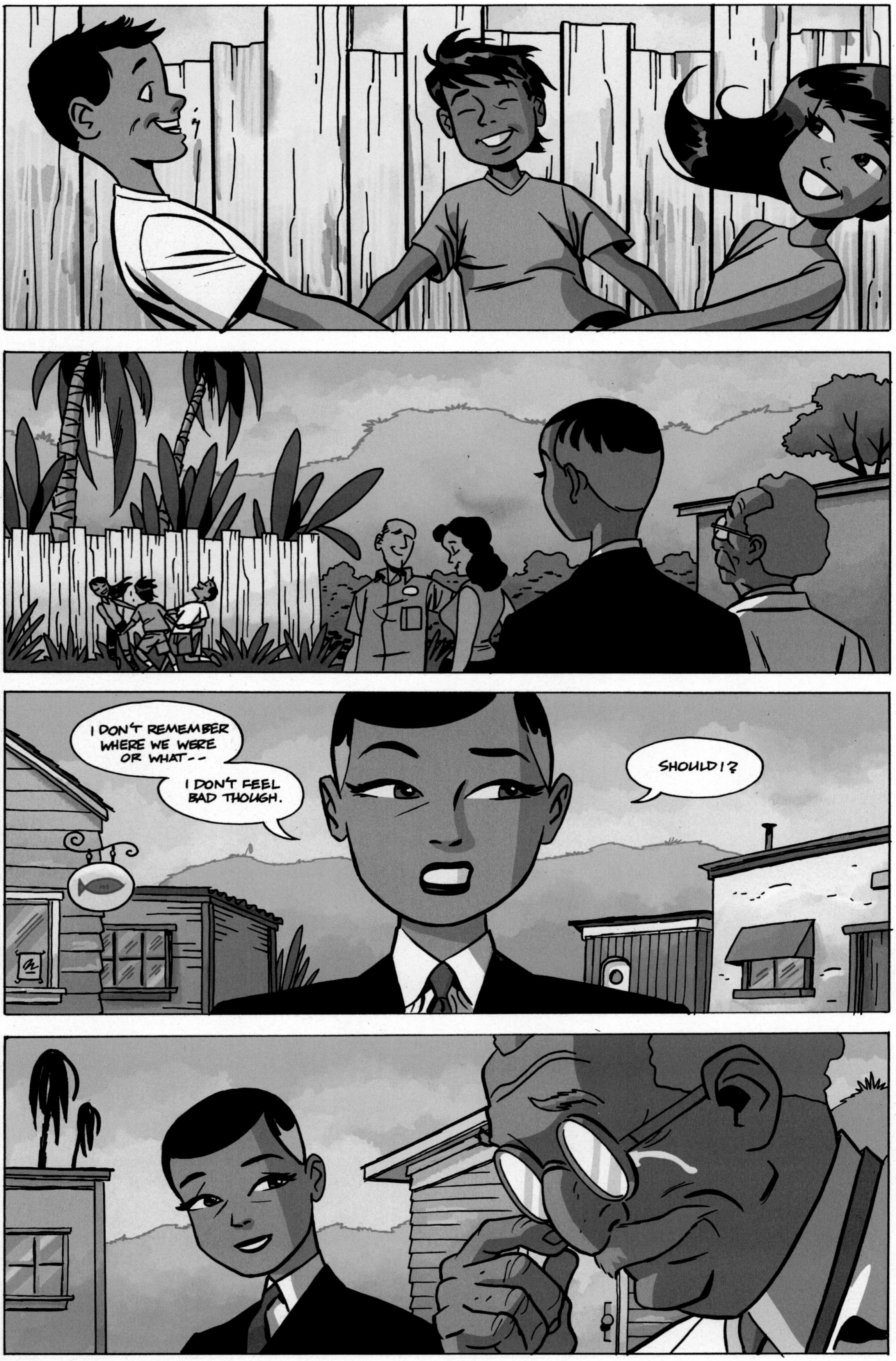
I DON'T REMEMBER WHERE WE WERE OR WHAT--
I DON'T FEEL BAD THOUGH.
SHOULD I?

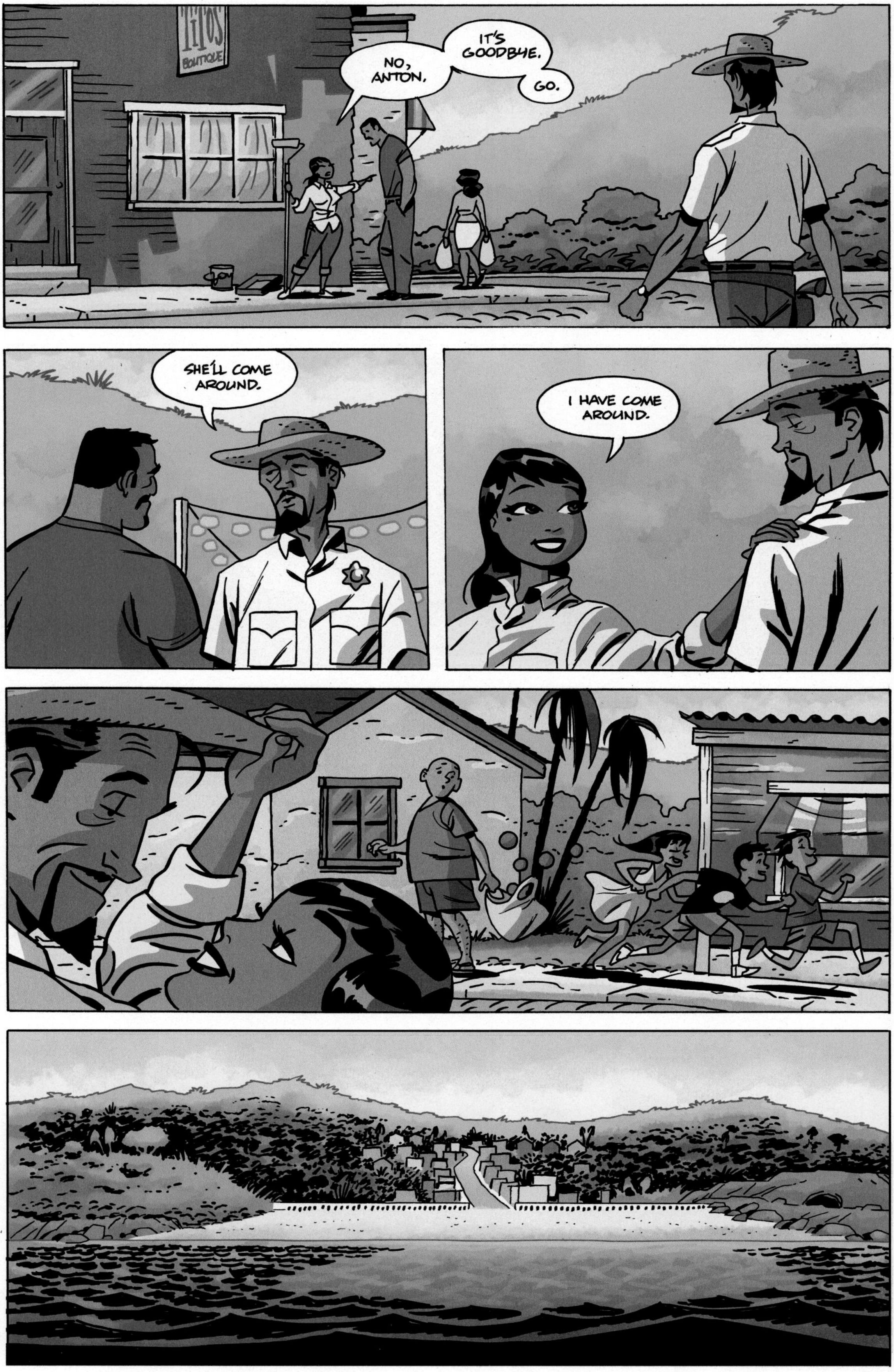
TITO'S
BOUTIQUE
NO, ANTON.
IT'S GOODBYE.
GO.
SHE'LL COME AROUND.
I HAVE COME AROUND.

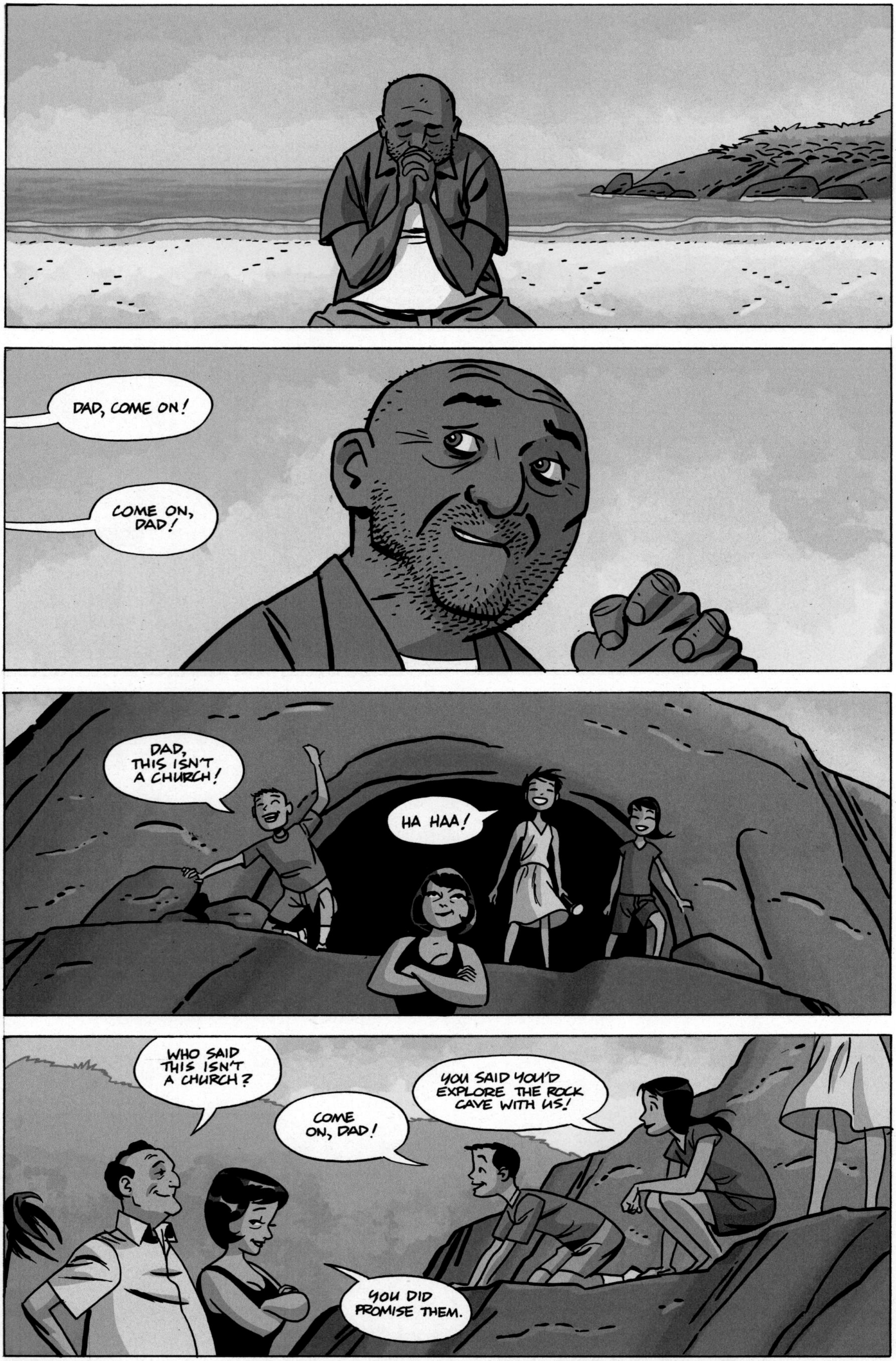
DAD, COME ON!
COME ON, DAD!
DAD, THIS ISN'T A CHURCH!
HA HAA!
WHO SAID THIS ISN'T A CHURCH?
COME ON, DAD!
YOU SAID YOU'D EXPLORE THE ROCK CAVE WITH US!
YOU DID PROMISE THEM.

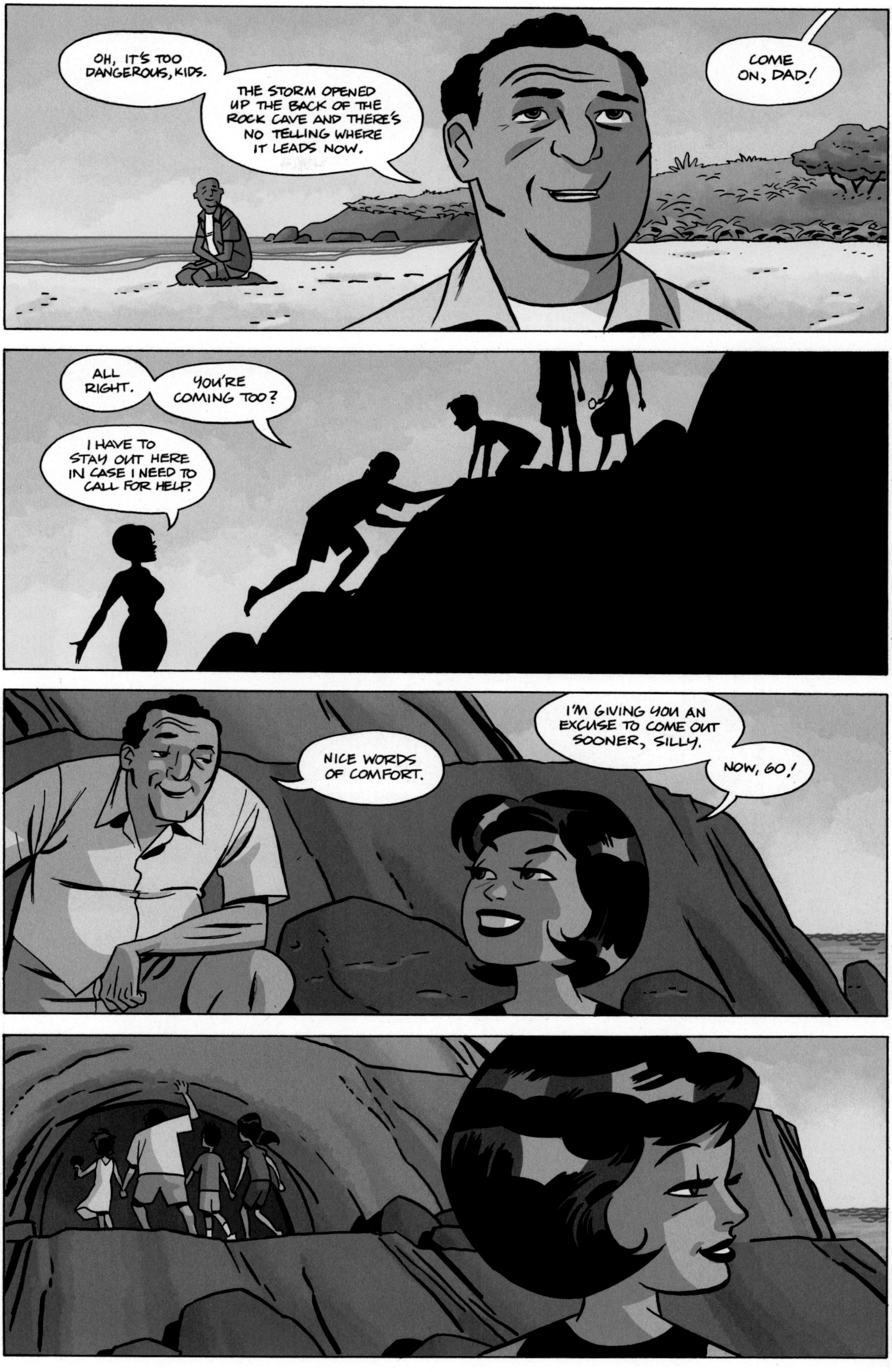
OH, IT'S TOO DANGEROUS, KIDS.
THE STORM OPENED UP THE BACK OF THE ROCK CAVE AND THERE'S NO TELLING WHERE IT LEADS NOW.
COME ON, DAD!
ALL RIGHT.
YOU'RE COMING TOO?
I HAVE TO STAY OUT HERE IN CASE I NEED TO CALL FOR HELP.
NICE WORDS OF COMFORT.
I'M GIVING YOU AN EXCUSE TO COME OUT SOONER, SILLY.
NOW, GO!

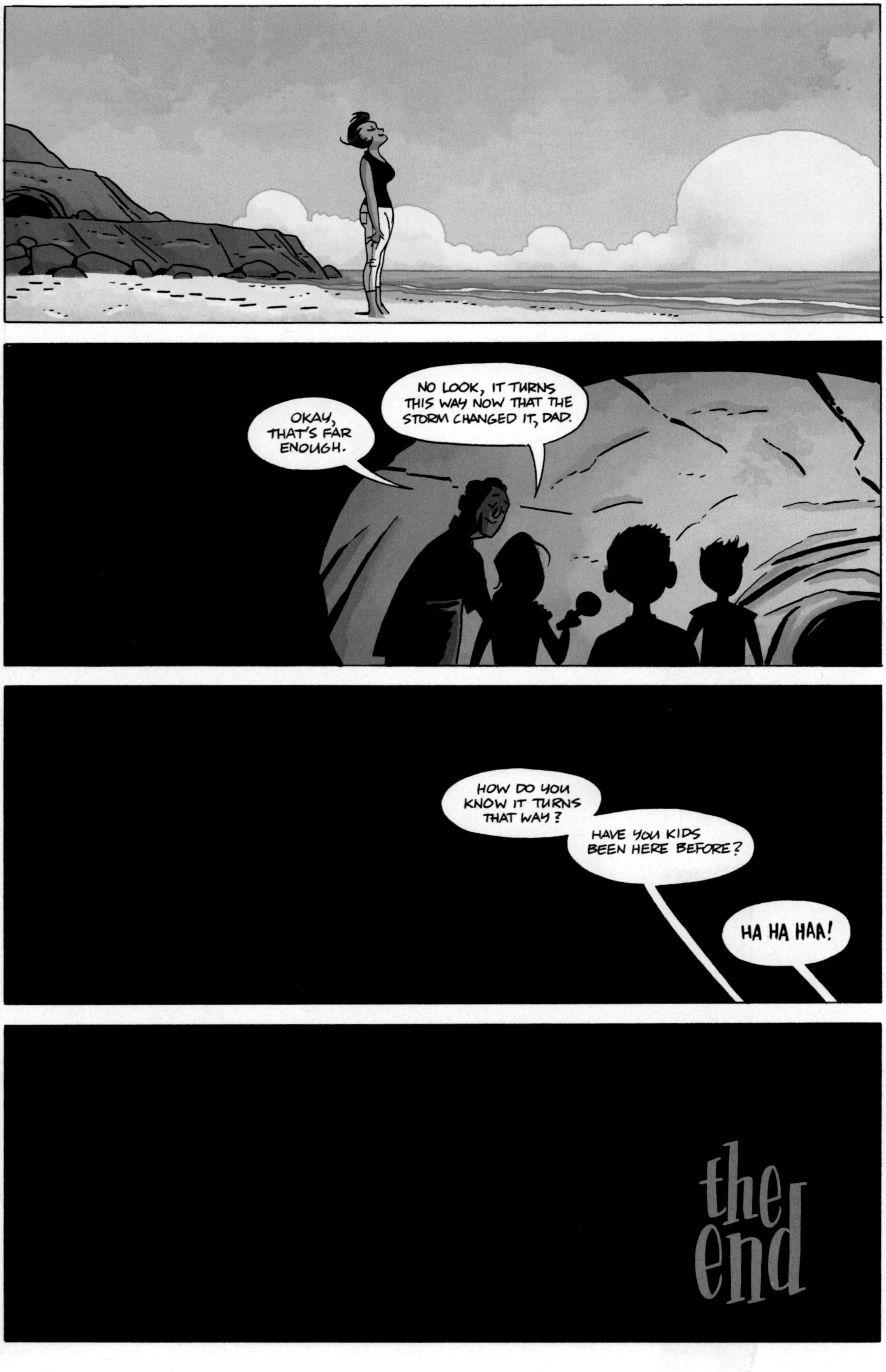
OKAY, THAT'S FAR ENOUGH.
NO LOOK, IT TURNS THIS WAY NOW THAT THE STORM CHANGED IT, DAD.
HOW DO YOU KNOW IT TURNS THAT WAY?
HAVE YOU KIDS BEEN HERE BEFORE?
HA HA HAA!
the end

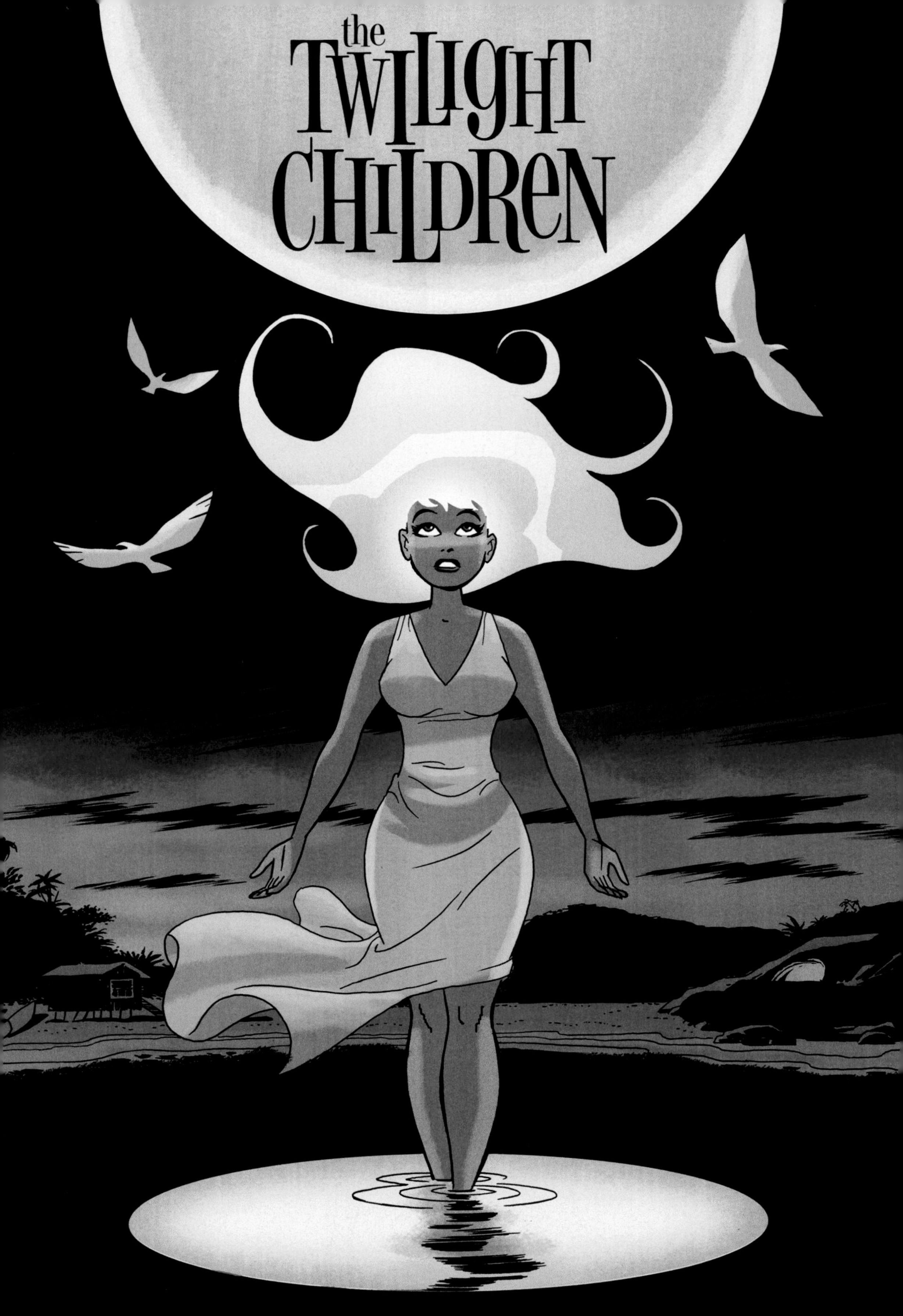

the
TWILIGHT
CHILDREN

Variant cover art for issue #1 by **Darwyn Cooke**

the TWILIGHT ZONE

Character designs
and page layouts by
Gilbert Hernandez

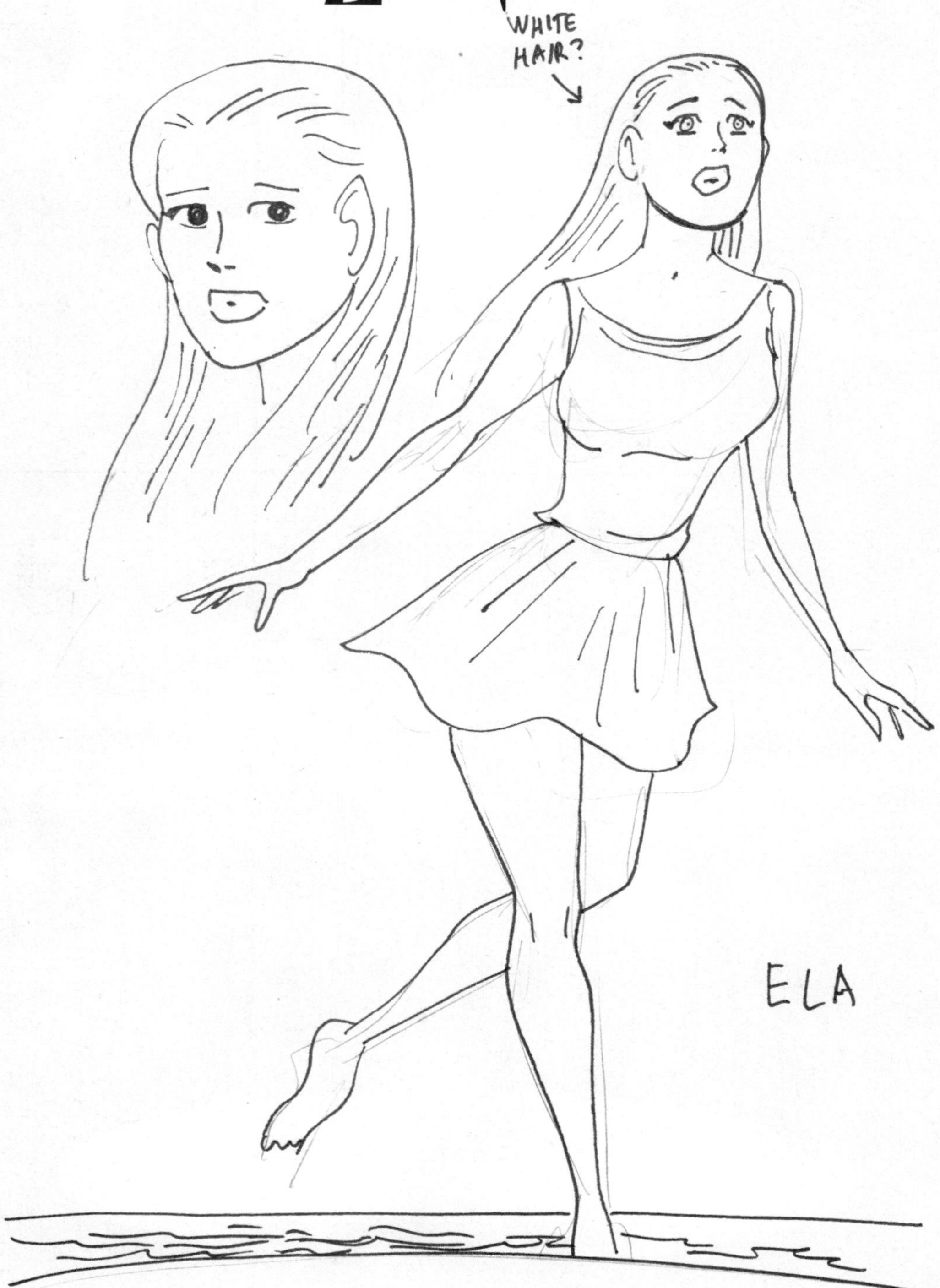

WHITE HAIR?
ELA

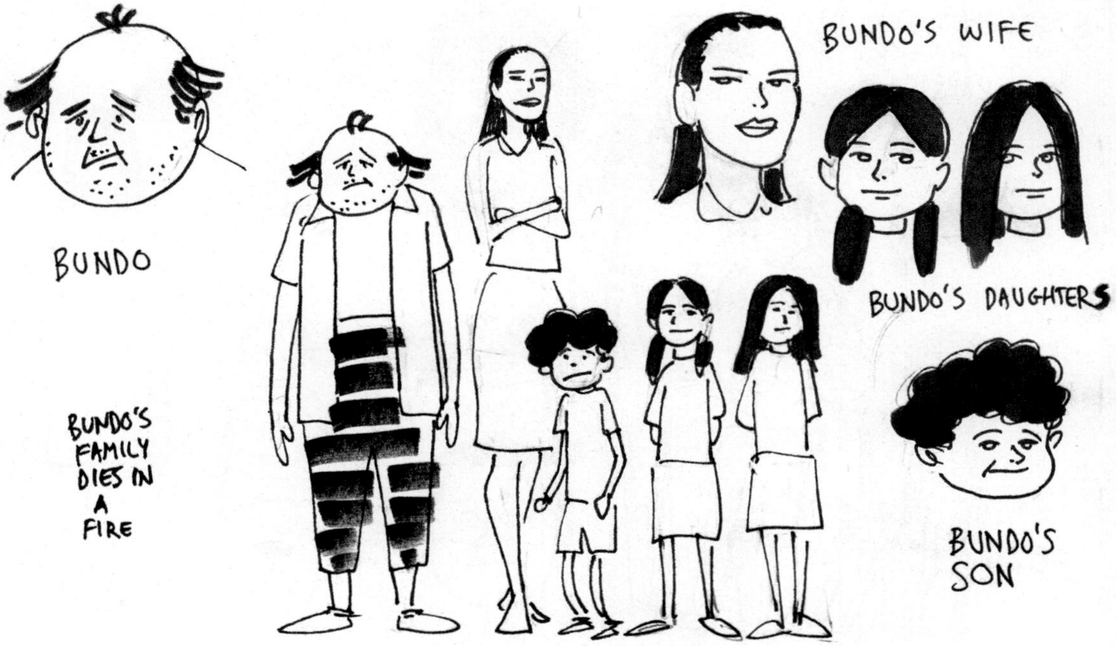
BUNDO
BUNDO'S WIFE
BUNDO'S DAUGHTERS
BUNDO'S FAMILY DIES IN A FIRE
BUNDO'S SON

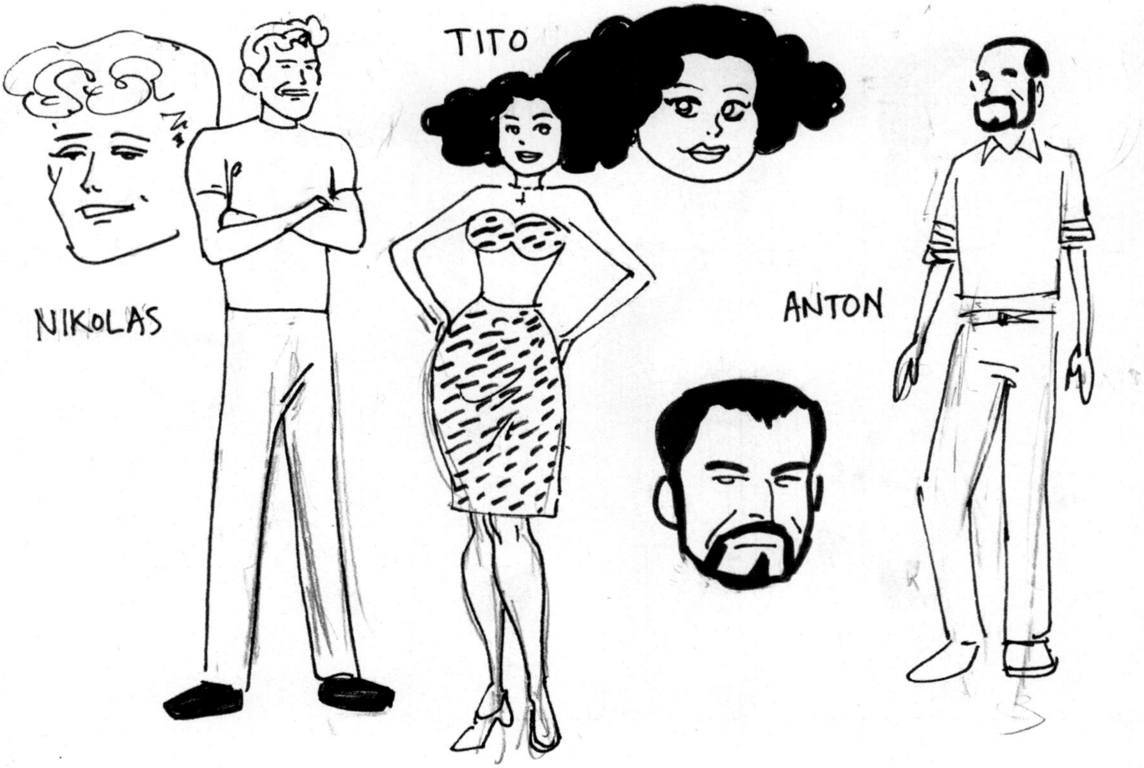
TITO
NIKOLAS
ANTON

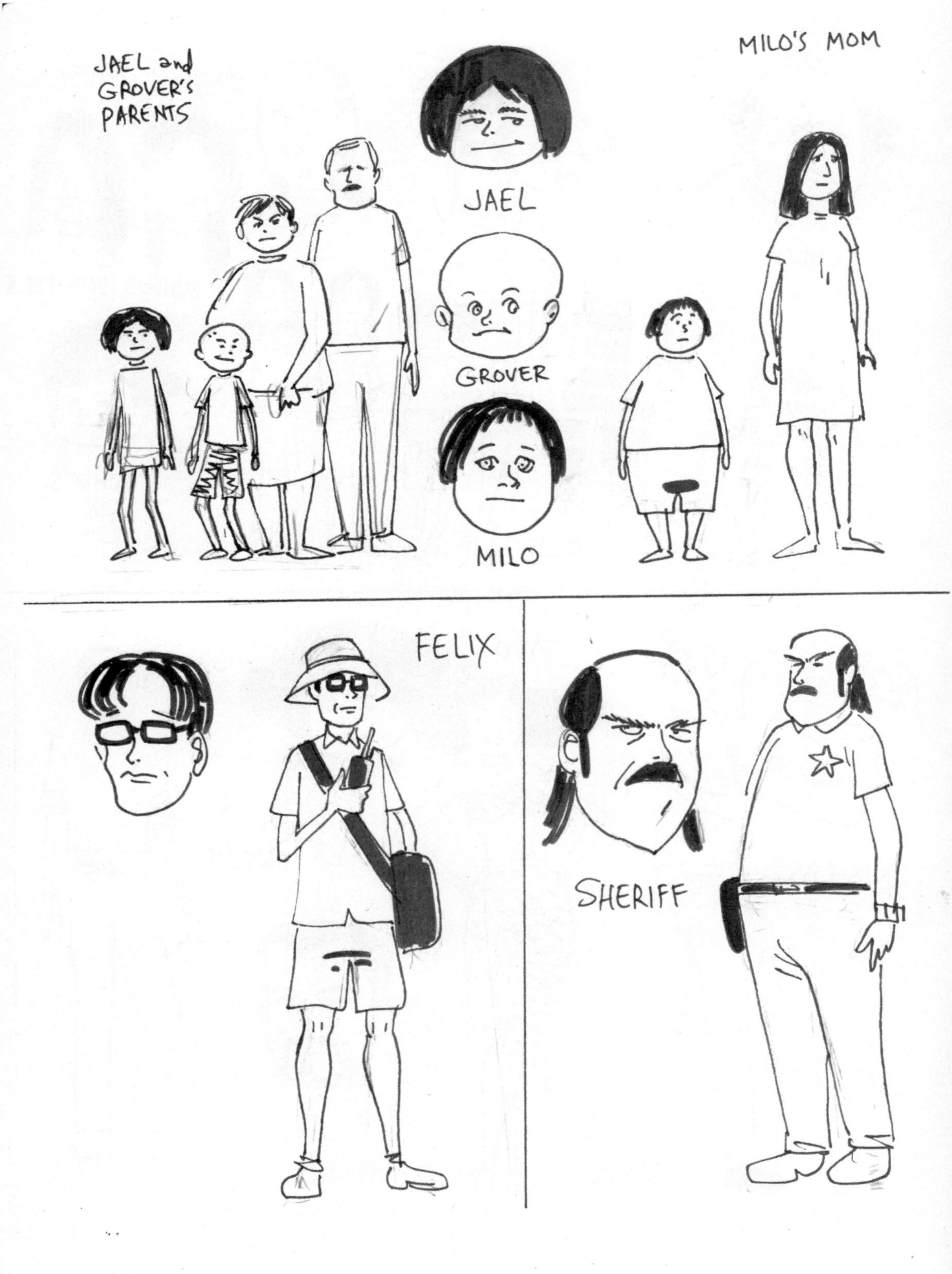
JAEL and GROVER'S PARENTS
JAEL
GROVER
MILO
MILO'S MOM
FELIX
SHERIFF

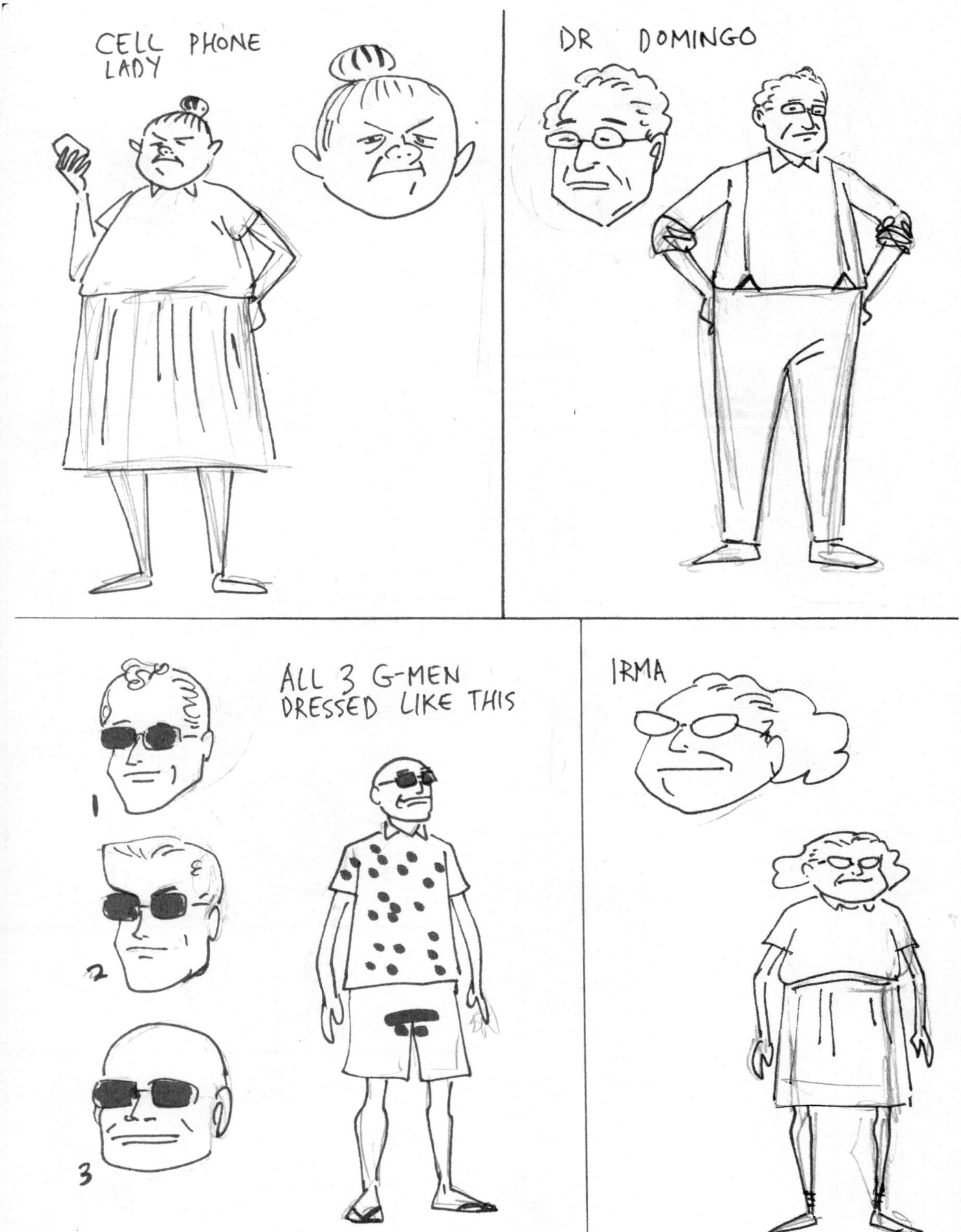
CELL PHONE LADY
DR DOMINGO
ALL 3 G-MEN DRESSED LIKE THIS
1
2
3
IRMA

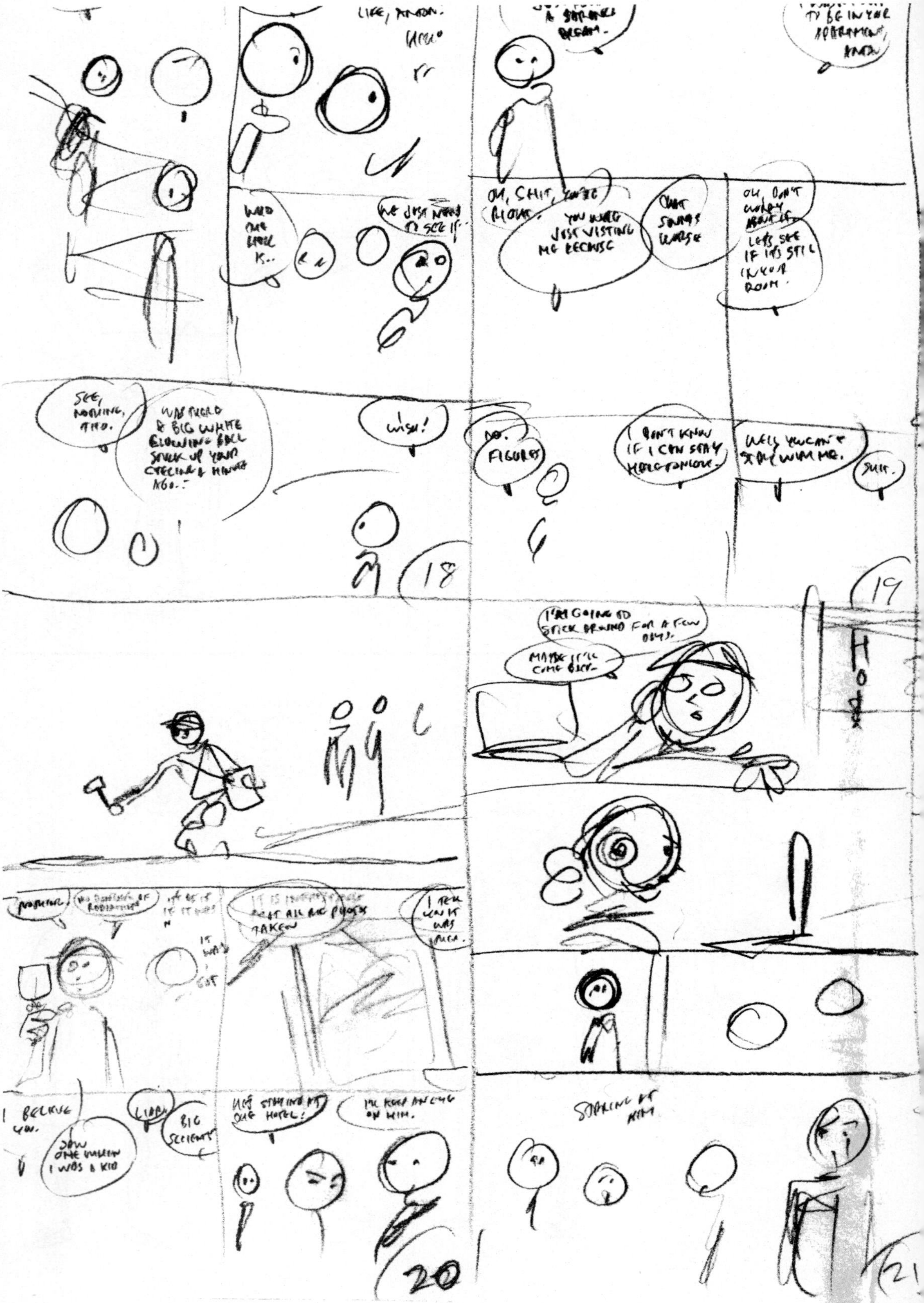
LIKE, ANTON.
A STRANGE DREAM.
OH, DON'T WORRY ABOUT IT. LET'S SEE IF IT'S STILL IN YOUR ROOM.
SEE, NOTHING, THO.
I WISH!
18
NO. FIGURES
I DON'T KNOW IF I CAN STAY HERE TONIGHT.
WELL YOU CAN'T STAY WITH ME.
SHIT.
19
I'M GOING TO STICK AROUND FOR A FEW DAYS.
MAYBE IT'LL COME BACK.
I BELIEVE YOU.
BIG SCIENTIST
HE'S STAYING AT OUR HOTEL!
I'LL KEEP AN EYE ON HIM.
20
STARING AT HIM
21

Thumbnails for issue #1, pages 18-25

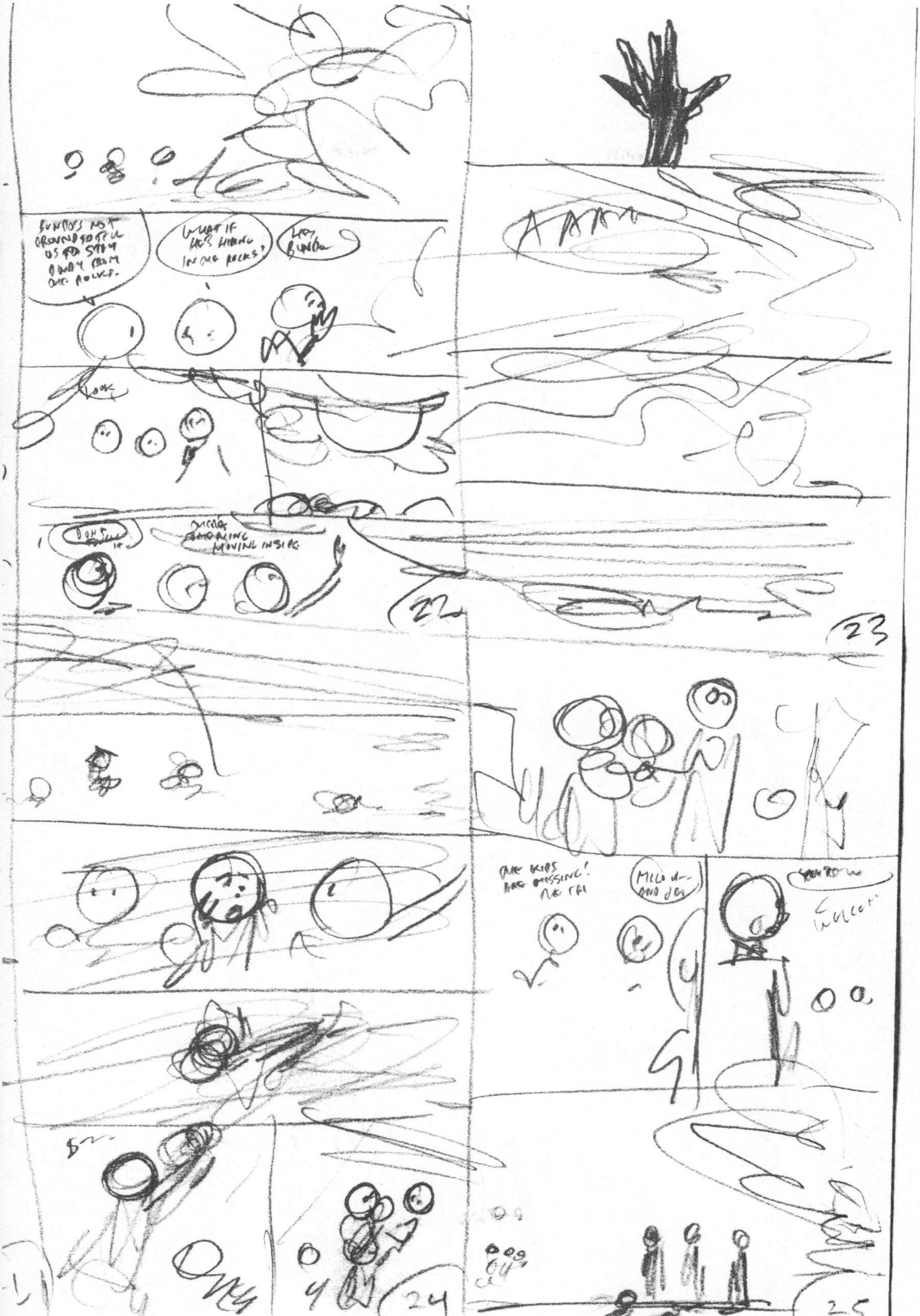
BUNDY'S NOT AROUND TO TELL US TO STAY AWAY FROM THE ROCKS.
WHAT IF HE'S HIDING IN THE ROCKS?
22
23
THE KIDS ARE MISSING!
24
25

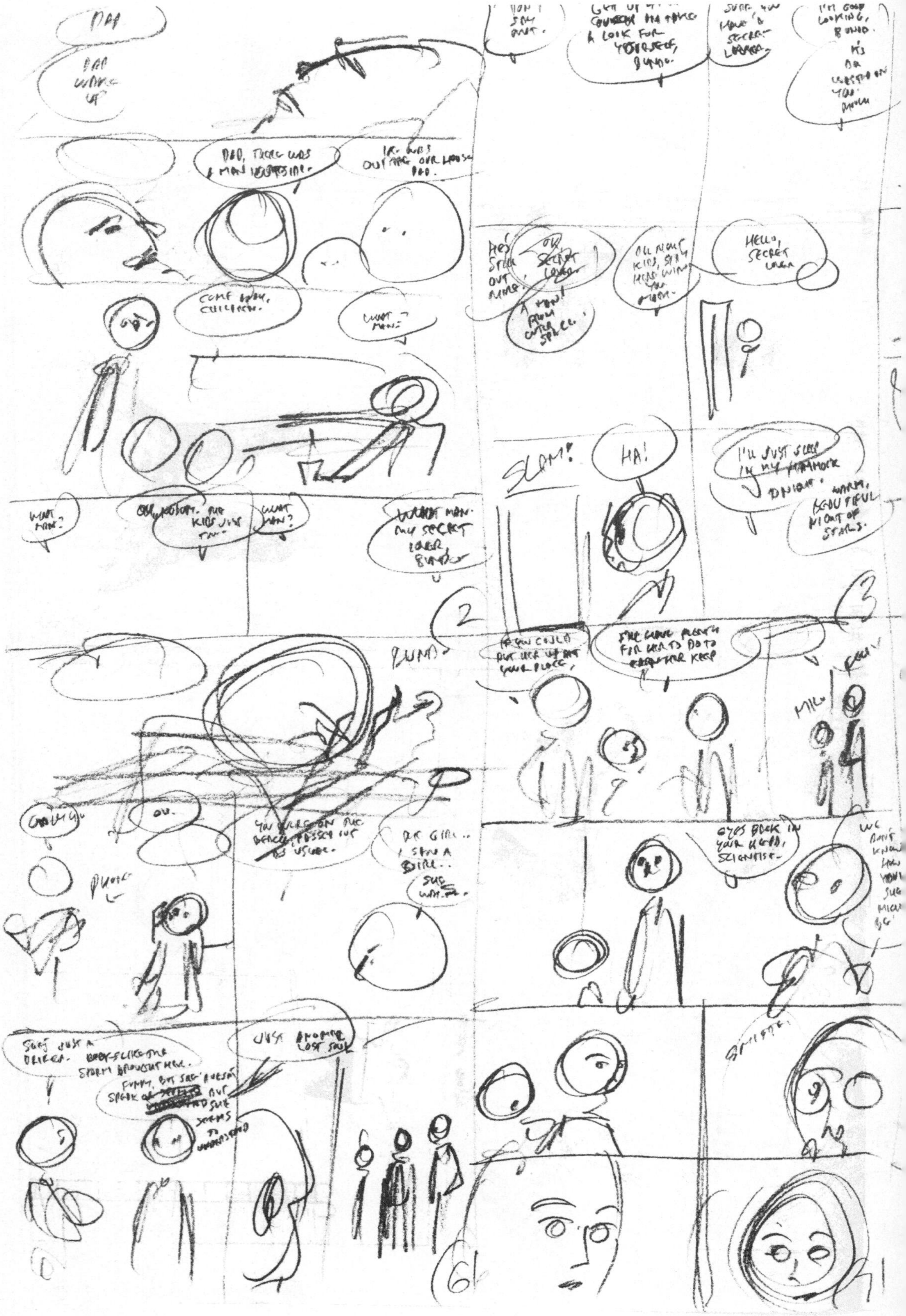
DAD
DAD WAKE UP
DAD, THERE WAS A MAN OUTSIDE.
COME AWAY, CHILDREN.
WHAT MAN?
HELLO, SECRET LOVER.
SLAM!
HA!
I'LL JUST SLEEP IN MY HAMMOCK TONIGHT.
2
3
BUMP
EYES BACK IN YOUR HEAD, SCIENTIST.
JUST ANOTHER LOST SOUL
6

Thumbnails for issue #2, pages 2-9

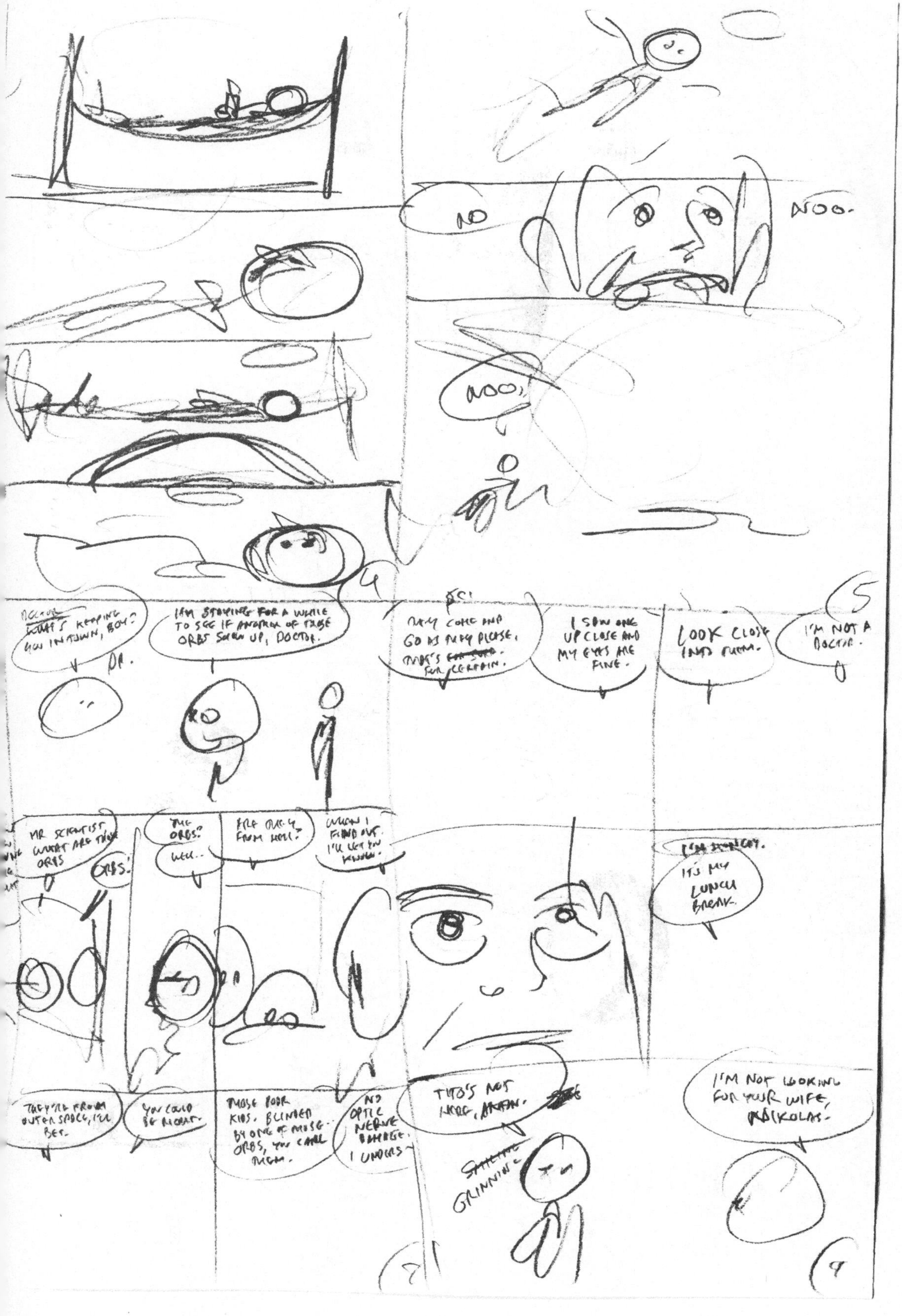
NO
NOO.
NOO.
WHAT'S KEEPING YOU IN TOWN, BOY?
I'M STAYING FOR A WHILE TO SEE IF ANOTHER OF THESE ORBS SHOW UP, DOCTOR.
THEY COME AND GO AS THEY PLEASE. THAT'S FOR CERTAIN.
I SAW ONE UP CLOSE AND MY EYES ARE FINE.
LOOK CLOSE INTO THEM.
I'M NOT A DOCTOR.
MR SCIENTIST WHAT ARE THESE ORBS
ORBS!
THE ORBS?
WELL..
WHEN I FIND OUT, I'LL LET YOU KNOW.
IT'S MY LUNCH BREAK.
THEY'RE FROM OUTER SPACE, I'LL BET.
YOU COULD BE RIGHT.
THOSE POOR KIDS. BLINDED BY ONE OF THESE.. ORBS, YOU CALL THEM.
NO OPTIC NERVE DAMAGE. I UNDERS~
TITO'S NOT HERE, AGAIN.
GRINNING
I'M NOT LOOKING FOR YOUR WIFE, NIKOLAS.
8
9

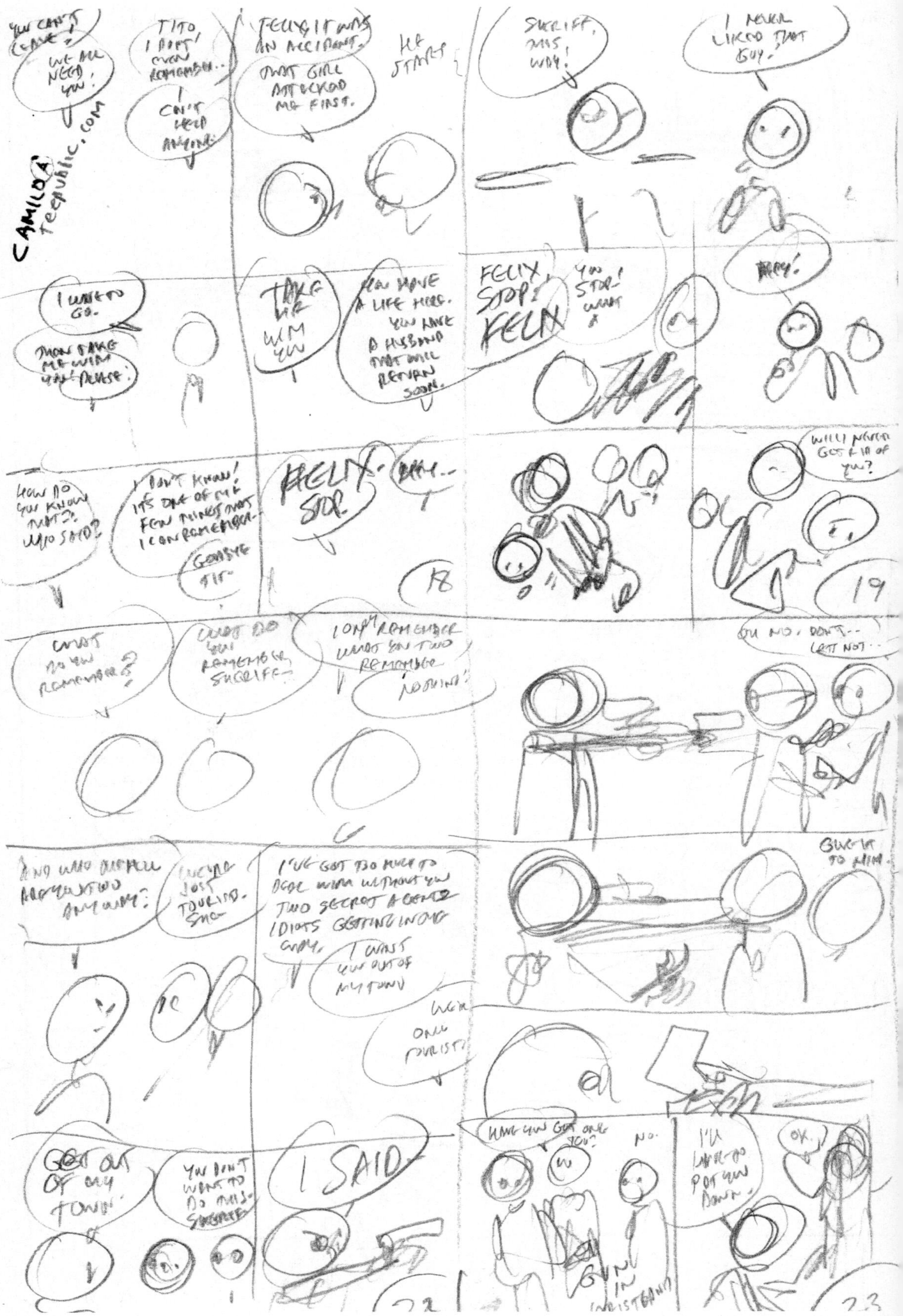
CAMILO@TEEPUBLIC.COM
I WANT TO GO.
THEN TAKE ME WITH YOU. PLEASE.
TAKE ME WITH YOU
YOU HAVE A LIFE HERE. YOU HAVE A HUSBAND THAT WILL RETURN SOON.
FELIX, STOP! FELIX
YOU STOP!
HOW DO YOU KNOW THAT?! WHO SAID?
I DON'T KNOW! IT'S ONE OF THE FEW THINGS THAT I CAN REMEMBER.
GOODBYE
FELIX. STOP.
18
19
WHAT DO YOU REMEMBER?
WHAT DO YOU REMEMBER, SHERIFF?
I ONLY REMEMBER WHAT YOU TWO REMEMBER
NOTHING!
I'VE GOT TOO MUCH TO DEAL WITH WITHOUT YOU TWO SECRET AGENT IDIOTS GETTING IN MY WAY.
I WANT YOU OUT OF MY TOWN
GET OUT OF MY TOWN.
YOU DON'T WANT TO DO THIS
I SAID.
OK.
GUN IN WRISTBAND
23

Thumbnails for issue #3, pages 18-25

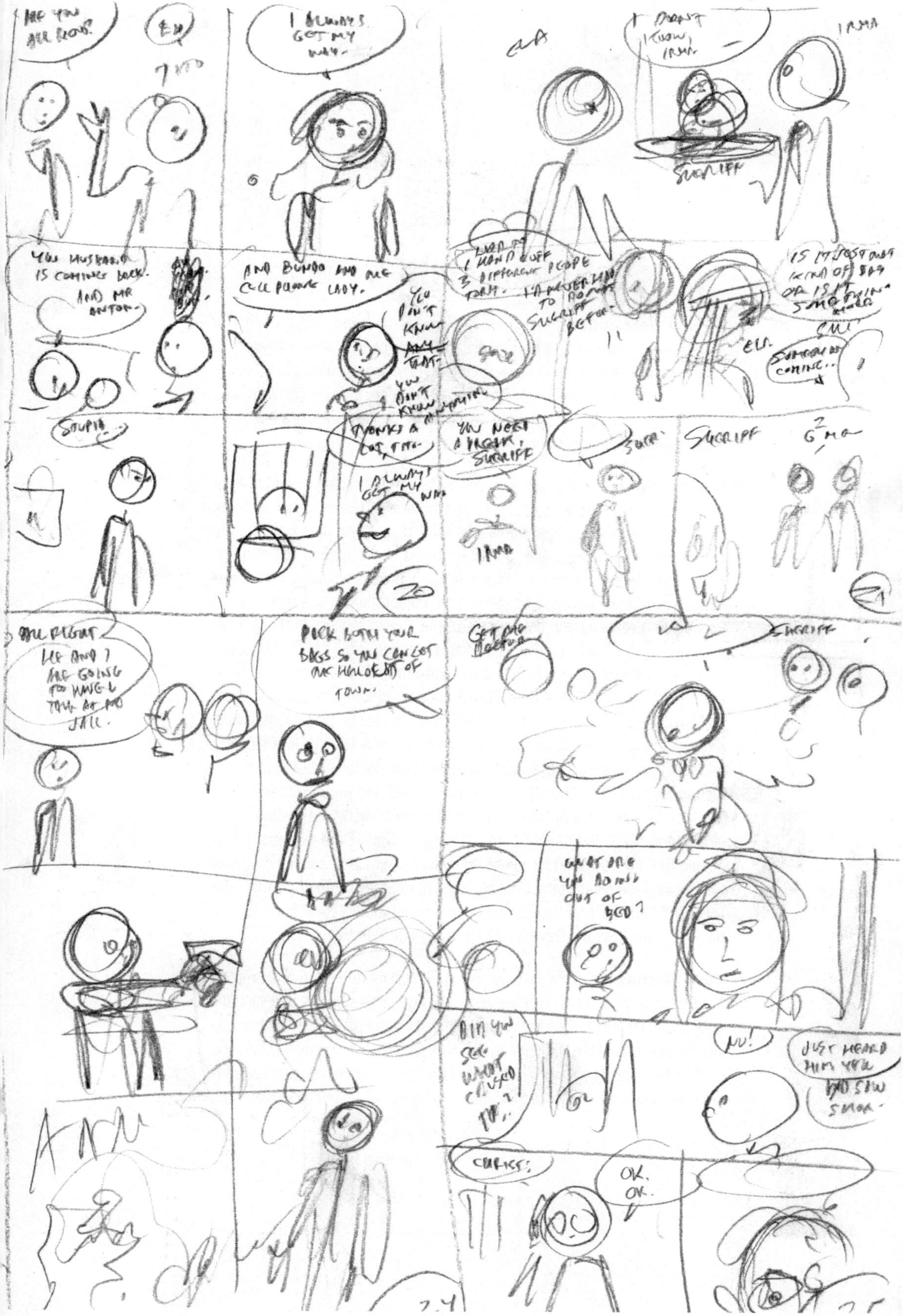
I ALWAYS GOT MY WAY.
I DON'T KNOW, IRMA
IRMA
SHERIFF
IS COMING BACK.
AND MR ANTON.
AND BUNDO AND THE CELL PHONE LADY.
YOU DON'T KNOW THAT.
YOU DON'T KNOW ANYTHING.
STUPID...
THANKS A LOT,
YOU NEED A BREAK, SHERIFF
I ALWAYS GOT MY WAY
IRMA
SHERIFF
SOMEONE'S COMING...
SHERIFF
ALL RIGHT
ME AND I ARE GOING TO HAVE A TALK AT THE JAIL.
PICK BOTH YOUR BAGS SO YOU CAN GET THE HELL OUT OF TOWN.
SHERIFF
WHAT ARE YOU DOING OUT OF BED?
DID YOU SEE WHAT CAUSED THE..?
NO!
JUST HEARD HIM YELL
CHRIST!
OK, OK.

BIOGRAPHIES

Gilbert Hernandez grew up reading comics and watching sci-fi/horror movies, so is it any wonder that he became a cartoonist? After 34 years, he continues to create comics for *Love and Rockets* (alongside his brother Jaime), and he's still going strong. His most recent projects include THE TWILIGHT CHILDREN from Vertigo (co-created with Darwyn Cooke), *Loverboys* from Dark Horse, and *Bumperhead* from Drawn & Quarterly.

Darwyn Cooke is an Eisner Award-winning cartoonist and animator. After spending several years as a magazine art director and graphic designer, Cooke switched careers and began working in animation, where he contributed to such shows as *Batman: The Animated Series*, *Superman: The Animated Series* and *Men In Black: The Series*. Following these successes, DC Comics approached Cooke to write and illustrate a project that he had submitted to the company years earlier, BATMAN: EGO. The critical success of this graphic novel led to more freelance work, including a relaunch of the CATWOMAN series with writer Ed Brubaker, which inspired Cooke to write and draw the graphic novel CATWOMAN: SELINA'S BIG SCORE, as well as assignments on *X-Force* and *Spider-Man's Tangled Web* for Marvel Comics. Cooke then spent several years writing and drawing the ambitious epic THE NEW FRONTIER, a six-issue miniseries bridging the gap between the end of the Golden Age of Comics and the beginnings of the Silver Age. He also illustrated and wrote (with friends) a highly acclaimed issue of DC's artist-centric series SOLO, and crafted a new incarnation of THE SPIRIT for DC. In 2012, he was one of the essential voices behind BEFORE WATCHMEN, one of the most talked-about comics events of the decade. His recent projects include *Richard Stark's Parker* for IDW, THE TWILIGHT CHILDREN for Vertigo and a month-long variant cover event for DC. He lives in Nova Scotia, Canada with his lovely wife Marsha.

Dave Stewart began his career as an intern at Dark Horse before moving on to coloring comics. An artist in his own right, Stewart's stunning and versatile work has made him one of the industry's most sought-after color stylists. His credits include BATMAN, SUPERMAN, BATMAN/THE SPIRIT, *Conan*, *B.P.R.D.* and *Hellboy*. His industry awards include nine Eisners and five Harveys. He currently resides in Portland, Oregon with his wife, Michelle, and three black cats.